CHINA
CROSSES THE YALU

The Decision To Enter the Korean War

CHINA
CROSSES THE YALU

The Decision To Enter the Korean War

※
※
※

ALLEN S. WHITING

Stanford University Press,   Stanford, California

Stanford University Press
Stanford, California
© 1960 by The RAND Corporation
Printed in the United States of America
First published in 1960 by The Macmillan Company
Reissued in 1968 by Stanford University Press
L.C. 68-13744

2-13-73

To
My Father
and Mother

PREFACE

※

THE KOREAN WAR of 1950–1953 is a major bench mark in the foreign policy of the People's Republic of China (PRC) during the first decade of Communist power. The conflict catapulted the new regime of Mao Tse-tung from the situation of a victor in civil war to that of a contender with the United Nations for control of Korea. It forced the Chinese and Russian Communists into closer political and military collaboration than had previously existed. It highlighted Peking's relations with New Delhi as India essayed the role of mediator between East and West. Finally, it affected the course of Chinese Communist relations with both the United States and the United Nations for many years to come.

These problems were thrust upon a new Chinese ruling group, inexperienced in foreign affairs. Equally important, that ruling group remained almost unchanged in composition long after the Korean War. It is fair to assume that the course of events and the consequences of policy in 1950–1951 conditioned the manner in which Mao Tse-tung and his associates subsequently evaluated the role of China in Asia, the nature of the Sino-Soviet alliance, and relations with the West, particularly with the United States.

The initial purpose of this inquiry, therefore, was to determine the extent to which later Chinese Communist policies emerged from developments attending the Korean War. In the course of research, an additional topic of interest appeared, namely, the way in which the Korean War illuminates the broader question of limited war.[1] Until October 1950, when Chinese Communist "volunteers" crossed the Yalu River, two important constraints had conditioned the course of the war. First, each side had enjoyed privileged sanctuaries from which it could supply the front, the Communists working from Chinese and Soviet territory bordering Korea, and the United Nations forces operating from bases in Japan. In addition, despite both Russian and American possession of atomic bombs, no nuclear weapons had been employed by either side. What import did these limitations have for the Chinese Communist decision to intervene? Did that decision leave room for maneuver in the event of miscalculation about the effect such intervention might have upon these limitations of combat? This case study offers clues concerning the stability of limitations, the problem of testing their observance by the enemy, and the question of how one side communicates to the other the conditions which might induce it to override such limitations.

This last problem raises still another aspect of limited war, namely, the role of expectations of enemy behavior. Such expectations may be derived from direct communication between belligerents or indirect communication through third parties, and from statements primarily designed for domestic audiences but monitored by the enemy. In addition, expectations may be inferred from ideological assumptions about the enemy and past experience of him. What are the enemy's war aims? How likely are they to fluctuate according to the shifting tides of battle? How credible are his deterrent threats or his hints of compromise? If the enemy signals a willingness to negotiate, how can his intentions be tested while safeguarding freedom of maneuver and advantages at the battle front? Some insight into these problems may be gained from study of the interaction between Sino-Soviet moves and United States decisions in the fateful months of August and September 1950.

These considerations have determined the framework within which the Chinese Communist decisions that led to Peking's involvement in the Korean War have been examined. This work does not, therefore, purport to analyze Chinese Communist military strategy per se, nor does it examine the Soviet strategy behind North Korean aggression. Even less is it a comprehensive history of the first six months of the war. Necessarily, however, it probes key Sino-Soviet decisions relating to Peking's reactions, and so may throw light on certain obscure aspects of the conflict about which there has been considerable speculation but little research. In particular, the postponement of Peking's attack against Taiwan, Chinese Communist charges of U.S. air violations across the Yalu River, the movements of the People's Liberation Army (PLA) into Northeast China, and the three-week break-off in contact between

Chinese Communist "volunteers" and U.N. forces in November 1950 are examined in detail for their relationship with the decision to commit Chinese Communist power in Korea.

A brief word on the analytical scheme may prove helpful. Developments attending the Korean War are viewed from the perspective of decision makers in Peking, in so far as that perspective can be reconstructed from Chinese Communist statements and behavior. Alternative courses of action open to the Chinese have been derived from the frame of reference within which the new regime evaluated events, alternative policy goals, and the available means of promoting policy. The logic behind final decisions has been deduced upon the assumption that the Chinese leaders calculated the expected costs, risks, and gains associated with alternative courses of action. In brief, it has been assumed that Chinese Communist behavior is rationally motivated.

This approach is intended neither to justify Chinese Communist decisions nor to find fault with U.S. and U.N. decisions. Such judgments lie beyond the scope of this inquiry.

It has been impossible to determine the role of individual Chinese leaders in framing decisions on the Korean War. It seems certain that differences of opinion existed. These differences may have played an important role, for instance, in delaying the final military intervention. The absence of reliable evidence on this point has compelled the author to use the terms "Peking" and "Moscow" instead of singling out Mao Tse-tung, Chou En-lai, or others.

In addition to the acknowledgments in the footnotes, certain assistance deserves special mention. Abraham M. Halpern initiated this study and offered valuable comments in its early stages. Alexander George, Victor Hunt, and Hans Speier reviewed various drafts of the manuscript and made critical suggestions. Richard Moorsteen offered comment on the economic analyses. Many participants in the events generously gave of their time for interviews, while others in government and private capacities commented upon the manuscript at various stages. Among these persons, my appreciation is particularly due Dr. E. Taylor Parks, Dr. John Miller, Brigadier General (Ret.) S. L. A. Marshall, Ernest A. Gross, Dr. Philip C. Jessup, Howard Boorman, Philip Manhart, Theodore Wertheim, Wallace Gibson, and Paul McPherson. Ian Graham, editor for the Social Science Division of The RAND Corporation, was both conscientious and considerate in his comments, while Brownlee Haydon suggested further stylistic improvements. Mrs. Joanne Bobo did the final typing. Mrs. Joan Culver produced the index and bibliography. Special gratitude is acknowledged for the assistance provided by The RAND Corporation in making this study possible, and especially for the administrative help of Jeffrey C. Kitchen, Joseph M. Goldsen, Arnold Mengel, and John Hogan. As always, the author bears sole responsibility for whatever errors or shortcomings occur in the study.

This study was prepared as part of the continuing program of research undertaken for the U.S. Air Force by The RAND Corporation.

CONTENTS

※

MAPS

※

TABLES

※

I

THE FRAMEWORK
OF POLICY

※

BEFORE MOVING into the events of 1950, it is necessary to reconstruct the framework of policy within which Mao Tse-tung and his associates approached the Korean War. On October 1, 1949, this new elite proclaimed the establishment of the People's Republic of China (PRC). For twenty-eight years the Chinese Communist Party (CCP) had struggled as an armed minority to seize power. Victory brought not only the elation of success but problems of responsibility. Achieving political unity in a turbulent and underdeveloped country, building a planned industrial society on a shattered agrarian economy, and restoring China's long-lost power in Asia confronted the regime with staggering and unfamiliar tasks. The Korean War, an added burden, appears in retrospect to have posed well-nigh insuperable problems for the CCP leaders. Some of their successes in coping with this array of problems as well as some of their failures, may be better understood if one first examines the foundations of PRC policy.

The new leadership possessed a frame of reference with three main components relevant to our analysis. First, the Chinese component, operative for the Manchu and Kuomintang as well as for the Chinese Communist elite, stemmed in part from the environment, in part from the continuity with which successive Chinese regimes viewed that environment. Second, the ideological component, derived from the canons of Marxism-Leninism, was consciously adopted by the CCP as its basic creed. Finally, the experiential component resulted from the years of

CCP struggle against Chinese and Japanese opponents. These three influences help to explain the domestic and foreign policies adopted by Communist China in 1949–1950, including its reaction to the Korean War.

The Chinese Component

The Chinese component of the Chinese Communist outlook combines xenophobic attitudes with expansionist tendencies. Both elements stem in part from the problem of territorial security, prominent in China's history. The symbolic importance of this problem was enhanced by the traditional Chinese allocation of authority and legitimacy to the regime that could lay claim to the so-called "Mandate of Heaven." Such a claim was dependent upon the regime's ability to defend the frontiers against "barbarian" incursions while maintaining the peace against domestic insurrection.

The Mandate of Heaven and Irredentism

Without explicitly supporting the Mandate of Heaven definition of legitimacy, twentieth century Chinese elites turned to the extensive empire of the Middle Kingdom for their delineation of China's territorial sovereignty. Both Nationalists and Communists have variously included among "lost territories" portions of contemporary Russia, India, Burma, and Viet Nam. Some of these claims derive from tenuous historical relationships involving suzerainty and military protection, often manifested by little more than ceremonial exchanges of "tribute." Alternatively they are based upon disputed texts of maps and unsurveyed frontiers.[1]

In 1936 Mao Tse-tung upheld this tradition, projecting his future rule over considerably more land than lay under *de facto* Chinese control at the time:

It is the immediate task of China to regain all our lost territories. . . . We do not, however, include Korea, formerly a Chinese colony, but when we have re-established the independence of the lost territories of China, and if the Koreans wish to break away from the claims of Japanese imperialism, we will extend them our enthusiastic help in their struggle for independence. The same thing applies for Formosa. . . . The Outer

Mongolian republic will automatically become a part of the Chinese federation, at their own will. The Mohammedan and Tibetan peoples, likewise, will form autonomous republics attached to the Chinese federation.[2]

Mao's assumptions about Mongol, Mohammedan, and Tibetan attitudes ignored more than a century of anti-Chinese revolts among these peoples.[3] However, by insisting on recovery of "lost territories," by pledging Chinese rule over the borderlands of the old empire, and by hinting at a sphere of influence in Korea and Taiwan (Formosa), Mao spoke the language of Middle Kingdom rulers.

"Restoration" of Chinese control over Tibet, for instance, was politically both just and necessary, for Mao Tse-tung as for Chiang Kai-shek, Sun Yat-sen, and other claimants to leadership. The important difference lay in Mao's ability to implement his words where his predecessors had failed. Viewed from Peking, this was not invasion of a neighboring state but re-establishment of legitimate sovereignty; viewed from the outside, it exemplified the expansionist element in the Chinese component of policy.

Strategic Considerations

The symbolic authority and legitimacy embodied in the Mandate of Heaven are not alone in prompting Chinese expansionist moves. The lack of natural lines of demarcation along most of China's frontier has given the borderlands a recurring strategic importance. Only along the Sino-Soviet frontier in the northeast do rivers provide a readily definable boundary. In contrast, the line separating China from Outer Mongolia runs through the Gobi Desert and along the Altai Mountains. In the west and south, China is separated from Russia, Afghanistan, and India by lofty mountain chains, infrequently broken by passes. Jungles as well as mountains cover the Burmese and Indo-Chinese borders.

Most of this extensive frontier was never adequately surveyed. Many points lay beyond effective Chinese power during the nineteenth and twentieth centuries. As a result, French pressure from Indo-China, British pressure from Burma and India, Russian pressure upon Sinkiang, Mongolia, and Manchuria, and Japanese pressure upon Korea, Manchuria, the Liu-chiu (Ryukyu) Islands, and Taiwan all combined to evoke an image of China being carved like a melon at the will of foreign powers.

In addition to the symbolic requirements of legitimacy, then, expansionistic tendencies in the Chinese component stem also from determination to advance disputed and vulnerable boundaries so as to recover strategic points of control. Weaker neighbors, such as India and Burma, offer opportunity for such forward pressure. Until 1960 both Nationalist and Communist maps either drew them well below those shown on Indian and Burmese maps, or showed southern boundaries as "still to be delimited." Similarly the two rival Chinese regimes agreed in identifying islands in the South China Sea, off Borneo and the Philippines, as under Chinese sovereignty. Even islands in the Amur River claimed by Russia appeared as Chinese on Peking's maps. While Soviet cartographers clearly indicated the Sino-Mongolian border, their Chinese counterparts termed it "still to be delimited." [4]

Xenophobia

Recurring xenophobia accentuated the expansionist element in Chinese foreign policy. This springs in part from traditional Chinese assumptions concerning the innate superiority of the Middle Kingdom as contrasted with "foreign barbarians." However, it has more objective causes, too, such as the erosion of territorial sovereignty under foreign pressure and the ideological penetration of Western commercial and missionary groups under the enforced protection of extraterritorial privileges. Peking was occupied in 1860 by European forces and in 1900 by American as well as European troops. Such expeditions extracted concessions and special privileges without reciprocity. Even as a member of the victorious coalitions in World Wars I and II, China had to cede control of territory to its allies, to Japan in the first case and to Soviet Russia in the second.

Manchu injunctions against "foreign devils" are amplified in Communist attacks against "foreign imperialists." Thus the cause of China's ills is persistently explained in terms of external enemies. Even Chiang Kai-shek, seldom without outside advice and assistance, blamed foreign powers for the collapse of traditional Chinese society and institutions.[5] Whatever truth there may be in these accusations, foreign scapegoats serve both internal psychological needs and external political goals.

Chinese hostility to foreigners has existed at various levels of society. Over the past century foreign troops in China repeatedly abused the populace and affronted Chinese dignity. The resulting hatred manifested itself in popular accounts of atrocities allegedly perpetrated by foreign missionaries and soldiers, and in sporadic but violent anti-foreign riots. At higher levels, official suspicion of Western governments fed on alleged injustices at the Versailles and Yalta conferences, following secret agreements among China's allies in the two world wars.

By 1949 xenophobia provided a ready audience in China for this typical Communist diatribe against the external threat:

> They [the imperialists] will not only send their running-dogs to bore inside China to carry out disruptive work and to cause trouble. They will not only use the Chiang Kai-shek bandit remnants to blockade our coastal ports, but they will send their totally hopeless adventurist elements and troops to raid and to cause trouble along our borders. They seek by every means and at all times to restore their position in China. They use every means to plot the destruction of China's independence, freedom, and territorial integrity and to restore their private interests in China. We must exercise the highest vigilance. . . . They cannot possibly be true friends of the Chinese people. They are the deadly enemies of the Chinese people's liberation movement.[6]

In sum, the expansionist and xenophobic elements in the Chinese component of policy provided three important points of reference for the new elite:

(1) reassertion of Chinese control over areas historically within the empire but under non-Chinese rule for more than half a century;

(2) redress of past injustices suffered at the hands of foreign powers;

(3) suspicion of foreign powers and, in particular, opposition to any implication of inferior status for China.

On this basis Russia was for many Chinese no less the target of criticism than other powers. Czarist practices in Sinkiang, Mongolia, and Manchuria exemplified foreign imperialism.[7] After World War II, Soviet stripping of factories in Manchuria and retention of railroad and military-base privileges in this area aroused concern in China. This concern persisted during the first years of the PRC, with open resentment expressed against Sino-Soviet joint-stock companies in Sinkiang and against reliance upon Russian economic and technical assistance.[8] At the official level, however, Mao's regime steadfastly countered all criticism of Soviet Russia. This showed the dominant role of ideology in the new policy frame of reference.

The Ideological Component

The ideological component reinforced some elements and modified others in the Chinese component of policy. It fostered the expansionist element through its messianic mission to spread Communism throughout the world. It reshaped the xenophobic element to exempt Soviet Russia and "socialist" countries from attack, while intensifying hostility against the United States and "capitalist" countries. Finally, it abandoned traditional Chinese assumptions concerning the desirability of compromise, by introducing a new element into the frame of reference: the inevitability of conflict among classes and nations.

Assumptions of Conflict

The ideological component is rooted in the articulated Communist credo of the new elite. As Mao Tse-tung declared in 1945, "From the very beginning our Party has been a party based on the theory of Marxism-Leninism, for Marxism-Leninism is the crystallization of the most correct and most revolutionary scientific thought of the world proletariat." [9] Foremost in this ideology is the goal of world Communism. Even in 1931, as a small armed band besieged by Nationalist armies in South China, the CCP proclaimed that it would, "under no condition, remain content with the overthrow of imperialism in China, but, on the contrary, will, as its ultimate objective, aim at waging a war against world imperialism until the latter is all blown up." [10]

This aggressive element in the Communist component is bolstered by a set of assumptions basic to Marxism-Leninism. These posit the destruction of capitalism as not only necessary to safeguard the existing socialist center but also desirable in order to create the universal good society. In the long run, only realization of the maximum goal of world domination will assure the minimum goal of Communist survival. Behind this argument is the assumption of omnipresent conflict. At the highest level, according to the Marxist-Leninist credo, conflict in the international arena brings capitalism and Communism into a life-and-death struggle. Although this conflict may be postponed and "peaceful co-existence" secured temporarily, the capitalists constantly seek to destroy Communism because of the challenge it poses to their own system.

As early as 1926, Mao echoed Lenin's doctrine of a bipolar world divided into two mutually antagonistic camps: "The present world situation is one in which the two big forces, revolution and counter-revolution, are engaged in the final struggle. . . . There is no room for any to remain 'independent.' " [11] Mao's denial of possible "independence" of the two warring camps led to repeated denunciations of neutralism or "a middle way." As a corollary Mao enunciated his famous "lean to one side" policy of exclusive alliance with the Soviet Union.

In 1940 his essay "On New Democracy" warned:

In the international situation of today the "heroes" in the colonies and semi-colonies must either stand on the side of the imperialist front and become part of the force of world counter-revolution or stand on the side of the anti-imperialist front and become part of the force of world revolution. They must stand either on this side or on the other, for there is no third choice.[12]

After Yugoslavia's expulsion from the Cominform in 1948, Liu Shao-ch'i, leading CCP theoretician, wrote:

If one is not in the imperialist camp, assisting American imperialism and its agents to enslave the world or one's own people, then one must be in the anti-imperialist camp. . . . To refrain from lining up on one side or the other and to keep neutral is impossible. . . . So-called neutralism . . . is nothing but deception, intentional or otherwise.[13]

The Soviet Alliance

Opposition to the "imperialist" camp and denial of a "neutral" path was paralleled by alliance with the Soviet Union. In 1940 Mao argued:

All the imperialist powers are hostile to us; if China wants independence she can never attain it without the aid of the socialist state and the international proletariat . . . without the assistance of the Soviet Union and the assistance given through anti-capitalist struggles waged by the proletariat in Japan, Britain, the United States, France, Germany, and Italy. . . . In particular, aid from the Soviet Union is an absolutely indispensable condition for China's final victory in the War of Resistance. Refuse Soviet aid and the revolution will fail.[14]

On the eve of victory he restated his policy in unmistakable terms:

You lean to one side. Precisely so . . . Chinese people either lean to the side of imperialism or to the side of socialism. To sit on the fence is impossible; a third road does not exist. . . . Internationally we belong to the anti-imperialist front headed by the U.S.S.R. and we can look for genuine friendly aid only from that front, and not from the imperialist front.[15]

The ideological component drastically modified a traditional Chinese admonition to "use barbarians to control barbarians." The Soviet Union was no temporary ally against more immediate enemies. Instead, an immutable, exclusive alliance was to bind China to Russia. Playing off one "barbarian" against another reappeared, however, in Mao's attention to "the universality of contradiction in imperialism." [16] Again following Lenin's lead, he wrote in 1940, "Our tactical principle remains one of exploiting the contradictions among them [the imperialists] in order to win over the majority, oppose the minority, and crush the enemies separately." [17]

The ideological component, then, provided the following assumptions underlying Peking's policy:

(1) the world is divided into a socialist or anti-imperialist camp and a capitalist or imperialist camp, each hostile to the other;

(2) neutrality is a camouflage for membership in the capitalist camp;

(3) alliance with the socialist camp is necessary to the success of the revolution in China and to its survival;

(4) alliance with the socialist camp is essential to promoting revolution throughout the world;

(5) the inevitable conflict between the two camps may be postponed temporarily by strengthening the unity of the socialist camp and by exploiting contradictions within the capitalist camp;

(6) the final victory inevitably belongs to Communism.

The Experiential Component

From its inception in 1921 to its seizure of power in 1949, the Chinese Communist Party developed in an environment singularly isolated from world affairs. It encountered little evidence to challenge a priori assumptions, while much of its experience reinforced stereotypes embodied in the ideological component. This was to influence the regime's reaction to the Korean War.

Limited Information and Contacts

Mao Tse-tung had never left China prior to his trip to Moscow in December 1949. The majority of his colleagues had never visited Western countries. Those who had been abroad in the early twenties associated largely with radical intellectual or workers' groups.[18] Nor was information about the outside world readily available to the CCP guerrilla bases. Between its break with the Kuomintang in 1927 and its re-establishment of a united front in 1937, the party relied exclusively on Soviet broadcasts for foreign news.[19] During World War II, the CCP headquarters in Yenan reported only dispatches from the Soviet news agency, TASS. An Englishman there at the time commented later on "the distorted view" of his associates, and concluded, "Up to 1948 . . . the Chinese Communist leadership was very badly informed on world affairs." [20] Only Chou En-lai, who represented the CCP in Chungking during the war, might be excluded from this judgment.

Isolation and misinformation may explain some of the distortion in CCP analyses of world affairs. In 1936 Mao discussed international problems at length with correspondent Edgar Snow, showing much interest but little grasp of facts.[21] His reliance on simplistic Soviet interpretations was reflected in his dismissal of Hitler as "a mere will-less puppet of the reactionary capitalists" and in his insistence that "Indian independence will never be real without an agrarian revolution." Equally fallacious was his prediction: "The Japanese revolution is not only a possibility but a certainty. It is inevitable and it will begin to occur promptly after the first severe defeat suffered by the Japanese Army."

Acceptance of Own Propaganda

Perhaps Mao spoke propagandistically while retaining more sophisticated judgments privately. The consistency of the bias in his erroneous forecasts, however, makes probable his wholehearted acceptance of Communist assumptions concerning world affairs. For instance, in 1940 Mao claimed that a lessening of "contradictions between Great Britain and America on the one hand and Japan on the other" might force China, under the leadership of Chiang Kai-shek, to "become engaged in a war against the Soviet Union through the provocation of Great Britain and America." [22]

Mao's misreading of international relations was shared by other CCP leaders who appeared to accept uncritically Soviet analyses. After World War II they depicted a United States tottering on the brink of economic collapse and facing imminent conflict with other capitalist countries as it wrested away their colonial holdings. Typical was this CCP statement in January 1947:

> The American economic crisis will arrive this year or next. . . . The American people, including enlightened members of the American bourgeoisie represented by Wallace, will certainly rise for a determined struggle with the reactionaries. . . . In the future, the possibility exists of America's inciting aggressive wars against other capitalistic countries (first of all Great Britain).[23]

Reinforcing Experiences

This distorted view of the world was reinforced by experiences which made this view seem correct. From 1937 to 1941 Western governments vacillated over resistance to Japan while Soviet Russia provided the sole military support for beleaguered China. This gave weight to CCP preconceptions concerning relations between "imperialist and semi-colonial countries."

Similarly, United States involvement in Chinese politics toward the close of World War II appeared to support Chiang Kai-shek and the Kuomintang (KMT) against the Chinese Communists. That this stemmed inevitably from the legal position of Chiang as head of the Republic of China made little difference to CCP analyses which ascribed

U.S. policy to "reactionary" machinations. Experience reinforced suspicion in Yenan, as is manifest in Mao Tse-tung's comments of 1945:

The U.S. Government's policy of supporting Chiang Kai-shek in the struggle against the Communist Party shows the rampancy of the American reactionaries. . . .[24]

[Ambassador to China] Hurley bluntly declared that the United States would cooperate only with Chiang Kai-shek but not with the Chinese Communist Party. This, of course, is not only Hurley's personal opinion but the opinion of a group of people in the U.S. government. . . . If Hurley's policy continues, the U.S. government will fall hopelessly into the deep, stinking cesspool of Chinese reaction. . . . It will place a crushing burden on the government and people of the United States and plunge them into endless woes and troubles.[25]

Despite the inconsistencies of subsequent U.S. moves in China which at times opposed Chinese Nationalist interests, the over-all impression of American support for Chiang seemed to confirm CCP expectations of imperialist hostility. Yet experience was selectively perceived. At this same time, Soviet depredations in Manchuria were explained away or excused as actions of "White Russians and ex-convicts freed from prisons in order to win a new life serving in the Red Army" and as "Russian customs which are different from Chinese customs." [26]

Provocative CCP Behavior

Experience reinforced in still another way the a priori assumptions of the ideological component. Many CCP actions exacerbated relations with the non-Communist world. When Nationalist forces evacuated Manchuria, United States consular officials remained in Mukden to maintain formal contact with the new regime. Within a month Red authorities placed all American diplomatic personnel there under house arrest. Eight months later several of the detainees were imprisoned and tried for alleged abuses of their servants. Meanwhile, in Peking and Tientsin, officials seized Economic Cooperation Administration stockpiles without prior negotiation and without receipts for the seized supplies. Throughout this period Communist communications media maintained a virulent anti-American propaganda campaign. Even the so-called "White Paper," which the State Department published in 1949 to refute critics demanding further American support for Chiang Kai-shek, was dismissed by Mao Tse-tung as fresh evidence of American enmity:

> Disrupt, fail, disrupt again, fail again, till their doom—that is the logic of imperialism and all reactionaries in the world. They will certainly not go against this logic. This is a Marxist law. We say: "Imperialism is very vicious." That means that its fundamental nature cannot be changed. Till their doom, the imperialist elements will not lay down the butcher's knife, nor will they ever turn into Buddhas.[27]

Such words and deeds aroused congressional and public opinion in the United States, leaving the Truman administration little choice but to withhold recognition from the People's Republic of China. This non-recognition policy, largely a result of Chinese Communist behavior, was in turn taken as further confirmation of Mao's strictures against American imperialism. These developments influenced the later interaction between Peking and Washington in the Korean War by reinforcing the xenophobic and aggressive elements in the Chinese and ideological components of policy.

Thus, past experience affected the outlook of the new regime in several ways:

(1) for most of its existence, the CCP leadership had seen the world through Soviet glasses, receiving information and interpretations of events chiefly from Moscow;

(2) lack of contact with the outside world permitted uncritical acceptance of Communist propaganda as reflecting reality;

(3) distortions of interpretation were reinforced by foreign behavior vis-à-vis China in general and the CCP in particular which "proved" the validity of Marxist assumptions concerning the capitalist world; and, finally,

(4) CCP actions toward their presumed enemies, of whom the United States was regarded as leader, exacerbated relations with these countries so as to provoke behavior which further strengthened CCP confidence in their assumptions about Western hostility and the need for Soviet support.

This schematic reconstruction of the frame of reference within which the new elite formulated policy in 1949–1950 leaves undetermined the relative weight of each component and its various elements. Without access to further materials on the actual formulation of policy, it would be impossible to determine the degree to which one or another factor received priority in Chinese Communist decisions. However, indirect evidence on this question is offered in the specific domestic and foreign policies adopted. After examining these policies for the light they throw on goal priorities, which in turn reflect the various influencing components, we shall have completed the background against which the Chinese Communist reaction to the Korean War can be more clearly understood.

II

PROBLEMS AND POLICIES

※

INAUGURATION OF THE People's Republic of China came amidst difficult domestic and foreign circumstances. At home the new regime faced a wholly stagnant economy, disrupted by more than ten years of foreign invasion, civil strife, and severe inflation. Chinese Communist Party land reform, with its wholesale transformation of the rural social and economic order, added still another disruptive element to production and distribution problems. Remnant Nationalist forces and hostile landed gentry engaged in armed opposition to Communism throughout the central and southern provinces. Chiang Kai-shek's aircraft conducted desultory raids over Shanghai and other cities, while his troops dominated Chinese coastal waters from widely scattered offshore islands. Taiwan and Hainan still stood as Nationalist bastions of some magnitude. Finally, Tibet remained in limbo, neither fully independent nor securely under Chinese control.

In the world at large, the so-called "cold war" pitted Soviet power against that of the United States in a wide arc extending from Berlin to Tokyo. Throughout much of this arc, crumbling colonial empires and newly independent countries offered fruitful ground for sowing seeds of Communist revolt. This international tension and instability, however, gave "new China" cause for anxiety over its own security. As an ally, Soviet Russia offered important political and material support, but the alliance was one of unequal partners, with the imbalance of power leaving China at a disadvantage. As an enemy, the United States posed a major threat with its avowed policy of "containing" international

Communism. This policy was manifested in Asia by the gradual transformation of Japan from vanquished foe into potential friend of America. Overshadowing the entire postwar scene was the ominous threat of
the atomic bomb, long available to the United States but only recently
developed in the Soviet Union.

We do not know the degree of optimism or pessimism that may have
colored Chinese Communist evaluation of these problems in 1949. It is
likely, however, that domestic and foreign policies were weighed with
due regard for the means available. In contrast with the precipitate
course of events that had catapulted the Bolsheviks to power in 1917,
the costly and prolonged struggle to win control of China equipped the
CCP leadership with ample experience of the need to correlate resources
with strategy. By reviewing the new regime's assessment of domestic
economic and military problems, we can sense some of the constraints
that may have influenced foreign-policy goals.

No single policy was dictated a priori by domestic conditions. On the
one hand, a limited, almost passive, international posture would permit
concentration of attention and energies on reconstruction of China's
shattered economy. On the other hand, a bold, aggressive foreign policy
might enhance the domestic prestige of the new regime. Similar alternatives arose for domestic policies. Some clues to the construct of policy
goals are provided by Peking's statements and actions during the winter
of 1949–1950. The handling of international recognition, negotiation
of the Sino-Soviet alliance, and Peking's self-proclaimed role in Asian
revolutionary movements provide our principal points of focus. While
it is impossible to determine the precise relationship between these matters and planning of the Korean War, alternative hypotheses on this
last problem will be reviewed in the light of our general reconstruction
of policy.

Economic Problems

In 1949 natural disasters hit the Chinese economy, already crippled
by more than a decade of foreign and civil war. Summer and fall rains
broke ten-year records, while pests and drought afflicted areas not hit by
floods.[1] Approximately forty million persons suffered from these phe-
nomena. The loss of an estimated six million tons of grain caused wide-

spread famine. Emergency relief measures strained transportation lines in disrepair from war and neglect.

Declining Productivity

Chinese Communist analysts painted a dark picture of economic stagnation. Agricultural acreage was less than two-thirds of prewar tillage, while output fell by more than 40 per cent.[2] Only half the prewar draft animals remained. Declines in hogs, sheep, and fertilizer reached 80 to 90 per cent. Farm tools were fewer by 40 to 60 per cent, depending upon the area. The estimates for 1950 postulated no more than a partial recovery, with output of important items, such as grain and cotton, well below prewar peaks.

Industrial production also declined, as shown by the following table:

TABLE 1

PHYSICAL OUTPUT IN CHINA IN 1949 COMPARED WITH
"PRE-LIBERATION" PEAKS

("Pre-liberation" Peak = 100)

Commodity	Percentage	Base Year
Power	72.3	1941
Coal	50.1	1942
Petroleum	38.1	1943
Pig iron	13.6	1943
Steel	17.2	1943
Cement	28.8	1942
Metal-cutting machines	29.4	1941
Cotton yarn	73.7	1933

SOURCE: *Communiqué of the State Statistical Bureau of China on the Development of National Economy and the Results of the Implementation of the State Plan for 1954*, issued by the State Statistical Bureau, Peking [1956?], as translated in *Current Background*, No. 382, American Consulate General, Hong Kong.

Following World War II, spiraling inflation swept China and further disrupted living standards. In December 1949, just prior to Mao Tsetung's departure for Moscow, an authoritative report warned, "The depreciation of the currency and the rise of commodity prices since mid-October have caused great losses to the people throughout the country, especially to the millions in the People's Liberation Army and the working people who live on wages." [3] The report blamed expanded military and governmental staffs required by the "newly Liberated Areas," together with low productivity, for the imbalance between currency in circulation and commodity supplies. Only a cut in government payrolls, chiefly military, and a rise in productivity, could remedy the crisis. The report concluded, "The burdens can be removed only when the entire country has been liberated, when the reactionary KMT troops have been completely wiped out and when the war has been concluded. It will not be too long."

Continued Military Expenditures

Yet the draft budget for 1950 allocated almost 40 per cent of expenditures for military purposes, with an anticipated deficit of nearly 20 per cent to be covered by additional paper currency.[4] The sober mood of the regime and its concern over the political as well as economic consequences of the budget are reflected in the following remarks of the Minister of Finance, Po I-po:

We shall still have to ask the peasantry to share the burden. For twelve years the peasants have provided both manpower and money, have made the greatest contributions. We have to be grateful to them. In the 1950 budget revenue from grain tax still occupies first place, i.e., 41.4% of the nation's total revenue. This tax burden on the average peasant is 19% of his total agricultural income and in the old Liberated Areas it is even 21%. Yet, for the time being, we cannot lighten the peasant's burden, for the sake of winning the war and restoring our economy. . . . We must point out to the military, administrative, government and education workers that at present difficulties are met on the road to victory so they need not complain about their hard life.

Po's allusion to peasant problems and the complaints of the less burdened came as Mao was preparing to negotiate the Sino-Soviet alliance. In time, Russian assistance could be a critical factor in alleviating economic distress. Meanwhile, however, more immediate solutions had to be found. On December 6th Mao ordered a decrease in military expenditures and the transfer of troops to productive activity. Noting that "the revenue of the country is insufficient to meet expenditures," Mao declared: "The chiefs of all military areas must instruct the troops under them to take part in the work of productive construction and to save part of the State expenditure. . . . This should be made into a movement, and a long-term plan and concrete steps worked out . . . [for] agriculture, stock raising, fishery, irrigation works, handicraft, construction works, industry, and transportation." [5]

With a slackening of inflation in March 1950, Mao repeated his order: "The financial condition of our country has begun to improve. . . . However, in order to bring about a fundamental turn for the better . . . considerable retrenchment in military and administrative expenditures by the state [is necessary]." [6] Liu Shao-ch'i's May Day address predicted, "After Taiwan is liberated the enemy's blockade and bombing will naturally end, the country's military expenditures can be greatly reduced, a great increase in investment in economic construction can then be made, and our country can move ahead on the road to transitional economic reconstruction." [7]

As a consequence, the 1950 budget for the Northeast (Manchuria) allocated less than 10 per cent for military expenditures, compared with more than 40 per cent in 1949.[8] This was praised as making possible the region's "first balanced budget." In the Northwest, a March directive suspended recruitment and established agricultural production teams among the troops.[9]

Finally in June, Mao, seconded by the CCP Central Committee, initiated demobilization of the People's Liberation Army:

The PLA, while preserving its main forces, should demobilize part of its troops in 1950, but only on condition that sufficient forces to liberate Taiwan and Tibet are guaranteed as well as sufficient forces to consolidate the national defense and suppress the counter-revolutionaries. This demobilization must be carried out with care so that demobilized soldiers can return home and settle down to productive work.[10]

Halting Inflation

The deflationary fiscal policies pursued during the first quarter of 1950 resulted in declining price levels in the late spring. By June the program had progressed to the point where the People's Bank of China could embark on a program of credit expansion both to state and to private investors.[11] Thus military retrenchment, austerity, and fiscal measures succeeded in checking inflation to the point where fresh monetary expansion could encourage expanding investment. The program of fiscal stability and increased productivity was based on a continuing decline in military expenditures. Beyond the announced campaigns against Tibet and Taiwan, it would appear that there was no anticipation of major military commitments in 1950, at least as far as Peking's economic planners were concerned.[12]

One final economic development pertinent to our study was the emphasis given industrialization of China's Northeast provinces, adjacent to North Korea. In 1949 the area had already proved its agricultural value by exporting 2.6 million tons of grain to deficient regions south of the Great Wall.[13] The 1950 harvest was expected to increase by 37 per cent. Similarly, 1950 output of machine tools, iron, and steel was to triple that of 1949, while coal and electric power were targeted at increases of 55 and 43 per cent respectively.

Even allowing for journalistic license, the following description of developments in Northeast China gives some measure of the area's importance in industrialization plans:

Northeast China holds the key to the industrialization of all China. This vast area constitutes a test-tube in which policies and methods for industrialization are being worked out, following which they will be applied extensively throughout the country. In addition the rest of China looks to Manchuria for the bulk of the machinery, steel, and other industrial goods needed to mechanize production during the coming years. . . . It has all the potential for becoming the Ruhr of Asia and one of the major industrial centers of the world.[14]

In short, Chinese Communist economic analyses indicated realistic appreciation of the immediate need for a stabilized currency, increased productivity, and lower military expenditures. Economic calculations may well have tempered the political elation of victory, introducing an element of caution into other areas of policy, lest they place added burdens upon the already strained resources of China.

Military Problems

In contrast with national economics, military problems offered a familiar challenge to the CCP leadership. For more than twenty years, Mao Tse-tung, Chou En-lai, Chu Teh, and the other Politburo members had literally fought their way to power. Now they commanded five million troops, equipped with Japanese supplies conveniently abandoned by the retiring Red Army in Manchuria and with American booty captured from Nationalist units.[15] From a purely guerrilla organization, the PLA had developed into a massive force capable of both positional and mobile warfare, unequaled in Asia.

Yet this force was not an unmixed blessing. In addition to the aforementioned economic problems that it posed, the PLA was too large for the available munitions industry to support over prolonged periods of action. Deficiencies were acute in heavy artillery, armored vehicles, and ammunition. Air power was conspicuous by its absence, as was naval power. Finally, the rapid expansion that had quadrupled the PLA in four years seriously diluted its political as well as its military reliability. Small wonder that Mao assigned troops to labor brigades pending gradual demobilization.

Nationalist Opposition

Several tasks remained, however, before demobilization. First, anti-Communists, ranging from traditional bandits to remnant Nationalist guerrillas, threatened much of central, southern, and western China. In Hunan, for instance, 200,000 PLA troops engaged in "bandit suppression" throughout the spring of 1950.[16] Similar resistance in Sinkiang, Kansu, Szechuan, and Yünnan compelled continued "pacification," despite Mao's claim of victory in the mainland civil war.[17]

Formal Nationalist opposition on the offshore islands, as well as Taiwan and Hainan, posed a different problem. Inexperienced in amphibious operations, PLA commanders warned of the difficulties confronting further moves against the Chiang Kai-shek forces. In February 1950, General Su Yü, addressing the Third Field Army assigned to attack the offshore islands and Taiwan, detailed the obstacles which lay ahead. His words merit quotation at length since they indicate the mood of authoritative estimates at the time:

I must first of all point out that the liberation of the islands along the southeast coast, especially Taiwan, is an extremely big problem and will involve the biggest campaign in the history of modern Chinese warfare. . . . [Taiwan] cannot be occupied without sufficient transport, suitable equipment, and adequate supplies. Furthermore a considerable number of Chiang Kai-shek land, sea, and air forces are concentrated there together with a batch of the most intransigent reactionaries who have fled from China's mainland. They have built strong defense works, depending on the surrounding sea for protection. At the instigation of the American imperialists, they have invited in a group of Japanese militarists. . . . One must realize these are new difficulties that have arisen in the course of our war. Only when we have fully prepared the material and technical conditions for overcoming these difficulties can we smoothly carry out this tremendous military assignment and thoroughly eradicate the KMT remnants.[18]

General Su's remarks jibed with PLA experience up to that time. In October 1949 a Communist assault upon the island of Kinmen (Quemoy) had been smashed by well-entrenched Nationalist defenders. Furthermore, in early 1950 a serious epidemic of schistosomiasis infected thousands of Third Army troops training along the streams of Chekiang and Fukien for amphibious landings on Taiwan.[19]

In April, however, crack units from General Lin Piao's Fourth Field Army climaxed their swing down through central China with invasion of Hainan Island. By the end of the month, a Red victory was assured. Third Field Army units, "entrusted with the task of liberating Taiwan, sent delegations to Hainan to study the successful operations there." [20] One month later, General Su's forces seized the Chusan Islands, near Shanghai. The authoritative *Jen Min Jih Pao* (People's Daily) hailed both operations as harbingers of victory against Taiwan, "the last battle in completing the liberation and unification of our country." [21]

Taiwan and Tibet

The delay in pursuing the Nationalists from the mainland to Taiwan seems to have been dictated by the logistics of attacking across more than one hundred miles of open water. In addition, hope of political subversion on Taiwan may have argued for postponement of the difficult amphibious operation. During early 1950, Nationalist counter-intelligence agents discovered Communist activity in high military circles and may have nipped in the bud an insurrection essential to Peking's plans.

Communist concern over the reaction of the United States is one factor, however, which does not seem to have deterred Peking from this venture. General Su made no reference to American military opposition as such. He apparently took at face value President Truman's disclaimer of "any intention of utilizing armed forces to interfere in the present situation. The United States Government will not pursue a course which will lead to involvement in the civil conflict in China. Similarly the United States will not provide military aid or advice to Chinese forces on Formosa." [22] Peking's propaganda charged that a "secret treaty" pledged American assistance to Taiwan in return for bases, but the charge was groundless. Down to June 25, 1950, no United States military activity occurred on Taiwan.

In short, the evidence makes credible the proclaimed intentions of the Chinese Communists to invade Taiwan in 1950. Hong Kong dispatches correctly described Third Field Army training for this task. The build-up of transport was reflected in an informed summary of United States intelligence reports to the effect that by June "virtually all preparations had been completed for the invasion of Formosa." [23] Peking's exhortations to units stationed opposite the island paralleled those broadcast prior to the Hainan invasion as the time of attack approached.

In addition to Taiwan, increasing attention was given to the imminent invasion of Tibet. This required less preparation, however, and faced less formidable resistance. The assignment lay well within the capability of forces already in South China. As of June 1950, the bulk of the PLA seemed scheduled for "pacification" and economic construction assignments, pending gradual conversion to civilian status. Although this is a speculative reconstruction of Chinese Communist military plans for 1950, it is compatible with the regime's economic calculations, its announced intentions, and its disposition of forces.

Northeast Build-Up

In mid-1950 a somewhat ambiguous movement of troops into Manchuria took place. In April redeployment of the Fourth Field Army from terminal assignments in South China and Hainan shifted units back to their starting point in Northeast China. The month-long journey from Canton to Mukden returned these troops to permanent bases where they joined other Fourth Field Army detachments in agricultural, forestry, and construction tasks.[24] Between the middle of May and early July, more than 60,000 troops entered the Northeast Region, adjacent to North Korea, bringing the total strength there to approximately 180,000 men.[25] This redeployment implemented directives on assignment of units to construction projects. It was paralleled by troop movements elsewhere, returning units to points of origin from which they had begun pursuit of Nationalist forces, or to permanent bases in designated army command areas. No troops other than those from the Fourth Field Army entered Northeast China at this time.

This does not exclude the possibility, however, that the build-up in Northeast China just prior to the North Korean attack served additional functions beyond those attending redeployment for peaceful purposes. It placed Peking's best troops in a position to backstop Pyongyang, in the event North Korean plans went awry. Further consideration will be given to this possibility when we review alternative hypotheses concerning China's relationship with the outbreak of war in Korea. At this point, however, it is important to note the military concentration in Northeast China as possible evidence of early Chinese participation in planning for the Korean War.

Diplomatic Problems

The foreign policy of the People's Republic of China can be divided into two parts, diplomatic and revolutionary. The first concerned formal relations with other countries, involving such matters as exchange of recognition and negotiation of the Sino-Soviet alliance. The second, the revolutionary aspect, concerned relations with Asian Communist parties and insurrectionary movements. A review of developments in these two areas during 1949–1950 will facilitate analysis of Peking's general foreign policy on the eve of the Korean War.

Recognition

On September 29, 1949, the Chinese People's Political Consultative Conference proclaimed a "Common Program" which contained, *inter alia,* a statement of foreign-policy principles.[26] Article 2 pledged to "unite with all peace-loving and freedom-loving countries and peoples throughout the world, first of all with the USSR, all Peoples' Democracies and all oppressed nations. It [the PRC] shall take its stand in the camp of international peace and democracy, to oppose imperialist aggression, to defend lasting world peace."

This declaration set the tone for other points in the "Common Program." The regime was to "abolish all the prerogatives of imperialist countries in China" (Article 3) and "examine the treaties and agreements concluded between the Kuomintang and foreign governments" in order to "recognize, abrogate, revise, or renegotiate them" (Article 55). Diplomatic relations "on the basis of equality, mutual benefit and mutual respect for territory and sovereignty" would be negotiated with those governments which "have severed relations with the Kuomintang reactionary clique and which adopt a friendly attitude towards the People's Republic of China" (Article 56). For "commercial relations," however, only "a basis of equality and mutual benefit" was a prerequisite (Article 57).

The attack upon "prerogatives of imperialist countries" reflected the Chinese component of policy in its insistence on eliminating past marks of international inferiority. This was equally manifest in the pledge to "abrogate, revise, or renegotiate" existing treaties. It was the Communist component, however, which postulated a "camp of international peace and democracy" opposed to one of "imperialist aggression." Peking's handling of recognition seems to have been conditioned primarily by this latter, divisive principle. Bloc countries consistently received favored treatment, manifested by PRC acknowledgment of offers of recognition, the conclusion of agreements to exchange representatives, and the arrival of PRC envoys.

By the end of October 1949, an exchange of representatives had been agreed upon with all the Communist-bloc countries but Albania. Yet the Yugoslav recognition offer of October 5th was not even acknowledged by Peking, officially or unofficially. To be sure, Tito had "severed relations with the Kuomintang reactionary clique" and manifested "a friendly attitude towards the People's Republic of China" as dictated by the "Common Program." His expulsion from the Cominform in 1948, however, left him beyond the pale as far as the "camp of international peace and democracy" was concerned.

Within the bloc, Sino-Soviet relations received prior attention. On October 16th the U.S.S.R. ambassador accepted accreditation in Peking as the first foreign envoy to the PRC. On November 3rd his Chinese counterpart was received in Moscow. Not until July 1950 did PRC representatives arrive elsewhere, appearing in Mongolia and Poland that month. Nearby Pyongyang did not receive a PRC ambassador until August 13, 1950. By June 1950 formal relations had been established between the PRC and twenty-five countries, of which eleven were Communist controlled. Among the fourteen non-bloc countries, five had agreed to an exchange of representatives, namely, Sweden, Denmark, India, Burma, and Indonesia, in that order. When the Korean War began, the Swedish, Danish, and Indian representatives were the only non-Communist envoys in Peking. The Burmese ambassador arrived August 7, 1950. Chinese envoys to all five countries except Indonesia arrived during September and October 1950.

Great Britain's offer of recognition on January 6, 1950, was rejected in an official protest against British consular activity on Taiwan, British failure to support PRC admission to the United Nations, and questions of property control in Hong Kong. Peking seemed willing to forego the advantages of trade and prestige that would accrue from British recognition, in order to give a practical demonstration of respect for the Communist categorization of countries as "peace-loving" or as "imperialist." Later that spring a Chinese "friendship delegation" in England reflected this hostile attitude. Appearing almost exclusively before Communist-front groups, it declined invitations from other sources. Its chairman, Liu Ning-i, saw Labour Government officials once. Speaking before them at a luncheon, he sharply attacked Labour policies in an address that he immediately issued to the press.[27] As for the United States, recognition from Washington was made impossible by the incessant attacks against American policy as well as by the abuses against American personnel and property mentioned in Chapter I.

The deliberate twisting of the lion's tail was exemplified by Peking's choice of January 6, 1950, the previously announced date of British recognition, for posting notices on the British and American consulates general, and on the French and Netherlands embassy offices, declaring that after seven days, "former military barracks" of these governments would be "requisitioned." On January 14th the properties were seized. They had been held through treaty provisions. None of the Dominion governments followed the British lead in offering recognition, perhaps because of this move.[28]

In short, Peking seemed to disparage recognition in so far as it depended upon favorable relations with non-Communist governments. Officially it claimed that British abstentions in the United Nations on the question of admitting the People's Republic of China impeded relations between the two countries. Yet by rejecting recognition the Chinese Communists further reduced the prospects for British support in the U.N. Nor were France and America likely to support Soviet resolutions in the Security Council on behalf of PRC admission after the seizure of their properties in China.

The new regime did not wholly ignore the United Nations. On November 15, 1949, and on January 8 and January 15, 1950, Chou En-lai cabled Lake Success demanding the ouster of "Kuomintang reactionary clique representatives" from international organs.[29] Domestic propaganda featured Soviet activities in the U.N., including the January departure of Jacob Malik from the Security Council in protest against the presence of T. F. Tsiang, appointed by Chiang Kai-shek's regime. The Soviet boycott of Lake Success continued throughout the spring, remaining in effect at the outbreak of the Korean War.

It is difficult to determine the precise importance accorded the U.N. in Chinese Communist policy. Perhaps inexperience prompted Peking to expect immediate admission, regardless of its diplomatic posture. Whatever its expectations, the results of its actions were of lasting importance. First, the new leadership remained personally isolated from almost the entire non-Communist world during the first months of the Korean War. Second, the increasing international criticism of PRC attitudes and actions reinforced a priori CCP assumptions concerning the hostility of the non-Communist world. These developments made Sino-Soviet relations of unique importance for the People's Republic of China.

The Sino-Soviet Alliance

In contrast with its somewhat dilatory handling of world recognition, the new regime gave immediate attention to Sino-Soviet relations. On December 16, 1949, Mao arrived in Moscow on his first known trip abroad. More than Stalin's birthday dictated his visit. In response to a TASS inquiry concerning the duration of his stay, Mao replied: "I have come for several weeks. The length of my sojourn here depends in part upon the amount of time which it will take to solve the questions of interest to the People's Republic of China." [30] He elaborated briefly: "Among them, first of all, are such questions as the existing treaty of friendship and alliance between China and the USSR, the question of Soviet credits to the PRC, the question of trade and a trade agreement between our two countries, and others."

Mao's words implied that prolonged negotiations might be necessary to reach agreement on these issues. Thus his stay would not follow the pattern of short visits by East European leaders for summary acceptance of Soviet terms. Mao's ten weeks in Moscow, supplemented on January 21, 1950, by the arrival of Chou En-lai and others, took on added significance in view of the array of problems in Peking which demanded attention. Not until March 4th did the Mao-Chou entourage return to the affairs of state in the PRC.

Among the many issues lumped under Mao's vague allusion to "other" questions, the Korean problem may have held high priority. Yet there is no direct evidence on the negotiations beyond the official documents, and these cover only those matters referred to explicitly in Mao's statement. His reference to the 1945 Sino-Soviet treaty, concluded with the Chiang Kai-shek government, touched on the most far-reaching matter under discussion.[31] That pact bound the two countries to mutual military assistance in the event of an attack upon either party by Japan. This was significantly changed in the 1950 treaty to include attack "by Japan or any state allied with it." Foreign Minister Chou En-lai explicitly identified the target of this phraseology as "American imperialism." [32] The problem of U.S.-Japan relations as they affected Sino-Soviet relations will be examined more fully in the next chapter. Yet it must be noted at this point that the extended conditions of Soviet military support probably represented China's most important gain at the Moscow conference. Given the doctrinaire mistrust of imperialism and the association of the United States both with Chiang Kai-shek and more recently with a resurgent Japan, this reassurance of Russian protection undoubtedly made the Soviet alliance seem worth whatever material or political costs it might entail.

That Russian support was not an unmixed blessing for Mao was evident from the need to refute "anti-Soviet" criticism, both before and after this trip.[33] Chinese objections to Soviet troops in Port Arthur, Russian-leased facilities in Dairen, and Soviet advisers in the Northeast Region may have strengthened Mao's position in prompting Stalin to assuage Chinese sensitivities by modifying the 1945 agreements. In any event, the established thirty-year terms for "joint" Sino-Soviet control of the Port Arthur naval base, of the harbor at Dairen, and of the Chinese Changchun Railway disappeared. Instead, exclusive Chinese ownership of all facilities was guaranteed "immediately on the conclusion of the peace treaty with Japan, but not later than the end of 1952." The delayed transfer of control may have been a compromise between the Chinese desire to regain immediate possession and the Chinese need to gain experience in the various enterprises, especially the naval installations.

While the railway facilities were to be turned over "without compensation," payment was necessary for the naval properties at Port Arthur. The disposition of Dairen harbor, the only warm-water port available to Russia on the Pacific, was to be settled only after "conclusion of the peace treaty with Japan." Furthermore, elimination of Soviet controls in the Northeast was offset somewhat by establishment of Sino-Soviet joint-stock companies in Sinkiang for petroleum, nonferrous and rare metals, and civil aviation.[34] Their duration, thirty years, was identical with the abandoned 1945 terms for "joint" operations in Manchuria.[35]

These provisions show evidence of bargaining. We do not know how, if at all, the "war booty" seized by Russia in Manchuria during 1945–1946 entered the discussions. The replacement value of the removed Japanese industrial plant was estimated by a U.S. commission at $2,000,000,000. Perhaps this was set against the transfer of railway properties which, unlike the naval installations, required no compensation.

Mao's reference to "the question of Soviet credits to China" culminated in agreement for a Soviet loan of U.S. $300,000,000, repayable over ten years at interest of 1 per cent per year. Repayments were to commence not later than December 31, 1954. This assured reasonable terms for badly needed industrial equipment at a time when Peking had little prospect of credit elsewhere.[36] While it is difficult to assess the degree to which this satisfied Chinese Communist expectations, the loan probably provided additional proof of the advantages of alliance with Russia.[37]

Without access to further materials, one can only offer a tentative estimate of the Mao-Stalin exchanges. No publicity was given to important agreements concerning trade procedures, diplomatic immunities, property transfers in Manchuria, and the specific structure of the joint-stock companies.[38] This secrecy suggests that Russian bargaining power gained advantages for the Soviet Union on these matters. In particular, dissolution of the joint-stock companies by Stalin's successors, four years later, indicated that their establishment in 1950 had caused friction in Sino-Soviet relations.[39]

Yet whatever minor disappointments Mao may have suffered, he could well consider the basic agreement beneficial for "new China." Russia's modern military might offered protection against Japan, and perhaps against the United States as well. Delay in the Soviet withdrawal from Port Arthur anchored a line of security extending through North Korea to Vladivostok. Secret protocols for Russian assistance in reorganizing and re-equipping the PLA may well have been agreed upon at this time. Furthermore, a foundation for China's heavy industry was assured by the Soviet loan, while the Russians simultaneously abandoned economic controls in Manchuria. Against these gains, accession to Soviet demands for joint-stock companies in Sinkiang was a small price to pay.

The asymmetry of power in the relative positions of Stalin and Mao suggests that concern for Chinese xenophobia may have inhibited Stalin against forcing too hard a bargain lest latent "Tito-ist" forces strain the alliance. The treaty pledged co-operation "in conformity with the principles of equality, mutual interest, and also respect for national sovereignty and territorial integrity and non-interference in the internal affairs of the other party." This phraseology occurred in none of the agreements then in effect between Moscow and the East European regimes. Without knowledge of the initial Russian and Chinese drafts of the agreement, it is not possible to prove the significance of these words. However, they anticipated by six years similar Russian statements in 1956 on the principles governing bloc relations. It is likely that Stalin moved, however grudgingly, to strengthen the fledgling regime in pursuit of common ends. Ideologically, both countries shared the goal of advancing Communism in Asia; strategically, they faced a hostile United States moving toward alliance with a foreseeably re-armed Japan. Common aims and dangers gave substance to the new Sino-Soviet alliance, which also was basic to Mao's conception of Communist China's role in Asia.

Revolution in Asia

Peking proclaimed itself the leader of "national liberation" and Communist movements in Asia. With the apparent acquiescence of Moscow, this self-defined role was manifest in statements by the new elite as well as in its press treatment of other Asian regimes. Together with the Sino-Soviet alliance, this development indicated the degree to which ideology prevailed over traditional Chinese influences in the formation of policy.

On November 16, 1949, Liu Shao-ch'i addressed the Trade Union Conference of Asian and Australasian Countries in Peking, under the auspices of the Russian-directed World Federation of Trade Unions (WFTU). Next to Mao, Liu ranked as the foremost CCP theoretician, and his directive to Asian revolutionary movements clearly outlined their course according to the victorious strategy of the CCP:

The path taken by the Chinese people in defeating imperialism and its lackeys and in founding the People's Republic of China is the path that should be taken by the peoples of the various colonial and semi-colonial countries in their fight for national independence and people's democracy.[40]

He then detailed the "united front" that was to embrace all "who are willing to oppose imperialism and its lackeys" under the leadership of the Communist Party as opposed to "the wavering and compromising national bourgeoisie." In addition, "wherever and whenever possible a national army which is led by the Communist Party" was to conduct "armed struggle [which] is the main form of struggle for the national liberation of many colonies and semi-colonies."

Liu's formula followed, point by point, what has since become known in the West as "the Maoist strategy." [41] Its enunciation at this time (November 1949) and under WFTU auspices appeared to signal the resolution of differences in the Soviet Union as to the degree to which Chinese experience should serve as a model for revolution in Asia.[42] If so, then the Soviet leadership now accorded Mao a role consonant with Chinese aspirations for Asian leadership. The Communist interpretation of that role involved attacks upon already independent regimes, implementing ideological assumptions about the omnipresence of conflict and the world division into two camps. Peking jeopardized its acceptance by governments in South Asia, as well as their support in international matters, by urging revolt in all countries where the leadership had not expressly rejected the United States and accepted the Soviet Union.

For our purposes, the critical element in the "Maoist strategy" is its treatment of the "national bourgeoisie," or more generally, of non-Communist nationalist leaders.[43] This fostered presumptions and prejudices concerning such persons as Jawaharlal Nehru before the experience of dealing with them in the Korean War and its attendant negotiations. Just as Mao, Liu, and others had insisted over the previous decade that for China there was no "neutrality," no "third road," so now the line was drawn for other Asian leaders according to their stand on "international imperialism" and domestic Communism. The responsibilities of state and the acceptance of recognition from New Delhi did not mitigate Chinese Communist attacks upon Nehru as a "running-dog of British-American imperialists." [44] In April 1950, despite China's official ties with Burma, India, and Indonesia, one Chinese writer asserted that "Burma, Indonesia, Malaya, the Philippines, South Korea, etc. have large people's struggles within them, correctly and justly striving for liberation. India, Thailand, and Near

Eastern countries . . . are just beginning their liberation struggle."[45] He singled out Nehru as being "at the beck and call of the imperialists after his rise, in August 1947. . . . India's anti-Communist movement of the reactionaries is worked from behind the scenes by the American imperialists."

Charges of "American imperialism" dominated Peking's propaganda on Asia. *Jen Min Jih Pao* ridiculed those who relied upon the United States, which "talks with great hypocrisy about 'national independence' for the 'backward countries.' "[46] Only "leaning to one side," that is, affiliation with the Soviet bloc, could provide genuine independence. "This is especially significant for the people of Southeast Asia," Chou En-lai warned. "America . . . seized control over Japan and South Korea after World War II, but is also attempting to control China, Indonesia, Viet-Nam, Thailand, Burma, and India."[47] A book reflecting the official viewpoint included in the "imperialist camp" the ruling groups of India, Burma, Thailand, and the Philippines, who were said to be "dependent upon imperialism."[48]

China's revolutionary policy, frankly aiming at the overthrow of neighboring elites, precluded any successful bid for Asian leadership in the traditional diplomatic sense. Out of harmony with older Chinese values as it was, the policy was fully consistent with Communist values. Furthermore it was not countered by experience, for up to then the CCP remained wholly isolated from "bourgeois" Asian groups.

This policy was to change as non-Communist Asian leaders during the Korean War diverged sharply from United States policy. Until June 1950, however, Peking emphasized its revolutionary role in Asia. Despite recognition from neighboring regimes, Chinese Communist statements evidenced clear hostility toward all who refused to join the "anti-imperialist camp" against the United States.

Within the general framework of policy, a minimum-maximum program of objectives emerged, embracing both traditional and Communist elements. In the immediate future, territorial sovereignty was to be reestablished inside the imperial frontiers. This required the "liberation" of Taiwan and Tibet. In the intermediate future, China was to direct and assist "national liberation," that is, Communist subversion and insurrection, in Southeast Asia. This would extend Chinese as well as Communist influence. In the distant future, Peking would head an

Asian Communist bloc. So ran the pattern of Chinese aspirations and expectations.

Indispensable to this program was the Sino-Soviet alliance. Not only did its political prestige elevate Peking's international status as co-leader of world Communism. Its strategic and economic support safeguarded China's material advance toward primacy in Asia. The foreseeable future would heavily tax the energies and resources of the new regime if domestic political security and economic reconstruction were to be secured. China's dependence on the U.S.S.R. conditioned the degree of political, as distinguished from material, support she could furnish to Communist movements elsewhere in Asia. Yet in time even the Sino-Soviet alliance was to be reshaped so as to erode Russian dominance, both within and over China. Long before that point neared, however, serious miscalculations in Korea faced the new alliance with the unanticipated risks of a major war.

III

RUSSIA, CHINA,
AND THE KOREAN WAR

※

IN RECONSTRUCTING the Chinese Communist frame of reference for foreign policy, our analysis has been largely conjectural because of the fragmentary nature of the evidence. This is even more true of the relations among Moscow, Peking, and Pyongyang on the eve of the Korean War. In considering these relations, however, we may still weigh the available evidence against alternative hypotheses concerning Peking's responsibility for, and interest in, the Korean War.

First, we shall examine the problem of Japan as a possible factor in the origins of the war.[1] The documents published after the Mao-Stalin conferences expressed Sino-Soviet concern over the *rapprochement* of Japanese and American policy. A Communist victory in Korea would offset, and perhaps reverse, the trend in Washington-Tokyo relations. Second, we shall reconstruct the comparative influence of the Soviet and Chinese Communist parties upon North Korean developments prior to the war. The record suggests that, during the 1945–1949 period, Moscow steadily increased its control over Pyongyang to the detriment of Korean groups oriented toward the Chinese Communist Party. In fact, the newly established Democratic People's Republic of Korea (DPRK) was, from all available evidence, a full-fledged Soviet satellite.

This, in turn, raises the basic question of determining Peking's role in the planning of the Korean War. Russian and Chinese Communist materials on this subject are uniformly propagandistic, deny all Soviet or Chinese responsibility, and insist that Syngman Rhee's "puppet troops" began the conflict. Therefore we can only conjecture the answer to important questions concerning the inception of the Korean War. Did the Chinese Communists play a major role in initiating the North Korean attack? Did the Soviet Union assign them any responsibility for supporting that attack? Or were they aware of its imminence without having responsibility for its outcome? What was their interest, as differentiated from their responsibility, in the Korean War? To the degree that we can refine our understanding of these questions, we shall make easier our subsequent examination of the Chinese Communist reaction to the unfolding of the war in the summer of 1950.

Japan: The Common Problem

For more than half a century China's statesmen had turned to Russia for assistance against the threat posed by Japan, their common enemy. Li Hung-chang under the Manchus and Chiang Kai-shek as leader of the Kuomintang found this threat sufficiently critical to compel negotiations with the neighbor to the north.[2] Mao Tse-tung, as head of "new China," explained his alliance with Stalin in similar terms. By 1950 the danger was far less immediate, following the shattering defeat of Japan in World War II. But this by no means had eliminated the possibility of her return as a strong military power in northeast Asia. On the contrary, the prospect of a Japanese-American alignment raised the possibility that the two major industrial countries of the Pacific littoral would merge their might in an anti-Communist coalition.

American Occupation Policies, 1947–1949

To be sure, such an alignment was far from realization in 1950. Japan was still an unarmed, occupied nation, while United States military preparedness remained at a relatively low level. Yet more than past Chinese defeats by Japan and Communist revulsion against "the imperialist camp" underlay Peking's expressed concern over "American imperialism rearming Japanese militarism." By 1948 important changes had appeared in the policies of General Douglas A. MacArthur, Supreme Commander for the Allied Powers (SCAP). Chief of these was the shift from restriction to rehabilitation of Japanese industry, attended by the shift from encouragement to restriction of Japanese labor activity.[3] In view of the standard Marxist tendency to associate Japanese industrial interests with military expansionism, and in view of the postwar surge of left-wing influence in Japanese labor unions, it is no surprise that Russia and Chinese propaganda evidenced growing concern over these developments.

Moreover, Allied discussions in 1949 signaled readiness to conclude a separate peace treaty with Japan, by-passing Soviet obstructionist tactics which had stalemated negotiations on the parallel German question. Such a separate peace treaty might give rise to a totally different Japan from the demilitarized state envisaged in the postwar constitution.[4] Informed Tokyo press reports described SCAP headquarters as urging not only a separate treaty but also long-term American leases of air, land, and naval bases in Japan.

For Moscow and Peking this chain of developments took on added significance when placed beside events in Western Europe. Establishment of the North Atlantic Treaty Organization foreshadowed a military defense network, centered upon the United States, which would ultimately embrace a rearmed West Germany. In the Pacific, a prolonged American occupation of Japan, or an independent Japan containing United States military bases, could provide the basis for a similar network that would not only hamper Communist advances in Asia but might seriously threaten the new Chinese regime.

The Japanese Communist Party (JCP) was a weak instrument with which to counter American policy. In January 1949, JCP electoral strength reached its postwar peak of 9.5 per cent. This carried little weight against the overwhelming support enjoyed by the conservative Yoshida government, which hewed close to the United States line. For the JCP, the parliamentary road to power seemed long and uncertain. In late 1949 Moscow appears to have decided upon more direct pressure against Japan. If Nippon could not be won over through indigenous radical forces, she must be frightened away from America through exploitation of domestic opposition to "militarism" and to involvement in the "cold war."

The Soviet Response

In December 1949 Moscow manifested a new harshness by trying captive Japanese officers on charges of "bacteriological warfare." In January 1950 the Communist Information Bureau (Cominform) ordered the JCP to supplement peaceful parliamentary tactics with a militant attack against imperialism and capitalism, in the streets as well as in the press. In February the Soviet Union increased its criticism of the Yoshida government and demanded that Emperor Hirohito be tried as a war criminal. Concurrent with these developments were the Mao-Stalin conferences, climaxed by the Sino-Soviet Treaty of Alliance specifically directed against "the revival of Japanese imperialism and the resumption of aggression on the part of Japan or any other state that may collaborate in any way with Japan in acts of aggression." [5]

There is no reason to doubt Chinese Communist support for these Russian moves. When the JCP initially resisted the Cominform directive of January 6th, *Jen Min Jih Pao* administered a vigorous rebuff to the Japanese comrades, throwing its weight completely behind the call for renewed militancy.[6] Throughout the spring of 1950 Peking echoed Moscow's attacks against Yoshida and "the U.S. plot to revive Japanese imperialism." This served to strengthen the hostile image of the United States in CCP domestic propaganda by linking America with China's recent invader. It also probably represented a genuine conviction at higher levels that serious danger lay ahead if the course of Japanese-American relations were not reversed.

In view of the multiple pressures directed at Japanese foreign policy, the Communist leaders may have conceived the Korean War as serving ends beyond the immediate control of the peninsula. Military victories in Taiwan and Korea could be heralded as ushering in the Communist era in Asia, and as demonstrating the impotence of America's "puppets," Chiang Kai-shek and Syngman Rhee. The resultant effect upon Japan might swing opportunistic groups behind existing neutralist opposition to Yoshida and prevent his supporting American policy.

Should this political calculation misfire, there was a risk that Japanese opinion might be panicked into an early alliance with the United States. Yet two considerations may have made this risk seem tolerable. First, an eventual alliance was already foreshadowed by the events of

1948–1950; all previous efforts on the part of Moscow and the JCP had failed to stem this trend. Second, should Japan draw closer to the United States, the political losses might be offset somewhat by extending Communist control throughout the Korean peninsula. In conjunction with Sakhalin and the Kurile Islands, Korea completed a "defense perimeter" of considerable importance for Moscow and Peking. Defensively, it provided a forward shield protecting the industrial center of Manchuria and the political center of North China. Offensively, it provided advance bases for dominating the Sea of Japan and the East China Sea, as well as for attack on U.S. bases in Japan.

Prospects of North Korean Victory

Assuming, as our analysis has so far done, that the Soviet Union planned the attack in Korea, how might it have calculated the prospects of North Korean victory? In particular, how might it have viewed the probable U.S. response to a Communist crossing of the thirty-eighth parallel?

So far as a DPRK-ROK confrontation was concerned, Soviet planners were undoubtedly confident of an easy victory. Republic of Korea forces were markedly inferior in equipment, while espionage and subversion further reduced their effectiveness. Communist intelligence sources in South Korea presumably had good information on these matters. American newspaper reports painted a similar picture of ROK defenses and, in June 1950, Ambassador John C. Muccio expressly warned a congressional committee of the deficiencies in South Korean military preparedness. Since the withdrawal of American forces from the country in 1949, no significant strengthening of ROK units had occurred. Instead, congressional opposition to economic and military assistance for South Korea had thwarted Administration efforts in this direction.

The question of the likely U.S. response to an invasion of South Korea was more complicated, but there is good reason to believe Soviet strategy discounted it in advance. New U.S. military commitments in Western Europe and growing congressional parsimony with respect to Asia resulted in a defense posture unconducive to effective American military action in Korea. The available forces in Japan appeared to be too small to play a significant role in a short war, and serious logistical difficulties hampered quick reinforcement from bases in Hawaii and the United States. The allocation of American resources and manpower were frankly discussed during the spring of 1950 in a relatively public manner, making it credible that Soviet calculations followed some such reasoning as the above.[7]

In addition to these indications of American weakness in Northeast Asia, specific statements from high U.S. officials may have encouraged Soviet calculations to downgrade the likelihood of a U.S. military response in Korea. In 1949 General MacArthur had implicitly excluded South Korea from the American defense perimeter, noting, "Now the Pacific has become an Anglo-Saxon lake and our line of defense runs through the chain of islands fringing the coast of Asia. It starts from the Philippines and continues through the Ryukyu archipelago which includes its broad main bastion, Okinawa. Then it bends back through Japan and the Aleutian Island chain to Alaska." [8]

In 1950 Secretary of State Dean Acheson went further. Speaking on January 12th before the National Press Club in Washington, Acheson outlined the "defense perimeter" of the United States in the Pacific as including "the Aleutians, Japan, the Ryukyus, and the Philippines." [9] He continued: "So far as the military security of other areas in the Pacific is concerned, it must be clear that no person can guarantee these areas against military attack. . . . Should such an attack occur . . . the initial reliance must be on the people attacked to resist it and then upon the commitments of the entire world under the Charter of the United Nations."

Acheson's references to the U.N. warrant consideration of the role that body may have played in Soviet calculations. He claimed the U.N. had "so far not proved a weak reed." Yet its lack of armed units made it a body for political rather than military action. Furthermore, the paralytic effect of the Soviet veto upon Security Council decisions had demonstrated in the past that, unless action were taken outside the international forum, there was little chance for it to be taken at all. It is curious, in this regard, that Jacob Malik's boycott of the Security Council, begun in January 1950 in protest against the seating of T. F. Tsiang as the Chinese delegate, continued until August. His absence left the Council free to endorse U.S. proposals for military as well as political steps in Korea. The nature of these proposals and their prompt implementation, however, was without precedent and may not have been foreseen in Moscow.[10]

In sum, it would appear that Soviet reliance upon a relatively quick and easy North Korean victory was well founded, assuming that only ROK forces had to be faced. Soviet calculations about the U.S. and U.N. responses to invasion across the thirty-eighth parallel, while proved erroneous, appear no less realistic in the light of the situation that existed in the spring of 1950. The potential political and strategic gains, not only in Korea but also in Japan, must certainly have seemed to justify the costs and risks which the Soviet Union could reasonably have expected to bear.

Alternative Explanations of the North Korean Attack

Although the detailed examination of Soviet motives lies outside the scope of this inquiry, they must at least be reviewed for their possible relevance to China's interest in the war. One hypothesis, widely accepted in the West at the time, posited the North Korean attack as a test of U.S. response, to be followed by further Communist aggression in the event of success in the Korean venture. Some proponents of this analysis saw Iran, Yugoslavia, and West Europe as likely points of subsequent attack. Others emphasized Indo-China, Burma, and Indonesia as scheduled for "liberation" on the Korean model.

As a justification for the "testing-ground" theory of the North Korean attack, some Americans later claimed that the U.S. response in Korea had dissuaded Moscow from further aggression. Yet this was not the first such test. It was preceded by Iran in 1946 and by Berlin in 1948–1949. In both instances, apparent American willingness to use force had dissuaded Moscow from the further use of force. An American failure to respond in South Korea would not necessarily have indicated a sudden weakening of determination elsewhere. We have already seen how the disposition of U.S. forces and the allocation of funds indicated a prior interest in Europe. We have also cited statements from General MacArthur and Secretary Acheson that excluded South Korea from the U.S. "defense perimeter" in Asia but included other countries, such as Japan and the Philippines.

If there is merit in the "testing" hypothesis, it would seem to relate to Communist aims in Southeast Asia where indigenous armed revolt could have served as a springboard for Sino-Soviet military intervention. Had the United States remained inactive while South Korea was overrun, similar blows might have fallen in Burma, Indo-China, and Indonesia. Thus, the U.S. response may have altered subsequent Communist strategy. If this is true, CCP interest in the Korean War lay in its effect on future moves in Southeast Asia, a region that was primarily Peking's responsibility.

Alternatively, was the North Korean attack designed to tie down U.S. military strength in Asia so as to reduce resistance to Communist aggression elsewhere? The subsequent course of events would seem to rule out this interpretation. In 1950 American forces in Korea suffered two resounding, if indecisive, defeats. In July and August North Korean units smashed through to the toe of the Korean peninsula, inflicting heavy casualties on the thinly defended U.S. lines. While reinforcements were rushed from distant bases, it was feared that Moscow would attack elsewhere. It failed to do so. Again in November and December, Chinese Communist "volunteers" drove U.S. armies back from the Yalu River to the thirty-eighth parallel. Still no Russian moves occurred in the Middle East or Europe. In retrospect, it may be thought that only the deterrent force of America's long-range nuclear air arm explains the Soviet inaction in other theaters. Nuclear power, however, did not deter Chinese Communist intervention in Korea, although, as we shall see, it may have complicated the planning of that intervention. It may have played a minor role in discouraging Soviet aggression elsewhere, but the fact that the initial aggression took place at all, and so close to China's borders, suggests that Sino-Soviet strategy was not basically affected by American nuclear weapons.

An attempt has been made above to reconstruct the immediate context within which the war originated and to relate that context to Chinese Communist interest. These interests appear to have been primarily Asian, rather than world-oriented. In Asia, the problem of Japanese-U.S. relations appears to have been the most critical factor in Sino-Soviet policy. A second consideration may have been the desire to press the use of military force in advancing Communist power in Southeast Asia. Within this framework we must now weigh the relative Chinese and Russian interests in Korea itself, after which we shall

examine the question of China's contributions to the war as they may
have been envisaged in early 1950.

Russia and China: Influence and Interest in North Korea

Between 1945 and 1950 a proliferation of Soviet controls established
Russian direction over North Korea. At the same time, Sino-Korean
economic and military relations revealed both conflict and co-operation
between the two neighbors. While the DPRK emerged within the
Soviet sphere of influence, it clearly remained, as throughout its history,
within the Chinese sphere of interest.

The DPRK: A Soviet Satellite

Moscow enjoyed several channels of communication and control in
North Korea that rendered the DPRK a Soviet satellite in the fullest
sense of the word.[11] Immediately after the Japanese defeat, Russian
occupation forces installed in office Soviet citizens of Korean ancestry,
often as vice ministers under local figures with nominal power. With
the establishment of an independent North Korean regime in 1948,
these ex-Soviet citizens remained in responsible positions, presumably
as trusted supporters of Russian policy. In addition, a large Russian
embassy in Pyongyang with specialists in military, cultural, and economic affairs was supplemented by representatives of various Soviet
economic ministries to form the so-called Soviet Mission. This mission
placed advisers throughout the DPRK government, including the
cabinet, the National Planning Commission, and the Ministry of Defense. Virtually no decisions, certainly not that of the June 1950 invasion, could be made without Soviet knowledge and, in all probability,
Soviet advice. Some sectors of the economy, such as oil and shipping,
came under direct Russian control through joint-stock companies.

Finally, a ten-year economic and cultural co-operation agreement,
concluded March 17, 1949, provided for Soviet-Korean trade, technical
assistance, and credit arrangements. It is believed that a secret military
assistance pact was also signed at this time. Unlike other Russian satellites, however, the DPRK does not seem to have concluded a mutual
defense treaty with the Soviet Union, an interesting omission in view
of Moscow's presumed responsibility for the Korean War. Yet the

equipment and training of the DPRK armies, except those Korean troops transferred from the Chinese Communist forces in 1949–1950, was entirely Russian.[12] Not only was Soviet control represented through advisers attached to all levels of the armed forces, but gasoline supplies were reportedly kept down to one-month levels with reserves kept in the U.S.S.R. In April and May 1950, large Russian deliveries of tanks, trucks, and heavy artillery made possible the June invasion across the thirty-eighth parallel.

By contrast, possible points of Chinese influence appear to have been systematically eliminated during the postwar years. In the early 1940's a Korean Volunteer Corps (KVC) was organized in Manchuria to fight the Japanese. In 1946 when it was combined with other resistance forces to form the Korean People's Liberation Army (KPLA), the KVC seems to have suffered a decline in status relative to groups from Russian-controlled areas. At the same time, Korean Communists from Yenan, organized as the Korean Independence Alliance, won only secondary positions in the new Korean Labor Party (KLP). During the following years, purges and demotions persistently weeded out those Koreans who had returned from China.

Chinese-Korean Relations

Chinese interest, as distinct from Chinese influence, centered on economic relations with North Korea. In 1946 floods severely damaged the Suphong Dam, forty miles north of Antung on the Yalu River. Of two Soviet proposals for its reconstruction, Korean authorities chose the one that excluded Chinese participation, sealed the inadequately constructed Japanese gates on the Chinese side, and diverted all overflow to Korean territory. Peking's representatives in the adjoining Northeast Region protested that half the river was in Chinese territory and that the dam rested on Chinese soil. Nevertheless unilateral Korean construction began in 1948–1949. CCP authorities thereupon refused access to Chinese territory for workers and construction equipment.

Allocation of power from the dam had reportedly become a subject of such controversy that only Soviet intercession early in 1949 resolved the dispute.[13] As a result, North Korea apparently released the surplus electricity for Manchurian industry while China ceased obstructing construction of the dam. During the same year, however, the DPRK Minister of Communications reported, "The annual import plan was not basically completed because of the unsatisfactory work of Antung station in China, which systematically blocked the exchange of cars with the North Korean railroad, not accepting cars from Sinuiju."

The formal relations between Peking and Pyongyang present a mixed picture, but certainly not one of close harmony. On the one hand, recognition was immediately exchanged and, on December 25, 1949, agreements were concluded on postal, telephone, and telegraph communications. On the other hand, despite Pyongyang's proximity, its first envoy did not arrive in Peking until January 28, 1950, after the Soviet and Czech representatives. Even less haste was shown by the Chinese. Not until August 13, 1950, did the first Chinese ambassador present his credentials in Pyongyang, only to depart within a few months, leaving a chargé d'affaires to represent Peking until 1955.[14]

Western speculation about Sino-Korean collaboration prior to the 1950 attack has focused on the transfer of approximately 12,000 Korean troops from Chinese Communist territory to the DPRK during 1949–1950.[15] This group, part of the much larger KVC, remained in Manchuria after World War II to form the PLA 164th Division. Its valor won it considerable repute in the Chinese civil war. Upon its arrival in North Korea, the unit was redesignated the KPLA Fifth Division, and assigned to an advance position near the thirty-eighth parallel.

While this move suggests Chinese Communist participation in preparations for the North Korean attack, it is susceptible to alternative interpretations, although these are not necessarily mutually exclusive. If friction between Peking and Pyongyang was resolved through Soviet good offices at this time, transfer of experienced Korean fighting units from the PLA to the KPLA may have been part of a general settlement of outstanding differences. In addition, Chinese Communist concern over military expenditures and preparations for a cutback in its own armed forces during 1950 made such a transfer expedient from Peking's point of view.

In sum, what is known of Sino-Korean relations on the eve of the war suggests conflict over the allocation of electric power along the Yalu, possible co-operation in the transfer of Korean troops from the

PLA to the KPLA, and correct but distant relations at the level of state and party politics. Specific Chinese interest in matters pertaining to its territory adjoining Korea was undoubtedly coupled with general Communist concern for the viability of the neighboring regime. There is little evidence, however, that the Chinese commitments in North Korea compared in any way with those of the Soviet Union. In particular, there is no clear evidence of Chinese participation in the planning and preparation of the Korean War.

China's Interest in the War

At this point it will be worth while to review briefly the various hypotheses pertaining to Chinese interest in the Korean War as reflected in developments prior to June 25, 1950. The available evidence agrees with most non-Communist conjecture that the North Korean attack was planned and directed by the Soviet Union. There is no agreement, however, nor is there any direct evidence on the degree to which Communist China participated in this planning. It is possible that Stalin did not even inform Mao of the forthcoming attack during their weeks of conference in Moscow, although this is highly unlikely. The length of their discussions, the improvement in Sino-Korean relations during 1949–1950, and the transfer of troops from China to Korea all indicate that Peking knew of the North Korean invasion well in advance. Indeed, such knowledge may have hastened the redeployment of Lin Piao's crack Fourth Field Army from southern to northeastern China during May and June, 1950.

Beyond this, however, there seems little ground for concluding that China anticipated direct involvement in the war. Communist calculations could easily discount the probability of effective American intervention. Furthermore, the equipment and direction of the North Korean attack were exclusively Russian. For Peking, the main military problems remained the conquest of Taiwan and Tibet, the "pacification" of southern and central China, and the reduction of military expenditures so as to relieve inflationary pressures.

At the same time, a North Korean victory would serve Chinese Communist interests. It would deflate the image of Western, particularly American, power, both in China and in Asia. This would facilitate the collapse of Chinese Nationalist resistance, which still looked to the United States for support. Communist control of all Korea would prevent a resurgent Japan from gaining a foothold on the continent and might even halt the rising tide of U.S. influence in Japan itself. Coming close on the heels of Communist victory in China, a sudden, fresh success by Pyongyang could not help cementing Peking's claim that a "new turning-point in history" had arrived throughout "the colonial and semi-colonial world." There may even have been thought, if not discussion, in Peking of an eventual Sino-Soviet division of Asia into spheres of influence, with Russia dominant in Korea and Japan, China in Southeast Asia. China's available means were then inadequate for such maximally defined ends, but a North Korean victory would do much, politically, to advance these ends. Thus the People's Republic of China had a strong interest in the attack of June 1950 but lacked direct responsibility for its initiation or outcome.

IV

PEKING'S REACTIONS:
JUNE–JULY

※

AT DAWN on June 25, 1950, North Korean infantry and armored units attacked in force across the thirty-eighth parallel, quickly overrunning Republic of Korea defenses. Within a week, the United States and the United Nations had reacted powerfully and set in motion developments that were gravely to affect Chinese and Russian interests, as well as those of the Democratic People's Republic of Korea. A review of events in the three weeks after the attack suggests that the Communist planners had to re-examine their initial expectations at this early stage in the war.

SELECTED CHRONOLOGY OF NON-COMMUNIST MOVES CONNECTED WITH THE KOREAN WAR, JUNE–JULY 1950 *

June 25   U.N. Security Council adopts U.S. resolution "noting with grave concern the armed attack upon the Republic of Korea by forces from North Korea"; calls for immediate cease-fire and withdrawal of DPRK forces behind thirty-eighth parallel; requests U.N. members to assist in execution of resolution and to give no support to DPRK.

Soviet Union boycotts meeting: Norway, Egypt, India abstain; Yugoslavia casts the only negative vote.

* Although this chronology is based on Eastern Daylight Saving Time in the United States, subsequent references to Chinese moves will be based on Peking time, twelve hours ahead of EDST.

June 27   President Truman orders U.S. sea and air units to render fullest possible support to ROK; instructs U.S. Seventh Fleet to prevent all military action in the Taiwan (Formosa) Strait as a "neutralization" move; U.N. Security Council adopts U.S. resolution noting DPRK refusal to abide by June 25 resolution and recommending that U.N. members furnish "such assistance . . . as may be necessary" to the ROK.

Soviet Union boycotts meeting; Egypt, India abstain; Yugoslavia casts the only negative vote.

June 30   President Truman orders U.S. ground forces to join sea and air units in support of ROK.

July 1   Indian ambassador in Peking secretly suggests admission of the PRC to the Security Council and termination of Soviet boycott in order to find "solution of Korean question."

July 13   Prime Minister Nehru offers Indian proposal in letters to Premier J. V. Stalin and Secretary of State Dean Acheson.

These developments posed serious problems for Peking and Moscow. How would U.S. forces affect the prospects for North Korean success and how would the bloc counter them? What would Peking's role be? How would the Seventh Fleet's "neutralization" of the Taiwan Strait affect the projected Communist invasion of Taiwan? What was the significance of U.N. endorsement of the U.S. position in Korea and of Indian attempts to mediate the dispute on terms favorable to the bloc? What changes, if any, occurred in Sino-Soviet attitudes to these questions as a consequence of further developments in July?

Problems of Chinese Communist Policy

We have already seen how, prior to June 25th, Peking probably anticipated a quick and decisive North Korean victory, accompanied or swiftly followed by the invasion of Taiwan. The United States and United Nations moves of June 25–30, however, raised doubts on both points. These doubts, in turn, gave rise to decisions that affected China's domestic development and world posture. An understanding of the various issues confronting the new regime at this time may provide insights into Peking's reactions throughout the critical months of 1950.

Taiwan

The Truman order of June 27th abruptly changed the Taiwan situation. Only six months previously the President had declared that the United States would avoid further involvement in the Chinese civil war. Renewed American political, economic, and military support for Chiang Kai-shek now seemed certain. Instead of ending resistance on Taiwan through subversion and a token invasion, the People's Liberation Army now faced the United States Seventh Fleet in addition to reorganized Chinese Nationalist forces. In the United Nations, Secretary General Trygve Lie had been skillfully attempting to break the East-West deadlock on Chinese Communist representation. Now the Chinese Nationalist delegate seemed secure in his place on the Security Council, unless U.S. policy changed or suffered a setback in Taiwan itself.

The alternatives facing Peking were few, clear-cut, and dismal. It could go forward with its planned invasion. The Seventh Fleet might be unable to meet both the Taiwan and the Korean commitments. Postponement of the Taiwan "liberation" would incur immediate political costs and long-term military risks. Substitution of propaganda for a military attack against the U.S. in the Taiwan Strait would call attention to "new China's" impotence on its very doorstep. Words alone would not remove Chiang Kai-shek and his supporters from either Taiwan or the United Nations. Nor would Nationalist resistance ever again be as weak as in 1950, given the prospect of renewed American training and assistance. Furthermore, with America's supply lines being extended and her military units below full strength, a simultaneous invasion of Taiwan and of South Korea might succeed in overwhelming resistance.

On the other hand, Communist desire to avoid general war, particularly with the U.S. atomic superiority, may have outweighed the above considerations. China's vulnerable coastal concentration of industry and transportation made the risk of U.S. air and sea attack extremely hazardous. Should the invasion fail, the political repercussions would be costly for Peking, especially in the coastal, southern, and inner provinces where Nationalist and anti-Communist guerrilla forces still operated. All such risks had to be seriously examined in the light of miscalculations that had preceded the North Korean attack. International reaction to that attack had proved more serious in its political and military consequences than had been anticipated. A Chinese Communist invasion of Taiwan might be interpreted in the West as proof of a co-ordinated offensive in Asia by the Soviet bloc. U.S. retaliation against mainland China could inflict heavy damage, and Soviet assistance might be slow in coming over the lengthy, strained transport lines, vulnerable to air and sea interdiction. In China's existing condition, an immediate invasion of Taiwan posed far-reaching hazards to the Moscow-Peking axis.

Korea

In addition to the Taiwan problem, Peking faced the prospect that Pyongyang's victory would be delayed, if not altogether thwarted, by U.S. "intervention." While this may have been primarily of Soviet concern, given Russian ascendancy in North Korea, it affected the People's Republic of China to only a slightly lesser degree. Communism was too recently victorious in China to ignore a setback across the Yalu that might reawaken U.S.-Nationalist activities throughout the mainland. Nor could Peking aspire to Asian leadership so long as it appeared unwilling, or unable, to influence events on its border. Should Syngman Rhee as well as Chiang Kai-shek survive because of U.S. military protection, the rising tide of Communist influence might be reversed from the Philippines to India. Japan would then fall securely into the "imperialist camp."

Thus both strategic and ideological considerations argued for maximum support of North Korea against "American aggression." Yet any Chinese assistance, whether propagandistic or military, entailed serious risks for Peking. Manchuria, China's vital industrial base, lay within easy reach of U.S. bases in Japan. Military aid to Pyongyang might invite damaging retaliation. A lesser level of support, limited to propaganda and diplomatic activity, would probably not affect the outcome of the war. In view of the widening international opposition to the

North Korean attack, such support might only jeopardize Peking's efforts to enter the U.N. Even inaction carried liabilities for China. At best, stalemate in Korea would increase the likelihood of an American-Japanese-South-Korean defense system. At worst, the "imperialist camp" might feel encouraged to counterattack the Sino-Soviet bloc on its vulnerable Asian flank.

Could the Korean War be terminated short of total North Korean victory without engendering enemy hopes of Soviet bloc weakness and schism? Would prolongation of the war eventually sap American willingness to fight far from home in a country only recently identified with U.S. interests? Or would it sooner exhaust North Korean strength, increasing the need for bloc support of Pyongyang? China's resources already faced heavy demands of industrial recovery, agricultural reform, and political consolidation. Participation in the Korean War, particularly against growing U.S.-U.N. forces, might strain these resources to the breaking point.

Finally, Peking had to weigh these alternatives against the interests of its Soviet ally. In Korea, the initial responsibility clearly lay with Moscow. Soviet membership in the U.N. gave Moscow a voice in international affairs that China lacked. China could not even resolve the question of Taiwan independently, since only Russian air power could protect the PRC should the United States actively support Chiang Kai-shek. The asymmetry of power within the Sino-Soviet alliance gave Mao Tse-tung little leverage for advancing Chinese policy where it ran counter to that of Stalin. Thus, some of the basic decisions may have been Russian, regardless of the degree to which they affected Chinese interests. It is possible to summarize known Russian moves and to infer Soviet decisions from the events immediately within our focus. The present treatment of Soviet strategy in Korea, however, must necessarily be related primarily to the question of Peking's role in that war.

China and the Korean War: The Evidence and Its Analysis

The complex and diverse problems just described confronted Peking simultaneously. Not susceptible to quick and final solution, they remained fluid throughout the summer of 1950. Estimates and tentative decisions made immediately after the initial U.S. commitment in June required re-examination during July, as U.S.-U.N. resistance increased. Furthermore, objective obstacles to the solution of China's problems may have been accompanied by subjective limits on decision making, such as rigidity in Moscow or inexperience and insufficient information in Peking. Russian behavior toward allies, Communist or non-Communist, had been characterized by inadequate communication and unilateral decisions. In this context the secrecy surrounding Sino-Soviet communications and decisions presents formidable problems to the analyst.

For the sake of clarity it will be well to consider separately the issues of Taiwan and Korea, although it must be remembered that Peking saw them as connected. An attempt will be made to define periods in the Korean War according to the shifts in Sino-Soviet strategy. Although this somewhat oversimplifies the complex and gradual evolution of policy that actually occurred, it will facilitate an understanding of the changes apparent in Chinese estimates of the situation.

Four types of evidence support the present analysis of evolving Chinese policy. First, the PRC leadership issued official statements, primarily for foreign consumption, as formal messages to the U.N., as declarations of Mao Tse-tung and Chou En-lai, and as authorized pronouncements from the Ministry of Foreign Affairs. Second, Chinese Communist communications, designed primarily for domestic audiences, reveal official thinking about developments in Korea and Taiwan. Serious analyses by and for the Communist elite appeared as anonymous commentaries in the authoritative daily newspaper *Jen Min Jih Pao* (People's Daily) and in the weekly journal closely associated with the Ministry of Foreign Affairs, *Shih Chieh Chih Shih* (World Culture). Propagandistic interpretations appeared in newspapers, magazines, and radio broadcasts, all closely controlled by the Chinese Communist Party. Third, contemporary U.S. intelligence reports and subsequent unit histories, with their accounts of Chinese Communist prisoners captured in Korea, enable us to reconstruct PLA troop movements. Finally, PRC diplomatic activity, particularly vis-à-vis India and the U.N., offers clues to Sino-Soviet strategy.

None of these sources provides a comprehensive picture of decision making in Peking, nor is the evidence always subject to one exclusive interpretation. At some points, the four types of data each support incompatible hypotheses. At important junctures, however, they suggest a pattern of policy clearly and consistently enough to constrict the range of reasonable explanation for Chinese Communist actions.

One final analytical caution is necessary. Considerable reliance has been placed upon content analysis, both quantitative and qualitative, for inferring shifts in Chinese Communist estimates, strategy, and tactics. The author fully recognizes the risk in attempting to determine the degree to which propaganda reflects the views of the regime, as distinct from the views it is designed to generate among its audiences. Where public communications suggested changing Chinese estimates, these were checked against actual diplomatic or military behavior, which might be expected to reflect such changes. Clues to changed official views occur in shifts of terminology, and in patterns of news omission and emphasis. Frequently their meaning is ambiguous, and other evidence fails to clarify their significance. To the degree that the gleanings from propaganda are borne out by political behavior, however, one may rely upon content analysis.[1]

Peking's Initial Reactions: Korea and Taiwan

Chinese Communist press treatment of the North Korean attack exhibited several characteristics during the period June 27–July 30, 1950. Initial reports of the war appeared belatedly and were quickly relegated to secondary positions in the newspapers. Cautious warning of unfavorable consequences from the entry of U.S. armed forces into Korea accompanied propagandistic assertions of confidence that Pyongyang would ultimately triumph. Throughout this period Peking appeared to avoid any specific and immediate commitment to assist North Korea, but instead placed Taiwan, as the primary Chinese problem, ahead of the neighboring war. At the same time, preparations for invading Taiwan slackened, and PLA redeployment suggested planning for future contingencies in Manchuria or Korea. No actual assistance, however, was furnished DPRK forces, which fought desperately to push U.N. units from their toehold in South Korea before the build-up around Pusan could secure a base for counteroffensives. For Peking, the period appears to have been one of watchful waiting, permitting evaluation of rapidly moving events and their possible consequences. Active responses to U.S. and U.N. moves in Korea appear to have been determined in

Moscow, while Peking's primary responsibility continued to be Taiwan.

The Outbreak of War and the U.S.-U.N. Response

No Peking newspaper reported the war for forty-eight hours following the North Korean attack. The silence may have been politically determined, since at least one Shanghai newspaper, on June 26th, carried a front-page story, complete with map, headlined, "Southern Puppet Army Attacks North Korea at Three Points, Public Announcement Warns Puppet Government to Stop Advance or Decisive Steps Will Be Taken." [2] The account told of DPRK "police guards" waging "a severe defensive war."

On June 27th *Jen Min Jih Pao* devoted most of page one to NCNA dispatches from Pyongyang, Kim Il-sung's "call to arms," and background information. Yet its editorial assurance of "the certain victory of the Korean people in their struggle for unity and independence" carried no note of immediate concern for Chinese readers. Syngman Rhee was dismissed as "less expert" than Chiang Kai-shek in military and political affairs. No mention was made of the initial Security Council resolution of the previous day, calling upon the DPRK to withdraw above the thirty-eighth parallel. In this as in subsequent Chinese reporting in the U.N., a time lag of at least forty-eight hours preceded publication of the news. Some U.N. events were suppressed even longer, suggesting reliance upon Russian interpretation of these matters.

From June 30th to July 6th, Korea disappeared into the back pages of *Jen Min Jih Pao,* except for a story on the Han River crossing and a summarized speech from Pyongyang. This probably reflected uncertainty over the American military impact, rather than lack of interest in the war. Thus, the initial *Shih Chieh Chih Shih* comment predicted, "The complete liberation of South Korea is not far off." [3] Similarly, on July 3rd, *Jen Min Jih Pao* expressed perfunctory confidence in North Korean victory. On July 6th, however, the newspaper changed its tone. Its second front-page editorial on the war termed it "the central problem of international relations," and warned that Washington was unlikely to "concede defeat." Citing additional American troops, planes, and ships heading for Korea and U.S. pressure upon other nations to join the action, the paper admitted that these "difficulties" would make Communist victory, although certain, "come not so fast." No alarm was sounded nor was any Chinese commitment to relieve the "difficulties" implied. However, this editorial evidenced the first concern over the possible effects of United States actions.

This concern became increasingly manifest in anonymous military commentaries appearing in *Jen Min Jih Pao* at roughly two-week intervals throughout the summer. Bereft of propagandistic bombast, these commentaries struck a consistently more sober note than did general articles on the war. Thus, on July 13th, the military writer noted that "more than forty" U.N. members "appear to be in the American gang." After adding that some "express only a 'limited type of support,'" he differentiated countries that, like France, India, and Denmark, had refused military assistance, from those that, like Great Britain and Thailand, had offered armed units. Despite the likelihood of increasing U.N. resistance, he concluded, "The imperialists look strong on the outside but are weak on the inside . . . [being] only 'paper tigers.'"

This mixture of caution and confidence reflected the confusing and fluid situation in Korea. On the battle front, the rapid North Korean advance encouraged optimism, but Sino-Soviet awareness of the impending U.S.-U.N. build-up introduced a pessimistic note. On the one hand, DPRK troops captured Seoul within three days of crossing the thirty-eighth parallel, forcing the ROK government to flee southward to Taejon. Red armies drove fifty miles in the first week to capture Suwon and Wonju, forty miles the second week to Chonan, and eighteen miles the third week to engulf more than half of South Korea. On the other hand, U.S. troop movements indicated the significance of the rear-guard action of American units, slowing the DPRK advance while stabilizing a toehold at the base of the Korean peninsula.

Meanwhile, U.S. Army and Marine units in Okinawa, Hawaii, and at home were publicly reported mobilizing for air and sea transport to Korea, to arrive in early August.[4] At the front, U.S. artillery increased in numbers and size, moving from 105- to 155-mm. howitzers by mid-July, while the new 3.5-inch bazooka proved its effectiveness against DPRK tanks in the battle for Taejon. In addition to the U.N. control of the air, intensified bombardment from American naval forces brought Communist coastal lines of communication under heavy attack.

TABLE 2

CHRONOLOGY OF UNITED STATES TROOP ARRIVALS IN KOREA,
JULY 1–18, 1950

Date	Unit	Embarked from
July 1–2	One-half battalion combat team from 21st Infantry Regiment, 24th Division	Japan
July 4–9	Remainder of 24th Division	Japan
July 9–12	25th Division	Japan
July 18	1st Cavalry Division	Japan
TOTAL	.... 30,000 troops	

SOURCE: *Korea—1950*, Department of the Army, Washington, D.C., 1952. No figures of unit strength are included, but references support the approximate total of 30,000 troops given in Karig, *et al.*, *Battle Report*, p. 89.

"Prolonged War" in Korea

On July 20th the first major battle between DPRK and U.S. forces ended in the Red capture of Taejon. No note of triumph, however, appeared in Chinese Communist commentaries. On the contrary, one week later *Jen Min Jih Pao* analyzed the first month of war in sober tones, reporting two additional American divisions en route to Korea, mobilization of fresh American mechanized units, White House demands for emergency defense appropriations, and increased United States pressure for men and material from other U.N. members. Again the warning sounded: "This doubtless increases the difficulties facing the Korean people." Adjoining columns graphically described the devastation of Korea from U.S. napalm bombings.[5]

Almost simultaneously, *World Culture* introduced a phrase of special significance for its Chinese readers, predicting, *inter alia*, "A prolonged war of attrition will naturally increase the difficulties of the Korean people but it will increase the difficulties of the American imperialists much more."[6] In 1938 Mao Tse-tung's classic study *On the Protracted War* had mapped the years of struggle from material inferiority to superiority, applicable both to China's war against Japan and to the civil conflict between the Chinese Communist Party and the Kuomintang. To depict Pyongyang's future in these terms suggested serious consideration at higher levels of an eventual stalemate, if not possible defeat, in Korea.

The gradual but persistent change in tone of these authoritative commentaries, moving from unqualified confidence in late June to prediction of "prolonged war" in late July, paralleled growing American confidence that a line could be held near the port of Pusan that would permit a perimeter defense protecting the vital build-up area. Informed U.S. reports predicted that out of this area an eventual U.N. counter-offensive would be launched in conjunction with amphibious landings behind North Korean lines higher up the peninsula.[7]

Yet nowhere did Peking's statements hint at the necessity for Chinese assistance to North Korea. On July 17th a radio broadcast linked a frank warning against undue optimism with assertions of North Korean self-sufficiency: "The American imperialists will not give up and admit defeat. They will strengthen their aggressive force. . . . The victory of the Korean people will come a little slowly [but] . . . there is no doubt that the Korean people . . . have sufficient strength to defeat imperialist aggression and eventually to attain national liberation." [8] Despite generalized exhortations to render "wholehearted support" to Pyongyang's cause, Chinese Communist propaganda seldom spelled out the implications of such support. Infrequently, it was specified as "moral." [9]

Alternatively, it was argued that by "actively preparing for the liberation of Taiwan, we shall be giving efficient aid to the support of Korea." [10] Rarely was the Korean War depicted in terms of China's immediate interests. In an exceptional article of July 26, 1950, *Jen Min Jih Pao* answered the query of why American armed forces were invading Korea, as follows: "To change it into a gangway of aggression for the United States on the borders of China and the Soviet Union."

Peking's broadcasts, then, gave no indication of Chinese Communist commitment to the Korean War. On the contrary, they and the newspapers stressed Taiwan as the only major responsibility confronting the PLA. This did not preclude secret military movements for future contingencies associated with the war, as we shall see shortly. So far as the Chinese people were concerned, however, the North Korean move, while encountering growing enemy opposition, offered no cause for anxiety or alarm.

Taiwan, India, and the U.N.

In contrast with the delayed and occasionally diffident treatment of the Korean War, Chinese Communist reaction to the June 27th order placing the U.S. Seventh Fleet in the Taiwan Strait was immediate and authoritative. Within twenty-four hours of the Truman statement, Foreign Minister Chou En-lai denounced the move as "armed aggression against the territory of China in total violation of the United Nations charter." [11]

Denying that the American move came as a "surprise," Chou declared: "All that Truman's statement does is merely to expose his premeditated plan and put it into practice. In fact, the attack by the puppet Korean government . . . at the instigation of the U.S. government was . . . designed to create a pretext for the United States to invade Taiwan, Korea, Viet Nam, and the Philippines." Chou pledged the PRC to "liberate Taiwan" regardless of any "obstructive action the United States imperialists may take." Later the same day, at a governmental meeting in Peking, Mao echoed this pledge.

Several points emerge from the timing and content of the Chou and Mao statements. First, the swiftness of the Chinese reaction to U.S. protection of Taiwan as contrasted with the slow response to the Korean War indicates a division of responsibility between Peking and Moscow. Chinese Communist pronouncements on Taiwan may not have required consultation with the Soviet partner, while those on the U.N. and Korea may have been subject to Russian review. Peking's first public comment on the Security Council resolution of June 25th came four days later. On June 29th *Jen Min Jih Pao* editorially attacked both this resolution and the Truman announcement on Taiwan of June 27th, but made no reference to the second Security Council resolution on Korea, also of June 27th. Messages to the U.N. bore out this pattern. Moscow delayed three days before officially protesting the June 25th resolution. No Chinese Communist protest was sent, perhaps because the issue concerned Korea exclusively. The second Security Council resolution elicited no Soviet response for one week. Then within forty-eight hours of Moscow's cable came a parallel protest from Peking, including, however, greater stress on Taiwan.

Aside from the timing, the content of Chinese references to the U.N., both in Chou's statement and in his cable of July 6th, raises a second point of interest. On the one hand, Peking employed the U.N. Charter as an acceptable reference to support its case against American action in Taiwan. On the other hand, Peking waited ten days before protesting the Truman announcement to the U.N., and then made no demand for action. In strong, almost insulting, language it charged: "By keeping silent on this act of open aggression, the Security Council and the Secretary General of the United Nations have forgone their functions and duties of upholding world peace and therefore have become pliant instruments to the policy of the United States government." [12]

While loath to dismiss the U.N. altogether, Peking neither acknowledged its authority in Korea nor demanded that it take measures on Taiwan.[13] In general, this seeming ambivalence resulted from Soviet policy. Moscow remained a member of the U.N. but boycotted its organs, including the Security Council, in protest against the "illegal" representation of the "Chiang Kai-shek clique." If the Russian absence compounded the "illegality" of resolutions passed in June, Peking could scarcely call for Security Council action in July when the Soviet boycott was still going on.

A more specific dilemma, however, confronted Peking. How could it support Pyongyang against U.N. opposition and still keep open its chances for admission to the U.N.? On July 1st this issue arose concretely when the Indian ambassador to Peking, K. M. Panikkar, called upon Vice Foreign Minister Chang Han-fu. Panikkar "put forward tentatively the suggestion that the question [of Korea] could probably be solved by referring it to the Security Council, with China taking her legitimate place, and consequently the Soviets giving up their boycott and returning to their vacant seat." [14]

This secret Indian move raised several problems for Sino-Soviet strategists. Only a short time previously Communist analysis had placed the Nehru government squarely in the camp of "American imperialism," castigating its "formal independence" and "playing at neutralism." [15] Yet Nehru had publicly called for PRC admission to the U.N., and Panikkar's proposal hinted that this might come as part of a "package deal" on Korea.[16] What further support for bloc goals might Delhi offer? True, it had moved from abstention to acceptance of the June 27th Security Council resolution authorizing military assistance to the

Republic of Korea. Yet an official explanation of this move had expressed "hope that even at this stage it may be possible to put an end to the fighting and settle the dispute by mediation." [17]

Peking's "two-camp" world view denied the possibility of disinterested mediation. Was Nehru finally joining the category, acceptable to China, of "national bourgeoisie opposed to imperialism?"

More than U.N. admission was at stake for Peking. Indian support on the Taiwan issue would be valuable for applying political pressure against the United States. Should PRC admission to the U.N. accompany settlement of the Korean War, Washington would have little justification for continuing its Seventh Fleet patrol of the Taiwan Strait. How vital these considerations were for Moscow is open to question. The fact remains that Peking made no response to Panikkar's proposal for ten days. On July 10th its favorable reply finally came, undoubtedly after consultation with its Soviet partner.

This delay in the Sino-Soviet response, paralleled in the handling of U.N. moves, may have stemmed from uncertainty over both Indian and Korean developments. If Delhi's motives puzzled Communist analysts, so did the import and outcome of U.S. action against Pyongyang. Thus Peking reacted slowly and cautiously to diplomatic as well as military developments. On July 9th *Jen Min Jih Pao* reviewed Indian policy without attacking Nehru but with skeptical reference to "Indian 'neutralism.' " Similarly, it depicted the U.N. as under "American domination" but cited the Charter as a basis for attacking "American imperialist aggression in Korea and Taiwan."

On July 13th, acting upon Peking's favorable response to the Panikkar proposal, Prime Minister Nehru sent identical letters to Premier Stalin and Secretary of State Acheson. He formally suggested that the PRC be admitted to the Security Council, thereby permitting the Soviet delegate to return, and that the United States, the Soviet Union, and People's Republic of China, "with the help and cooperation of other peace-loving nations," informally explore means to end the Korean War and to reach "a permanent solution of the Korean problem." [18] Stalin's prompt acceptance on July 15th contrasted with the Acheson rejection three days later.

The exchange revealed a new turn in Sino-Soviet strategy. Despite Nehru's public condemnation of North Korean "aggression," he clearly stood outside the "American camp," and to this extent was acceptable to the bloc. It was now possible to embarrass the United States diplomatically, for its prestige in Asia would suffer as long as Washington rejected Indian proposals endorsed by Moscow and Peking. If, on the other hand, Washington accepted these proposals, some goals of the Sino-Soviet bloc might be advanced without committing the bloc in advance to compromise on its other aims.

The following weeks gave increasing evidence of a change in bloc policy that utilized diplomatic means in conjunction with military action in Korea. As July drew to a close, Moscow announced that Jacob Malik would end his seven-month boycott of the Security Council on August 1st, when he would assume the President's seat according to regular rotation. In the meantime, Peking smoothed over the harsh image of Indian policy outlined in its earlier analyses. On July 13th *Jen Min Jih Pao* noted that Delhi offered "only a limited 'type of support' " for U.S. moves in Korea. After printing the Stalin note in full along with excerpts from the Acheson reply, the paper praised "the world-wide support for the peaceful proposals of J. Nehru and the reply of J. V. Stalin." [19] Its first editorial comment on the correspondence called the Indian move "of tremendous world-wide significance," despite the U.S. rejection. This "showed to all" the growing strength of "the forces of peace." [20]

By selectively quoting the Indian press, the Congress Party, the British Labour Party, and the American press, *Jen Min Jih Pao* depicted universal endorsement of the Nehru-Stalin exchange and opposition to the Acheson statement. Elsewhere the Indian ambassador was reported to have found Mao Tse-tung deeply concerned over Taiwan while viewing the Korean War as "a distant matter." [21]

The Indian *démarche* is of twofold importance. It brought about the first formal, public involvement of Peking in the Korean War. Admittedly, Peking was a passive bystander compared with Delhi, Moscow, and Washington. Yet the Panikkar-Nehru proposals established an important precedent by linking resolution of the Korean conflict with PRC representation in the Security Council. In a sense this legitimized Peking's interest in the war.

Even more significant, however, the Indian proposal challenged the Communist image of a world neatly divided into two warring camps with no "neutral" nations occupying a third position. Full appreciation of this may not have come immediately in Moscow or Peking. Nevertheless *Jen Min Jih Pao*'s gradual shift from criticism to praise of Nehru suggested at least a tactical modification of the "two camps" approach. Furthermore, Nehru's appeal for "mediation," backed as it was by terms initially acceptable to Sino-Soviet strategy, opened up the possibility of using diplomatic as well as military means for handling the Korean imbroglio. It may have helped to persuade Moscow to end its boycott of the Security Council and to return Malik as President of the Council in August. This will be discussed in more detail below. At present it is enough to emphasize that the Sino-Soviet reaction to the Indian proposals of early July stands as an important bench mark in the development of Chinese Communist policy, not only on Korea but on the broader problem of relations with Asia and the world in general.

Taiwan: Invasion Postponed?

The Chou En-lai statement of June 28th carried additional clues to Peking's policy that were borne out by subsequent communications to the elite and to the masses. His relative lack of attention to Korea as compared with Taiwan implied a differentiation of interest that was to characterize Chinese Communist comment on the two problems. This comment emerged initially amidst a previously planned campaign, scheduled for July 1–7, connected with a world-wide Communist movement, the so-called Stockholm Peace Appeal. The subsequent call of the World Federation of Trade Unions (WFTU) for international support of Pyongyang resulted in the formation of Chinese People's Committee for Resistance to United States Invasion of Taiwan and Korea. This committee set aside the week, July 17–24, to "unmask U.S. imperialism" and to "prove that the United States is not only not to be feared but that it can be completely defeated." [22]

Although the WFTU directive concerned Korea, Peking's implementation placed primary emphasis upon Taiwan, in the title of the campaign, in its inaugural manifesto, and in all following statements. No help for Korea was specified in the campaign literature other than "moral support" and "sympathy."

In the campaign title the Chinese term *fan tuei* (resist) connoted only attitudinal opposition. Significantly, this term was later changed during the celebrated "Resist-America Aid-Korea" campaign that accompanied actual intervention in Korea. In November 1950 it was succeeded by *k'ang yi*, connoting active opposition, exemplified by the war with Japan of 1937–1945 when this term appeared in Yenan's propaganda.

Did this attitudinal response, as contrasted with an active response, apply to Taiwan as well as to Korea? This raises the fourth and final point in Chou's statement on the Truman order to the U.S. Seventh Fleet. While expressing confidence "in driving off the American aggressors and in recovering Taiwan," he did not call for prompt invasion. Chou's remarks came in a propagandistic framework, addressed not only to China but to "all peoples throughout the world who love peace, justice and freedom and especially all the oppressed nations and peoples of the East."

A possible clue to the thinking behind Chou's phraseology occurred in a *World Culture* article on the new strategic situation and Taiwan. An unusually sophisticated analysis, it reviewed U.S. policy on China in the context of domestic Republican-Democratic politics, the State Department "White Paper," and the Truman-Acheson statements of early January 1950. It concluded that until June 27th, American support for Chiang Kai-shek had come as a reluctant Democratic concession to win Republican endorsement of aid to Syngman Rhee. The Truman-Acheson preferred policy was depicted as control over Taiwan either through trusteeship or through Taiwanese "independence." [23] The new Seventh Fleet order, however, had changed the entire situation. Now military considerations took priority over political preferences in U.S. policy. The writer drew the lesson soberly and succinctly for his readers: "Before June 27, the problem of liberating Taiwan pitted the strength of the PLA against the Chiang Kai-shek remnants, with the help of the American imperialists occupying a background position. Since June 27, the problem of liberating Taiwan pits the strength of the PLA against the American imperialists, with the Kuomintang bandit remnants moving into the background."

Like Chou, *World Culture* refrained from calling for immediate "smashing" of the American imperialists or for invasion. Instead, it predicted that a U.S. defeat in Korea would discourage further aid to

Chiang, unwillingly offered in the first place. This analysis tacitly argued for postponing the Taiwan invasion until after Pyongyang had forced the U.S. out of Korea. By implication, the analysis conceded the futility of attacking Taiwan as long as the threat of American interdiction remained. Further public indication that no immediate invasion was planned came from General Ch'en Yi, commanding the East China Military Area and the Third Field Army, which was assigned to the Taiwan operation. In May General Ch'en had exhorted his troops to train intensively in the removal of anti-invasion obstacles. On July 16th he declared: "While we intensify preparations to liberate Taiwan, we must not neglect our task of national economic recovery." [24] This minor shift of emphasis implied a major change in policy.

PLA Redeployment

Chinese Communist military movements provide additional clues to Peking's strategy on Korea and Taiwan. Between mid-May and mid-July, more than 60,000 troops from General Lin Piao's Fourth Field Army completed redeployment to their home base in Northeast China, after their victory in South China and Hainan Island.[25] This placed 180,000 of Peking's best troops within one month's march of the Korean battle front.[26] Yet these troops did not cross the Yalu River, nor did other units join the northeastern concentration until mid-September. Ostensibly this redeployment was routine, like other PLA moves throughout China that were designed to reduce military expenditures by assigning troops to economic construction. At the same time, one should not ignore the possible relationship of this particular move to the defense of Manchuria in the event of reversals in Korea, or to eventual assistance for the DPRK forces.

A similar relationship may be deduced from a simultaneous build-up in Shantung, midway between Shanghai and Mukden. Beginning in late June and early July, approximately 30,000 troops from Ch'en Yi's Third Field Army joined an equal number from the Fourth Field Army in this area. Few of the troops appear to have originated in the Shantung peninsula. Unlike other PLA units, these were not given economic assignments but received further training. This appears to have been a reserve force, positioned for contingencies connected with either Korea or Taiwan. Its location permitted quick land and sea movement to Northeast China, should the Korean War take a turn for the worse. In addition, it was readily available for movement through Northeast China into Korea, should Peking decide to reinforce Pyongyang. Finally, the Shantung group could respond quickly to a U.S.-Chinese Nationalist attack on the coastal provinces, or it could return to the Chekiang-Fukien area if the Taiwan invasion were rescheduled. Only a portion of the Third Field Army continued amphibious training during July and August, while a significant element moved up to Shantung.[27]

Thus, the PLA dispositions substantiated the clues in the public media that indicated an indefinite postponement of the invasion of Taiwan. The military moves, too, bear out public statements in suggesting that the Korean War was going contrary to initial calculations. Had a North Korean victory remained certain, albeit delayed by a few weeks, there would have been no reason to withdraw forces positioned opposite Taiwan. The context of the Seventh Fleet's orders gave credence to the *World Culture* analysis linking a U.S. defeat in Korea with a U.S. withdrawal from the Taiwan Strait. In the event of U.S. defeat and withdrawal, the invasion might be rescheduled according to the dictates of weather in the fall of 1950.

By reducing its strength opposite Taiwan, however, the Chinese Communist regime gave evidence of a major reappraisal of strategy affecting both Taiwan and Korea. The troop concentration in Shantung province and the forecast of a "prolonged war" indicated concern over the ultimate consequences of the U.S. moves. Although domestic audiences received little indication that Chinese interests were at stake, propagandistic attention to Taiwan and Korea established an atmosphere in which more threatening developments might be countered by Chinese Communist diplomatic or military moves. The Sino-Soviet response to Indian proposals for mediation, together with the announcement on July 27th that Soviet Delegate Jacob Malik would assume the Presidency of the Security Council in August, indicated that political measures would be tried first. While the PLA redeployment gave no immediate military support to North Korea, it left Chinese Communist forces favorably situated should military support prove necessary.

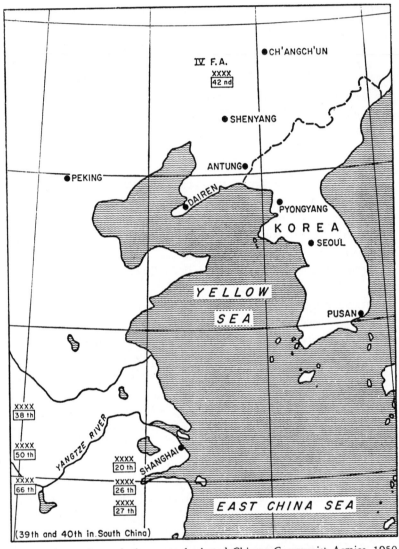

MAP 1. Approximate deployment of selected Chinese Communist Armies, 1950
Mid-May to June

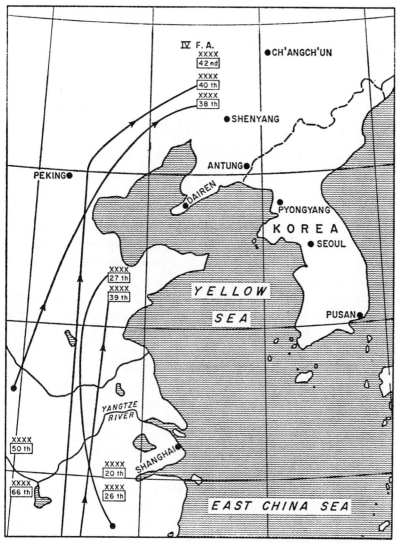

MAP 2. Approximate deployment of selected Chinese Communist Armies, 1950
Mid-June to July

V

AUGUST:
MILITARY AND
DIPLOMATIC STALEMATE

※

WE HAVE SEEN how events in June and July affected Peking's political and military posture without, however, involving the new regime directly in the Korean War. Before June the Chinese Communists had little, if any, responsibility in the planning of the war. Their military attention focused primarily upon Taiwan and Tibet, together with the "pacification" of resistance pockets throughout the mainland. In the first half of 1950 mobilization ended, accompanied by the redeployment and reassignment of People's Liberation Army units pending their gradual demobilization. Official policy stressed the need to shift manpower and resources from military to economic activity, so as to relieve inflationary pressures and facilitate reconstruction.

After June, however, political and military indicators evidenced a postponement of the Taiwan invasion for as long as the United States Seventh Fleet continued to shield Chiang's forces. The shift of the Fourth Field Army from South to Northeast China, begun previously, now took on added significance, for it strengthened the area bordering Korea. Furthermore, a new build-up in Shantung Province massed units from the Third and Fourth Field armies midway between Taiwan and Korea. Peking acknowledged that "a prolonged war" lay ahead, yet Chinese Communist communications nowhere presaged diplomatic, much less military, support to Pyongyang. Meanwhile the gradual slowing of the North Korean offensive paralleled a steady build-up of United Nations strength through the vital port of Pusan.

Like the military reactions, Sino-Soviet diplomatic responses changed slowly but perceptibly. India's proposal to mediate the Korean problem, contingent upon the People's Republic of China's admission to the U.N. and Soviet return to the Security Council, won a delayed but favorable response from Peking and Moscow. Chinese Communist press treatment of Nehru's policies shifted from ridicule to praise. At the end of July, Moscow announced that Jacob Malik would return to the Security Council despite the presence of the Taiwan delegate, which ostensibly had motivated the seven-month Soviet boycott. The miscalculations of Communist planners concerning the course of military and diplomatic events had been clearly demonstrated, and both Russia and China had been obliged to adopt new tactics.

The following chronology highlights the developments in August that marked the new course of Russian, and concomitantly of Chinese, strategy:

SELECTED CHRONOLOGY OF POLITICAL DEVELOPMENTS
RE TAIWAN AND KOREA, AUGUST 1950

August 1   Soviet delegate Jacob Malik returns to U.N. Security Council as President.

General Douglas MacArthur and Generalissimo Chiang Kai-shek issue joint communiqué after 48-hour conference on Taiwan.

August 4   Malik terms conflict "an internal civil war" and introduces resolution (1) to invite PRC representatives, as well as "representatives of the Korean people," for "discussion of the Korean question"; and (2) "to put an end to the hostilities in Korea and at the same time to withdraw all foreign troops from Korea."

August 9   Security Council members meet privately for "informal exchange of views."

August 10   U.S. delegate Warren Austin states goal of U.N. action is unified Korea.

August 11   U.K. delegate Sir Gladwyn Jebb calls upon North Korean troops to "go back whence they came' as a preliminary to further U.N. discussion of the issue; hints at *status quo ante bellum* as a basis for possible suspension of hostilities.

August 14   Indian delegate Sir Benegal Rau seconds Jebb proposal on DPRK withdrawal and proposes that committee of non-permanent Security Council members take up Korean problem after withdrawal.

August 17   Second private meeting of Council members for "informal exchange of views." Followed by open session at which Austin states objectives of U.N. action in terms of total victory over North Korea and unification of entire peninsula under U.N. auspices.

August 20   Chou En-lai cables Lake Success, endorsing Malik resolution of August 4 and demanding PRC representation at Korean discussions.

August 21   Third and final private informal meeting of Council members.

August 22   Malik warns, "Any continuation of the Korean War will lead inevitably to a widening of the conflict. . . ."

August 26   *World Culture* claims American action in Korea "seriously threatens the security of China in particular. . . . It is impossible to solve the Korean problem without the participation of its closest neighbor, China. . . . North Korea's enemy is our enemy. North Korea's defense is our defense. North Korea's victory is our victory."

Coincident with these developments, the balance of power at the battle front shifted steadily in favor of the United Nations. During the first two weeks of August the U.S. Second Division, the Fifth Regimental Combat Team, and the First Provisional Marine Brigade disembarked from points as distant as Hawaii and California. Regrouping and integrating Republic of Korea troops into American units provided still another source of manpower. While North Korea retained a significant advantage in reserves, U.N. front-line strength no longer suffered from markedly inferior numbers. Furthermore, what the defenders of South Korea lacked in manpower they made up in firepower. By the middle of August Red tanks faced equally strong U.S. armored units, while the Democratic People's Republic of Korea artillery sections were clearly outgunned.[1] Communist supply lines now extended hundreds of miles and were exposed to continual daylight bombing and night intruder attacks. Serious food shortages weakened Red troops already fatigued from long marches and incessant bombardment. Conversely, U.N. supply lines spanned only thirty to sixty-five miles from the main base at Pusan. No enemy attacks threatened U.N. communication lines either within the Pusan perimeter or between it and the sanctuary of Japan.

The shifting balance of military power became manifest during the second week of August. From August 7–11 twenty thousand American and ROK troops counterattacked the veteran DPRK Sixth Division near Masan, in the southwest portion of the Pusan perimeter. The battle ended in the first major U.N. victory, relieving the Eighth Army flank and forcing the enemy to abandon large quantities of equipment. Despite furious North Korean offensives against the entire line, no major breakthrough occurred. The key city of Taegu withstood repeated enemy attacks, while a Red crossing of the Naktong River failed to achieve any significant advantage.

It is no coincidence that in this critical period the anonymous military commentary in *Jen Min Jih Pao* was delayed.[2] On August 13th it finally reappeared, echoing the earlier *World Culture* forecast of "a prolonged war" and frankly admitting that the war was "in a new stage." This account, the most pessimistic yet to appear in the Chinese Communist press, undoubtedly reflected estimates at higher levels that provided a background for the Malik maneuvers at Lake Success. It detailed the American program of recruitment and mobilization. It gave the Chinese audience its first news of fresh international reinforcements for South Korea and noted that "Marshall Plan aid" had induced Great Britain, Australia, New Zealand, Thailand, Pakistan, Turkey, and other countries to contribute troops. It vividly described the havoc of napalm attacks upon DPRK communication lines and emphasized the ease of transport afforded the U.N. within the Pusan perimeter. Quoting General Walton Walker's order, "Do not retreat another inch!" the analysis concluded, "This undoubtedly increases the difficulties of the Korean people and cannot but compel the Korean people to prepare for a bitter and prolonged war." In short, victory was a slim hope, stalemate an imminent prospect, and defeat an unmentioned but obvious possibility.[3]

What recourse lay before Sino-Soviet strategists? Pyongyang's race against time to prevent a U.N. counteroffensive seemed to have been lost, although a few weeks remained for further efforts. Only military intervention by one or both of the Sino-Soviet partners, however, could guarantee victory for North Korea. Yet no such action was taken at this time, apparently because the risks were considered too great and because alternative courses of action offered an acceptable substitute for total victory.

The Indian proposal of July had already suggested that the Security Council, augmented by PRC representation, be the scene of a negotiated solution. This could be explored further without committing the Soviet Union to any particular position in advance. In addition political efforts might be aimed at deterring U.S. pursuit of U.N. objectives in Korea. Should those objectives be somewhat ill defined, Sino-Soviet pressure might exploit American unwillingness to fight a costly war, far from home, in order to win a compromise settlement. Only when these diplomatic alternatives had been exhausted would it be necessary to consider assuming the risks of active military support to North Korea.

Malik Maneuvers

On the surface, Jacob Malik's performance at Lake Success seemed designed for the twofold purpose of obstructing any U.N. action on Korea and of propagandizing Communist themes in the international forum.[4] Closer examination of his public speeches and his private, informal exchanges with other delegates, however, reveals clues indicating willingness to compromise. Malik never went beyond these initial exploratory efforts, perhaps because they were rebuffed by virtually all other Council members. Nowhere did he propose specific terms for ending hostilities. Adamant American opposition to Malik's position and to suggestions of compromise from other delegates signaled the failure of this phase of Soviet strategy.

"It Pays To Be Rude" [5]

The immediate impression given by Malik, from his arrival on August 1st until his departure four weeks later, was of uncompromising hostility to "the Anglo-American imperialist bloc and its aggressive policy in Korea." Both as President and as Soviet delegate, he pursued filibuster tactics so successfully as to prevent substantive voting throughout the entire month. His flagrant abuse of the President's powers and of parliamentary procedure resulted in the repeated defeat of his rulings. Despite his exploitation of the evident schism between Indian and American policies, Malik finally was warned by Sir Benegal Rau that two weeks of Soviet activity had increased, not lessened, international tensions.[6]

These tactics served propagandistic goals both within the Soviet bloc and abroad. Before August, United States spokesmen had acted almost without challenge in Council meetings. Malik's tirades furnished ammunition for Communist media to counteract the image of U.S.-U.N. unanimity. Any Indian support or British vacillation could be exploited to accentuate the theme of American isolation, which was dominant in Sino-Soviet propaganda. In addition, Malik's verbal attacks served to discourage "imperialist" hopes that his return signified Soviet weakness and a need to compromise. Beyond the ritualistic incantation of anti-American themes characteristic of Communist statements after World War II, the Soviet delegate was under a particular constraint not to speak softly in case he should encourage the "imperialist bloc" to bring further pressure against "the socialist camp."

Yet Malik's abusive behavior did not preclude a Soviet attempt to explore the prospects for a negotiated settlement in Korea. In 1949 Moscow's willingness to lift the Berlin blockade had been communicated indirectly through subtle hints and omissions scattered in seemingly routine Communist propaganda statements.[7] Confirmation of this vital shift in Soviet policy had come through informal conversations between the U.S. delegate to the Security Council, Philip Jessup, and his Russian counterpart, Jacob Malik. This precedent for Soviet reluctance to adopt traditional diplomatic procedures and channels to communicate with the West justifies examination of Malik's behavior in 1950 for similar evidence of a change in policy.

Hints of Change in the Soviet Position

The first move that compromised the previous Soviet position was, of course, Malik's return to the Security Council in the presence of the Republic of China delegate, T. F. Tsiang. Malik insisted that he returned only to assume the Presidency of the Security Council, which rotated among the permanent members and which had now fallen to Russia. Yet he spoke repeatedly as the U.S.S.R. delegate in addition to ruling as President. Furthermore, while terming all Council resolutions from January to July "illegal" because of his absence and Tsiang's presence, Malik proposed new resolutions for consideration with the Taiwan delegate in attendance. In short, his verbal and procedural attacks against Tsiang did not conceal a tacit acceptance of the situation that had previously been the occasion for a Soviet boycott.[8]

A second clue to the new Soviet strategy came on August 4th, when Malik introduced his main resolution, calling for invitations to the PRC and to "representatives of the Korean people" to attend the Council's discussions on Korea, and for "an end to hostilities" together with withdrawal of "all foreign troops." He did not request Chinese Communist representation except on an *ad hoc* basis, despite previous Sino-Soviet insistence that the permanent Chinese representatives on all U.N. bodies be those from Peking. Nor did Malik require the exclusion of Chiang Kai-shek's representative, who presumably would sit at the same table with the PRC spokesman. Finally, he made no mention of the Taiwan issue which had loomed so large in Chou En-lai's July 6th cable to Lake Success. *Jen Min Jih Pao* promptly offered editorial endorsement of the Malik proposal without, however, calling attention to his reformulation of the conditions under which Peking would participate in U.N. deliberations.[9]

The third evidence of a change in Soviet policy came in Malik's definition of "representatives of the Korean people" who, according to his resolution, were to attend Council meetings on the war. In contrast with the standard Communist formula of "the People's Democratic Republic of Korea against the puppet Syngman Rhee regime," Malik declared, *inter alia*, "There are in Korea two governmental camps, the North and the South . . . the authorities of the North and the authorities of the South. . . . An internal struggle and civil war has divided it into two warring and opposing camps, governmental camps. One governmental camp is headed by Syngman Rhee, and the other by Kim Il-sung." [10]

The repetitious references to two "camps" take on added significance when contrasted with the complete absence of similar terminology in other Communist communications. To the knowledge of the writer, never before had Soviet bloc statements awarded Seoul equal status with Pyongyang. Nor did Russian and Chinese comment at the time adopt Malik's phraseology. Yet his long statement was unambiguous on this point, amplified by his calling for invitations to "both the representatives of Syngman Rhee and the representatives of Kim Il-sung . . . both the representatives of the northern authorities and those of the southern authorities, regardless of their designation." On August 8th Malik reverted partially to the usual form, contrasting "the puppet Syngman Rhee regime" with "the People's Democratic Republic of Korea . . . which has the support of an overwhelming majority of the Korean people." [11] However, he repeated his invitation to "representatives of both parties, of the North Koreans and of the South Koreans."

Admittedly these clues permit contradictory interpretations. On the one hand, they may have represented a devious attempt to introduce the proverbial camels' noses under the tent. Peking clearly had no chance of gaining admission to the U.N. at this time as a full-fledged permanent member. Malik's resolution offered an opening wedge that might pry the door ajar more readily than Chou En-lai's truculent cables. Nor did Pyongyang enjoy any better prospect at Lake Success. All previous U.N. resolutions had designated the Seoul authorities as the only "lawful" government, referring simply to "forces" from North Korea.[12] On June 25, 1950, the ROK had been invited to send a delegate to Council meetings on the conflict, while the DPRK had been ordered "to withdraw forthwith all their armed forces to the thirty-eighth parallel." Malik now refused to honor this prior invitation to Seoul, insisting that ROK and DPRK representatives be invited simultaneously.

On the other hand, Malik did beat a retreat, both in word and deed, from his previous position. His return to the Council in the presence of Tsiang made him vulnerable to thinly disguised ridicule from the Western delegates, Austin, Jebb, and Chauval. His proposals for inviting the PRC and DPRK representatives to discussions on Korea left the decision to the Council and refrained from claiming their right to U.N. membership on the basis of national sovereignty. Furthermore, their mere presence would not solve the major problem confronting Communist policy; namely, how to end the Korean War short of total defeat without additional commitments of military force from the Sino-Soviet alliance. The question was no longer simply that of early 1950, to establish Pyongyang and Peking as the *de jure* Korean and Chinese spokesmen at Lake Success. Now it involved the search for a formula whereby a compromise settlement of the immediate problem, the Korean War, could be achieved on terms least unfavorable to the Sino-Soviet bloc. Malik's terming the conflict "a civil war" and his attribution of parity to Seoul and Pyongyang suggest a formula that side-stepped the embarrassing question of Russian responsibility for North Korean actions, a cardinal point of attack in all U.S. statements. Moscow would not be using its "good offices" to restrain Pyongyang, as requested by Washington on June 27th, but making a disinterested move in pursuit of peace.[13] At the same time, negotiations between South and North Korean representatives under the aegis of the Security Council could proceed according to the private dictates of the two senior partners on the scene, the United States and the Soviet Union.[14]

Furthermore, by terming the war a "civil conflict" Malik may have hoped to avoid the sticky question of North Korean responsibility, not only for the attack but for the flouting of Security Council resolutions. If Moscow were to concede the priority of the invitation to Seoul on June 25th, it would lose its ground for declaring illegal the main resolutions ordering the DPRK to cease fire and withdraw its forces. Reissuing the invitation to Seoul along with one to Pyongyang would implicitly redefine the nature of the problem before the Council in such a way as to free the bloc of any onus for "aggression."

Finally, nothing in Malik's position committed the Soviet Union to a specific settlement of the war, and by extending the Indian proposal to include the DPRK as well as the PRC at the talks he was merely amplifying a position already taken by a respected, non-Communist power. Should the Soviet resolution fail, little would be risked, while the potential gains were large. Should the resolution succeed, the intricate process of negotiation would reveal the extent to which the minimal goals of Soviet and American policy permitted compromise. The next move lay with the West.

The Non-Communist Response

The following two weeks of exchanges clarified the differing positions of the Soviet, American, British, and Indian delegates. These positions emerged in two ways. At open Security Council meetings, reported through television, radio, and press, acrimonious exchanges between Communist and non-Communist gradually raised the level of verbal violence. In addition, on August 9th, 17th, and 21st, the Council members met privately for "an informal exchange of views" with no official record and little political debate.[15] In these public and private meetings, the goals of the non-Communist members became increasingly explicit. Malik, however, elaborated only slightly upon his initial proposal of August 4th.

The British and Norwegian delegates, although wording their speeches so as to minimize differences from the Malik and Austin positions, defined the minimum U.N. responsibility as effecting the withdrawal of Communist forces above the thirty-eighth parallel before entering into discussions with North Korean representatives.[16] The Indian delegate proposed that after such withdrawal, a committee of non-permanent Council members consider the problem and "hear any person" on the dispute. This would remove it from a great-power context to the less volatile and more politically balanced group of Cuba, Ecuador, Norway, Egypt, Yugoslavia, and India.

Malik neither attacked nor accepted these proposals. On August 17th, at the informal meeting, he repeated his request for simultaneous invitations to both sides, adding that the Soviet Union could not accept the ROK representative at Council proceedings on the basis of the June 25th resolution, but that circumstances compelled Moscow to concede Seoul's right to be heard along with Pyongyang.[17] He pointed out that his resolution did not address itself to the validity of the earlier resolution but that it did permit ROK representation. Thus the positions of all parties would remain intact although the situation would be substantially altered. When questioned on his procedural formula for reinviting to Council debates a delegate already approved to attend, Malik parried by insisting that the group must first decide whether it wanted both sides to be represented. If this were agreed upon in principle, procedural matters could be settled afterward.

The apparent Soviet concern for its past public position on the alleged illegality of Council resolutions on Korea deadlocked discussion at this point. No other delegation implied willingness to cast doubt on the validity of the invitation of June 25th by reinviting the Seoul representative at this time. Malik made one last effort at compromise. According to his own account of the last informal meeting, on August 21st, he agreed to issue the invitation to Seoul immediately, provided it were agreed in advance that Pyongyang would receive a parallel invitation at a predetermined later date.[18] This appears to have been his maximum concession at this time. It fell markedly short of Indian proposals and remained wholly at odds with the American position, enunciated by Ambassador Warren Austin.

Austin's initial rebuttal, on August 10th, had attacked the Malik resolution along a wide front, remarking, *inter alia,* "This is not a battle for any fragment of the population; it is for the right of the Korean people to choose their own future." [19] On August 17th he expanded this statement in the most comprehensive summary of U.S. policy to date. His words merit quotation at length in view of their seeming insistence upon total North Korean defeat as the minimal condition for terminating hostilities. After "welcoming" Sir Benegal Rau's "thoughts" on the crisis, Austin addressed himself to the matter of further "discussions" and "examination" of the Korean question:

> The Security Council and the General Assembly have built already a firm base *for any future action* which might be decided upon to fulfill the objectives for which the United Nations is now fighting. The Security Council has set as its first objective the end of the breach of the peace. *This objective must be pursued in such a manner that no opportunity is provided for another attempt at invasion.* . . . The United Nations must see *that the people of Korea attain complete individual and political freedom.* . . . *Shall only a part of this country be assured this freedom? I think not.* . . . Korea's prospect would be dark if any action of the United Nations were to condemn it to exist indefinitely as half-slave and half-free, or even one-third slave and two-thirds free. . . . The General Assembly has decided

that *fair and free elections should be held throughout the whole of the Korean peninsula.* . . .

The United Nations ought to have *free and unhampered access to and full freedom to travel within all parts of Korea.* . . . We are waiting and while we wait the strength of the United Nations increases [italics added].[20]

Austin's words contained no hint of compromise. On the contrary, his references to "a firm base for any future action" and to increasing U.N. strength demonstrated growing American confidence in the Pusan perimeter defenses and the ultimate counteroffensive. Washington was clearly in no mood to invite Pyongyang, much less Peking, for talks on Korea. Malik's maneuver had failed.

Three days after Austin's statement the second phase of Sino-Soviet political strategy unfolded. On August 20th Chou En-lai addressed a cable to Lake Success, his first in more than six weeks, focusing this time not on Taiwan but on Korea: "Korea is China's neighbor. The Chinese people cannot but be concerned about solution of the Korean question. . . . It must and can be settled peacefully."[21] Seconding Malik's proposal of August 4th, Chou demanded PRC representation "when the Korean question is being discussed in the Security Council." Two days later Malik unleashed his most bitter and prolonged attack against American policy, warning: "Any continuation of the Korean War will lead inevitably to a widening of the conflict with consequences, the responsibility for which will lie with the United States and its Security Council delegation."[22]

Peking Enters the Scene

Although *Jen Min Jih Pao* had endorsed Malik's proposal on August 7th, Peking waited more than two weeks before officially notifying Lake Success of its interest in Korea. The sequence of events indicates that this delay was intended to test the U.N., and particularly the U.S., response to Malik's unilateral move. When his efforts seemed to have failed, additional pressure, now from China, attempted to persuade the West that a negotiated settlement of the war was preferable to pursuit of total victory. Such persuasion was to take the form of deterrence, embodied in the threat of Chinese intervention. That Peking's active interest came late and was revealed only gradually from August to October suggests that it was undertaken with reluctance. This conforms with the above analysis of Chinese Communist behavior in June and July. It is now time to examine Peking's posture in August for clues to the change in policy whereby Communist China declared itself an interested party in the Korean War.

Propaganda on Taiwan and Korea

Chinese Communist propaganda clues emerged through three separate, but related, developments. The first case, with the most voluminous material, related to the campaign whose slogan was, "Resist American Invasion of Taiwan and Korea." This began in July and continued in various forms into August. The second development centered on the fifth anniversary of North Korean "liberation," celebrated August 15th. Finally, the visit of General MacArthur to Taiwan from July 31st to August 1st elicited a response from Peking, but one that, significantly, was delayed.

We have already seen how the mass campaign, inaugurated on July 10th, shifted the stress from Korea to Taiwan and how its content advocated "resistance" in an attitudinal rather than a military sense.[23] These characteristics marked the propaganda throughout China at least until the celebrations of the founding of the Red Army on August 1st.[24] Once the designated time for featuring Taiwan and Korean material had passed, *Jen Min Jih Pao*'s attention quickly switched to other matters. Following the commemorative articles of August 1–7, hailing the Red Army, references to Taiwan almost disappeared from this newspaper. Except for Pyongyang's mid-month celebrations, Korean coverage in *Jen Min Jih Pao* fell more than two-thirds between its peak in the July campaign and the period August 18–25.

The fifth anniversary of North Korean "liberation" brought a temporary spate of articles and pictures in the Chinese press. It also marked an increase in Peking's public relations with Pyongyang. On August 11th Kuo Mo-jo and Li Li-san headed a "comfort mission" to the Korean capital, to "express our heartfelt salutations." [25] Kuo's parting remarks, however, gave no indication of substantive help but ritualistically reasserted "support" for "the just war of the Korean people and the revolutionary movements of all Asian peoples in their struggle for independence and emancipation." *Jen Min Jih Pao*'s editorial carried even less promise for the DPRK: "We joyously celebrate the victory that has been won by the Korean people. . . . Nevertheless, the Korean people must be fully aware that they still have many difficulties ahead, and must prepare to meet and overcome them. We believe the heroic Korean people have all the necessary forces for overcoming any difficulties." [26]

On August 13th the first PRC ambassador to North Korea finally presented his credentials. Neither his remarks nor the brief congratulatory telegrams from Mao and Chou offered any significant assistance to help Pyongyang overcome its "difficulties."

Mao's telegram had only one sentence, Chou En-lai's, two; both were couched in conventional Communist prose. To be sure, the "comfort mission" carried with it gifts "from the Chinese people" of medical equipment and money. North Korean propaganda, however, paid this scant heed compared with its lavish praise for past Soviet help. In fact, Radio Pyongyang's allusions to Chinese Communist "support" explicitly described its indirect nature: "The determination of the Chinese people for the liberation of Formosa is encouraging the Korean People more than anything else." [27] By contrast, DPRK strength was wholly attributed to "Soviet assistance," and "indeed, our friendship with the Soviet people is one of the guarantees for victory in the war." [28] In short, Peking appeared to be marking Pyongyang's anniversary with the minimum response commensurate with neighborly and "fraternal Communist" relations.

At no time during this period did Peking couch its propaganda on Taiwan and Korea in terms that implied imminent Chinese military action in either area. Even the observation of Red Army Day brought no such hint. Particularly striking in this respect was the failure to exploit the MacArthur visit to Taiwan for sharpening the image of "the American imperialist plot of aggression against China." Had mass mobilization been the goal of the "Resist American Invasion of Taiwan and Korea" campaign, MacArthur's forty-eight-hour visit with Chiang Kai-shek, capped by a joint communiqué implying complete harmony of aims, would have provided ample grist for Peking's propaganda mills. Yet not only was news of the trip suppressed in China, but editorial comment proved mild when it occurred. On August 5th *Jen Min Jih Pao* broke its silence on the matter, quoting part of the MacArthur-Chiang communiqué as evidence of "American aggression and invasion of Taiwan." This did not represent any threat to China, however, but only further obstruction to the "just and legal struggle to liberate Taiwan." That this obstruction might last indefinitely was implied by *Jen Min Jih Pao*'s comparing the inevitable "failure" of American policy in Taiwan with Japan's ultimate failure to hold Northeast China. The paper did not need to remind its readers that the earlier "failure" had succeeded for almost fifteen years.

Purposes of the Propaganda

In view of the above facts it would be difficult to cite the "Resist American Invasion of Taiwan and Korea" campaign as evidence of preparation for military intervention in the war.[29] The "hate America" theme served other purposes. So far as the mobilization of public opinion was concerned, the propaganda only indirectly prepared the Chinese audience for possible involvement at some later date without, at this point, indicating the time, place, or manner of involvement. In fact, the campaign appears in part to have aimed at countering anxiety over the threat of war, while breaking down remnants of pro-American feeling. *Hsüeh Hsi,* a leading theoretical journal, instructed Chinese Communist Party cadres on these "mistaken" concepts among the populace, and offered lines of counterargument.[30] It denied accusations that Russia and its allies were "aggressors," that "North Korea attacked South Korea ruthlessly and without provocation," and that the "United States intervened to defend the peace . . . as a United Nations police action." It warned: "There are some persons who take a fence-sitting attitude toward truth and falsehood. They doubt whether or not the Soviet Union-led anti-imperialist and peaceful democratic camp is definitely safeguarding long-lasting peace. They go so far as to consider both camps' talk of peace as being false, that both sides are preparing for war."

It is impossible to determine the extent to which such doubts prevailed on the mainland. Chinese Communist press references, however, indicate serious official concern over popular "fear" or "worship" of

America.[31] The carefully controlled propaganda on Taiwan and Korea countered such attitudes. On the one hand, it met them openly and did not attempt to ignore the genuine sources of domestic anxiety, perhaps magnified by rumor and misinformation. On the other hand, it did not stress the military threat posed by "American imperialism," but discounted the possibility of civil or foreign war returning to China. The United States was "a paper tiger." The image of MacArthur, conveyed in cartoon and caption, compounded ridicule with contempt, albeit infrequently linked with symbolic reminders of the atomic bomb.

A second target of the Taiwan-Korea campaign was anti-Communist opposition within China. Far from being anxious over the prospect of war with the United States, either in Taiwan or Korea, this opposition would welcome the "threat posed by American policy." By warning against the destructive role of "American imperialism and its agents" on the mainland, the regime could justify increased vigilance and repression, and hopefully explain away continued resistance to "liberation and pacification." By not portraying the situation as an immediate crisis, however, the regime could discourage dissident elements from prolonging resistance in expectation of imminent American support or general war. Anti-Communist opposition was no small problem. Peking later admitted that in Hunan alone, "during the five months from April to September 1950, altogether over 60,000 bandits were inactivated. . . . In October 1950 our Army launched a bandit-suppressing campaign along the border of West Hunan . . . and shattered Chiang Kai-shek's dream of setting up an 'anti-Communist guerrilla base.' " [32]

A third goal of the campaign was to spur reconstruction and land reform, the two major economic programs of 1950. Workers' meetings, mass petitions, and production charts geared "patriotic activity" to "resisting American aggression." In the countryside, those who obstructed land reform became "agents of American imperialism" and were eliminated in summary fashion. Shortcomings in either program were blamed on the foreign scapegoat, deflecting criticism from Communist rule.

This, in turn, suggests a fourth gain from the campaign: it provided additional means of organizing mass activity through innumerable committees and meetings. These *ad hoc* organizations, formed at the local level to promote the so-called Stockholm Peace Appeal in May and June, remained to mobilize "volunteers" for the Korean front in November and December. We do not know how much of their expanding work was anticipated by the regime at the outset. Yet, in retrospect, the propaganda movement in July and August can be seen to have served both immediate and longer-range political and organizational goals.

In sum, the Resist-America campaign did not mobilize the populace for war in Korea. At best, it prepared the climate of opinion for any eventuality and tried to arouse hostility against the United States without alerting the country for action. The general design of Peking's propaganda at this time indicates that military action, particularly war with the United States, would have been undertaken with considerable reluctance on the part of both the regime and the people.

The New Posture

Suddenly Peking's posture changed and a new note of determination entered its utterances on Korea. We have already examined Chou En-lai's cable to Lake Success of August 20th as the first manifestation of this new posture. Followed within forty-eight hours by Malik's harsh attack against U.S. policy, the Chou cable signaled a new course in Sino-Soviet strategy whereby Peking was to become increasingly involved in efforts to deter the U.N. from pursuing the war to total victory.

World Culture, having been first to hint at a postponement of the Taiwan invasion and first publicly to prognosticate a "prolonged war" in Korea, once again broke new ground by spelling out for the discerning reader the implications of the change in policy. The article merits quotation at length as the initial warning from the regime of serious responsibilities ahead in Korea:

The barbarous action of American imperialism and its hangers-on in invading Korea not only menaces peace in Asia and the world in general but *seriously threatens the security of China in particular.* The Chinese people cannot allow such aggressive acts of American imperialism in Korea. To settle the Korean question peacefully, first the opinions of the Korean people and next the opinions of the Chinese people must be heard. . . .

No Asian affairs can be solved without the participation of the Chinese people. *It is impossible to solve the Korean problem without the participation of its closest neighbor, China. . . .* North Korea's friends are our friends. *North Korea's enemy is our enemy. North Korea's defense is our defense.* North Korea's victory is our victory [italics added].³³

By implication, North Korea's defeat would also be Red China's defeat. Reluctance to state this unequivocally, at least to foreign audiences, may explain the deletion in broadcasts to North America of the important lines, "North Korea's enemy is our enemy. North Korea's defense is our defense. North Korea's victory is our victory." ³⁴ Suppression of these words suggests the meticulous manner in which Sino-Soviet communications only gradually raised the level of political pressure upon the United States. This avoided drawing a line so firm as to preclude flexibility in the event of negotiations or of miscalculation of the U.S. response. At the same time, a selected domestic audience was alerted to a basic change in Peking's policy.

As with Malik's earlier moves at Lake Success, however, the clues to a change in policy gave no insight into the precise content of policy. Thus a freshet of Communist cables, which flowed into Lake Success in the last week of Malik's Presidency, demonstrated new bloc pressure but did not define the desired U.N. response in a specific and credible manner. On August 24th Chou En-lai belatedly protested the Truman order of June 27th to the U.S. Seventh Fleet and demanded that the Security Council "condemn . . . and take immediate measures to bring about the complete withdrawal of all the United States armed invading forces from Taiwan and from other territories belonging to China." Presumably "other territories" referred to the Pescadores Islands and lesser offshore islands, still held by Chiang Kai-shek. While in effect proposing that Taiwan be included on the agenda, Chou did not insist on PRC participation in Council discussion of the matter. Set against the urgency of Korea, his introduction of Taiwan at this point gave the Sino-Soviet position a suspiciously propagandistic tone, obscuring any semblance of intent to negotiate that might have remained from Malik's earlier maneuvers.

This propagandistic appearance was accentuated by Chou's accompanying "demand" that the Council "stop the atrocities . . . of barbarous bombing" in Korea. Malik's sheaf of parallel petitions and cables from Communist groups throughout the world included an official protest against these "atrocities" from the Mongolian People's Republic. Yet there was obviously no more likelihood of Council action on this matter than on the "complete withdrawal" of U.S. forces from Taiwan. On August 26th still another cable from Peking named Chang Wen-t'ien as "chairman of the delegation of the People's Republic of China" to the forthcoming Fifth General Assembly.[35] Although the two earlier cables had compromised Peking's status by accepting Malik's proposal on conditional attendance at the Council discussion on Korea and by demanding Council action on Taiwan without PRC representation, Chou now insisted flatly that all Taiwan-appointed delegates be immediately expelled from the U.N. "as illegitimate delegates of the Chinese Kuomintang reactionary remnant clique." This demand, like the others, appeared so unrealistic in terms of the existing situation as to make questionable the seriousness Peking attached to any of its communications.

Despite the propaganda barrage, however, several developments command our attention. First, the Chou En-lai cable of August 20th and the *World Culture* article of August 26th declared China an interested party with respect to Korea in an unequivocal and unprecedented manner. Both the cable and the article, of course, must have been the outcome of decisions taken some days or weeks earlier. Second, these statements were accompanied by a warning from Malik against "continuation of the war" lest it "lead inevitably to a widening of the conflict." Third, these moves occurred one month after Peking's acknowledgment of the likelihood of "prolonged war" in Korea and at a time when a temporary stalemate had frozen the battle front, leaving North Korea in possession of almost all the peninsula but facing a rapid U.N. build-up in the Pusan perimeter.

In short, the emergence of China as one of the actively interested parties in Korea appears linked with the vain attempt by Malik to arrange negotiations to end the "civil war" between Pyongyang and Seoul under Security Council auspices. Realistically, the bloc could no longer hope to dictate the terms of settlement. It could, however, take soundings on enemy willingness to negotiate while the seeming advantage still lay with the DPRK and before the U.N. counteroffensive could expand enemy goals. Austin's speech of August 17th seemed to indicate that the U.S. would insist on uniting Korea, by force if necessary. Yet three other Council members had implied that the thirty-eighth parallel might provide a basis for ending hostilities on the *status quo ante bellum*. In this context Peking's new posture becomes more understandable. By enlarging upon the "contradictions" between Anglo-Indian and American policy, China as well as Russia sought to deter the U.N. from crossing the old dividing line in Korea.

Evidence of the new Chinese policy, then, appears early enough to suggest that Sino-Soviet agreement was reached on Chinese Communist involvement in Korea, at least of a political kind, in advance of the August 17th statement by Austin. The significance of this timing was obscured by a sudden increase in the level of verbal violence in the last week of August. In the U.S., Secretary of the Navy Francis P. Matthews, and in Tokyo, General Douglas MacArthur, both demanded a more aggressive military policy against the Soviet bloc. Close on the heels of these statements, Peking charged that U.S. aircraft strafed Chinese villages bordering the Yalu River. Chinese Communist reaction to these developments was immediate and militant, as will be seen in the next chapter. However, the initial militancy came from Peking *before* these provocations. Hence one must consider the possible reasons for Chinese Communist willingness to participate diplomatically, and perhaps militarily, in the Korean venture as early as the first two weeks of August.

Chinese Communist Considerations

In Chapter III we considered the possible relationship between the original goals of the North Korean attack and Chinese Communist interests, and found no significant conflict between them. On the contrary, DPRK success would benefit the PRC, through its probable impact on future U.S.-Japanese relations and on Communist influence in Asia. However, Peking had pressing political, economic, and military problems at home. These, together with Russian ascendancy in North Korea, made it unlikely that China would participate in the war. Pyongyang's victory was expected to be total and swift, with little or no U.S. opposition.

Now, however, stalemate if not defeat confronted Pyongyang. Moscow and Peking held the power that could tip the balance against the U.N. but both hesitated to commit that power. While the DPRK offensive gradually lost momentum, Communist China's best troops watched passively across the border. After the chances for victory seemed past, Peking suddenly identified itself with Pyongyang's cause, demanding participation in U.N. discussions on the war, but still withholding military support.

Peking's failure to act earlier or more vigorously is easier to explain than its decision to intervene politically in mid-August. We have already reviewed the salient domestic economic and political pressures that induced China to remain aloof from the war. That even her political involvement came late and developed gradually, in piecemeal fashion, is understandable. But what countervailing pressures brought it about at all? One answer may lie in the uncertainty and fear with which Peking viewed the expected U.N. counteroffensive. Would it stop at the thirty-eighth parallel? Whether or not Malik's maneuvers were designed to probe this question, they certainly elicited an answer to it: according to Austin, U.N. control over all Korea was the minimal objective.

Attainment of this goal would jeopardize Peking's position both at home and abroad. Domestic anti-Communists might intensify armed resistance to CCP rule. Japan might swing into an American-controlled Pacific defense pact. "Neutral" and anti-Communist forces throughout Asia might thereupon fall into line behind Washington. The "semicolonial and colonial national liberation movement" would be set back for years, perhaps decades. The military implications of a U.N. occupation of North Korea were as serious as the political. Might not U.N. forces push beyond the Yalu? Might not the MacArthur-Chiang Kai-shek accord include renewed air and land attacks against the mainland.

Such fears gained credibility from the image of MacArthur to be found in well-informed United States publications. Chinese Communist references to the *New York Times, Time,* and *U.S. News & World Report* reflected the careful perusal of American periodicals for information on U.S. intentions, as well as, of course, for derogatory matter to be exploited by Peking's propaganda. Thus information on MacArthur's views and his relations with Washington must be assumed to have contributed to Communist calculations. His seemingly unchallenged power in Japan, his reported flouting of White House advice, and his declared admiration of the Chinese Nationalists was reflected in authoritative dispatches throughout the summer of 1950. On July 10th *Time* recounted an alleged exchange of the previous week between Mac-Arthur and the Pentagon: " 'If such and such were undertaken, perhaps General MacArthur would like to do so and so?' The answer from Tokyo bounced back: 'No comment.' The Pentagon brooded for a while, then tried another approach: 'Do you desire any instruction?' The reply was terse: 'No.' " The same article asserted, "Last January, the State Department overruled MacArthur's urgent proposal that Formosa be defended." Such reports indicated MacArthur's key role in Far East strategy as well as his preferred policies.

The general's views on the Taiwan question were amplified in this issue of *Time,* "If we had dreamed that the Communists would take China, we would have swallowed Chiang Kai-shek, horns, cloven hooves, and all . . . if that was the way we felt about him. Personally I have great respect for Chiang." Two weeks later, *Time* (July 24th) described Chiang's reciprocal feelings, whereby his "unlimited confidence in MacArthur" made Chiang "happy to place the fate of Formosa and of Nationalist China in his hands. . . . No other American," according to the Generalissimo, "is [as] capable." This publication stated repeatedly that MacArthur's views differed from official policy, but suggested that the U.N. commander exercised considerable independence of judgment and action.[36] Communist assumptions about imperialist deceit and enmity fostered the most threatening interpretation on this evidence of "aggressive designs" in Tokyo and Washington.

A second factor that probably contributed to China's growing interest in Korea arose from those traditional influences that have been defined above as the Chinese component of Peking's policy. China, according to this scheme of thought, had a "right to be heard" on the Korean problem. For almost a century the "sick man of Asia" had been unable to prevent other nations from settling issues vital to China's interests without regard for Chinese views. Now the invasion of Taiwan had been postponed because of U.S. "interference." Were all Asian affairs, including those on China's borders, to be settled by American fiat? A conditional U.N. invitation was undoubtedly less desirable than permanent representation at Lake Success, but pending the preferred eventuality Peking's voice at the Council table would at least restore the image of China as an Asian, and perhaps a world, power. In Communist

China's absence, New Delhi continued to share the spotlight with Moscow and Washington, and India to serve as a self-appointed link between East and West.

Finally, Peking had to consider its Moscow ally. We know nothing of the actual exchanges that may have occurred between the two capitals at this time. Throughout August, reports from Hong Kong, Taipei, and Tokyo told of high level Sino-Soviet conferences.[37] According to a later account from a Chinese Communist prisoner of war, a Russian directive, communicated to Peking early in the month, outlined joint responsibilities whereby PLA manpower and Soviet firepower would furnish "volunteers" to Pyongyang in the fall.[38] It is impossible to verify these accounts, but Russian pressure undoubtedly was an additional factor contributing to Communist China's involvement in the Korean War.

This pressure may have taken both negative and positive forms. On the one hand, Moscow could withhold vital political and economic support from Peking. It could obstruct the transfer of industries and railroads in the Northeast. It might even hint that Soviet assistance to China under the 1950 mutual defense treaty would be more certain in the future if Peking actively supported Pyongyang's defense now. On the other hand, Soviet inducements may have included the assurance that a diplomatic show of force would suffice to swing neutral and moderate opinion in the U.N. away from the U.S. position, permitting a settlement on the *status quo ante bellum*. Russian pledges of military assistance, especially in air power, may have helped to persuade Peking that, in the unlikely event of war, the risks were tolerable. Finally, the Sino-Soviet treaty may have offered a firm guarantee of all-out Russian support should the U.S. attack mainland China in response to PRC intervention.

It is also possible, though highly unlikely, that Sino-Soviet decisions were made seriatim in response to external events, without advance planning or phased strategy. A point in favor of the theory is that no evidence has been found of Soviet re-equipping of the PLA during the summer of 1950, a logical preparation for combat with the superior firepower of U.N. forces. Furthermore, the disposition of Chinese Communist armies remained fairly constant from mid-July to early September; there was no major redeployment during this time. More striking still, Fourth Field Army units failed to cross the Yalu River before mid-October, although they might have been expected to prepare firm defense lines across the peninsula in anticipation of the U.N. advance.[39]

Yet the absence of military activity is inconclusive evidence of an absence of military planning. Sino-Soviet calculations may have erred in not allowing for so quick or so successful a U.N. counterattack as occurred in September. Meanwhile China and Russia may have hoped that verbal warnings and the presence of Peking's best troops in Manchuria would deter a drive to seize the entire peninsula. Plans for military intervention, in the event political measures failed, may have been limited at first to holding a small strip of territory from which the DPRK could maintain its existence and from which a prolonged war of attrition would erode U.N. resistance in the mountains of North Korea.

In short, the evidence on the degree to which Sino-Soviet decisions in August may have anticipated the course of events over the next two months is inconclusive. One point seems certain, however: Chou's cable of August 20th and Malik's warning of August 22nd ushered in a new, co-ordinated Sino-Soviet strategy. From this time forward the People's Republic of China was to become increasingly involved in the Korean War, culminating in the Chinese "volunteer" attack against the U.N. forces in mid-October.

VI

THE UNITED NATIONS
CROSSES THE PARALLEL

※

IT WILL be recalled that, on August 20, 1950, Chou En-lai cabled the United Nations, "The Chinese people cannot but be concerned about solution of the Korean question." On or about October 16, 1950, the first Chinese Communist "volunteers" crossed the Yalu River in secrecy. The following chronology gives the sequence of events between these two dates:

SELECTED CHRONOLOGY OF DEVELOPMENTS IN KOREAN CONFLICT,
AUGUST 25–OCTOBER 16, 1950

August 25　　U.S. Secretary of Navy Matthews calls for "instituting a war to compel co-operation for peace."

U.N. Commander General Douglas MacArthur says Taiwan is part of "the island chain" from which U.S. "can dominate with air power every Asiatic port from Vladivostok to Singapore."

August 25　　U.S. aircraft allegedly strafe Chinese villages bordering Yalu River.

September 1　　Commandant of U.S. Air War College suspended from post for remarks on strategy: "We're at war. . . . Give me the order to do it and I can break up Russia's five A-bomb nests in a week."

September 6	U.N. Security Council defeats (8–1, 2 abstentions) U.S.S.R. resolution of August 4 requesting DPRK and PRC participation in Korean debate, cease-fire, and withdrawal of "foreign troops."
September 11	U.N. Security Council defeats (6–3, 2 abstentions) U.S.S.R. resolution requesting PRC representation at meetings to consider charges against U.S. of air violation over Yalu River.
September 15	U.N. amphibious landing at Inchon in rear of DPRK forces, while U.N. counteroffensive begins at Pusan perimeter.
September 18	MacArthur charges Communist China gave "substantial if not decisive military assistance" to DPRK by transfer of ethnic Korean troops before June invasion.
September 19	U.N. General Assembly defeats (33–11, 8 abstentions) Indian resolution to admit PRC delegation.
September 22	Peking officially admits MacArthur charge of September 18; declares "will always stand on the side of the Korean people."
September 25	Acting PLA Chief of Staff, General Nieh Jung-chen informally tells Indian Ambassador Panikkar that PRC will not "sit back with folded hands and let the Americans come to the border."
September 30	Chou En-lai publicly warns: "The Chinese people . . . will not supinely tolerate seeing their neighbors being savagely invaded by the imperialists."
October 1	ROK troops cross thirty-eighth parallel as MacArthur gives ultimatum to Pyongyang "forthwith to lay down your arms and cease hostilities under such military supervision as I may direct."

October 2   Chou En-lai formally notifies Panikkar that if U.S. troops enter North Korea, China will intervene in the war.

                U.S.S.R. Foreign Minister Vyshinsky offers seven-point proposal at U.N. General Assembly for an immediate cease-fire and withdrawal of "foreign troops," followed by all-Korean elections.

October 7   U.S. First Cavalry Division crosses thirty-eighth parallel as U.N. General Assembly endorses "all appropriate steps to ensure conditions of stability throughout Korea."

October 10   PRC Ministry of Foreign Affairs spokesman stresses "peaceful" proposal by Vyshinsky and warns: "The Chinese people cannot stand by idly with regard to . . . the invasion of Korea by the United States and its accomplices and [with regard] to the dangerous trend toward extending the war."

October 16   First Chinese Communist "volunteers" cross into Korea in secrecy.

The swift collapse of Democratic People's Republic of Korea resistance following the Inchon landing accelerated Sino-Soviet efforts to halt the war short of North Korean territory. These efforts were two-fold. Russian maneuvers at Lake Success attempted to bring Pyongyang and Peking into U.N.-sponsored negotiations. On September 6th these maneuvers were defeated in the Security Council. Thereupon the Chinese increased their activity and issued warnings designed to deter the U.N. from crossing the thirty-eighth parallel. On October 2nd both partners brought their co-ordinated strategy to a climax with Chou En-lai's official warning to the United States through Panikkar and Vyshinsky's omnibus proposal to the General Assembly. Five days later U.S. troops crossed the parallel, signaling the failure of Sino-Soviet political strategy. At this point the Moscow-Peking axis turned to military action through Chinese Communist participation in the Korean War.

This chapter will probe Peking's known and conjectured reactions to the alleged air raids across the Yalu, U.N. rebuffs to Soviet proposals, and statements of intent from U.S. officials. As always, we are dependent upon clues in selective and mass communications, in diplomatic behavior, and in military movements for inferring high-level decisions. We do not know the full explanation for the two-month lapse between Chou En-lai's demand for the People's Republic of China's inclusion in U.N. talks on Korea and the initial contact between Chinese Communist "volunteers" and U.N. forces. However, closer examination of the interaction between Sino-Soviet moves and Korean developments will enable us to understand some, if not all, of the decisions that ultimately led to Peking's involvement in the Korean War.

Challenge and Response

We have already noted the new tone of belligerency in Chou En-lai's August 20th cable and Malik's speech of August 22nd, in response to the Austin statement of August 17th that had insisted on Korean unification under U.N. auspices. Chinese Communist propaganda gave this belligerent tone a fresh sense of urgency in the closing days of August after the U.S. air offensive apparently strayed across the Yalu River. If the Chou-Malik messages were intended to deter the U.N. from carrying the war to total victory, the border violations provided a convenient pretext for intensifying the signs of belligerency. At the same time Peking seems to have interpreted the pattern of U.S. political statements and actions during these weeks as a direct challenge to which a firm response was dictated both by national interest and by Communist ideology. The net affect was a sudden increase in the militancy of domestic propaganda, which, for the first time since the fighting began, alerted the Chinese populace to the specific possibility of war with the United States.

The "Imperialist Challenge"

Three types of "imperialist challenge" confronted Sino-Soviet analysts. The first consisted of demands from highly placed American officials for a more aggressive policy against the bloc. The second challenge consisted of alleged air intrusions over Chinese territory. Third, both Truman and Austin publicly warned Peking not to be become involved in the Korean War.

Among the American officials who called openly for a more militant policy, the first and most explicit was Secretary of the Navy Francis Matthews. On August 25th, speaking before 100,000 persons, Matthews advocated "instituting a war to compel cooperation for peace. . . . We would become the first aggressors for peace." [1] On the same day U.N. Commander Douglas MacArthur warned a veterans' organization against "misconceptions currently being voiced concerning the relationship of Formosa (Taiwan) to our strategic potential in the Pacific." [2] He stressed the "island chain . . . from the Aleutians to the Marianas . . . from [which] we can dominate with air power every Asiatic port from Vladivostok to Singapore." MacArthur called Taiwan "an unsinkable aircraft carrier and submarine tender" possessing "a concentration of operational air and naval bases potentially greater than any similar concentration on the Asiatic mainland between the Yellow Sea and the Strait of Malacca." A few days later Major General Orvil A. Anderson was suspended from command of the Air War College because of statements interpreted as urging war against the Soviet bloc.[3]

The White House swiftly repudiated those who hinted at the desirability of more aggressive strategies. General MacArthur withdrew his statement upon presidential order, although too late to prevent publication in the press. On September 12th Secretary of Defense Louis Johnson, reportedly behind the Matthews "preventive war" statement, resigned.[4] His replacement, General George C. Marshall, was seen as a close supporter of the Administration and more moderate in his approach to Communist China.[5] In addition, speeches by Truman, Acheson, and Austin emphasized that American military power pursued purely defensive aims and had no aggressive designs against any nation.

The top-level denial of aggressive intentions may have been interpreted in China as a crude effort to conceal the true aims of American imperialism, inadvertently "revealed" by military figures of high standing. On the other hand, it may have been accepted as evidence of "contradictions in imperialist circles" which might be scarcely less serious for China since MacArthur remained at his post and the Truman-Acheson administration was politically vulnerable. We do not know exactly how Peking and Moscow evaluated these developments. However, their occurrence at this particular time gave them special significance for Communist analysts.

Coincident with the political controversy over U.S. strategy came the first accusation of American planes over Communist China. On August 27th, according to official Chinese Communist statements, U.S. aircraft strayed across the Yalu River, machine-gunning the rail terminal and adjoining facilities at Talitzu as well as the airfield at Antung.[6] Peking reported three persons killed and twenty-one wounded, as well as minor damage to rolling stock. Within a few days U.S. authorities conceded the possibility of a "mistake" and offered compensation, provided appropriate inspection of the alleged damage could be made. Meanwhile, on August 29th, Peking charged a second border violation by U.S. pilots who allegedly fired on Chinese fishing boats in the Yalu River, killing four and wounding seven.[7] No American acknowledgment of this second incident was forthcoming.

We shall examine the Chinese Communist reaction to these events in the following section. At this point it suffices to note that they coincided with other developments contributing to an increased level of tension between Peking and Washington. Immediately after the air incidents described above, the following statement by General MacArthur was published: "It is in the pattern of Oriental psychology to respect and follow aggressive, resolute and dynamic leadership—to quickly turn from a leadership characterized by timidity or vacillation." [8] Addressing these words to the problem of influencing "continental Asia," the U.N. commander appeared to challenge Peking for the support of the Chinese people. Thus his policy on Taiwan and the alleged air intrusions along the Yalu may have been seen in Peking as part of an overall design to probe the vulnerability of the PRC and to seek its eventual overthrow.

The third type of "imperialist challenge" consisted of direct warnings against PRC involvement in the Korean War. On September 1st President Truman declared: "We do not want the fighting in Korea to spread into a general war; it will not spread unless Communist imperialism draws other armies and governments into the fight of the aggressors against the United Nations. We hope in particular that the people of China will not be misled or forced into fighting against the United

Nations and against the American people who have always been and still are their friends." [9] Four days later Ambassador Austin expressed concern in the Security Council over reports of heavy railroad traffic near the Korean-Chinese border.

While the ostensible purpose of the Truman statement was to reassure Peking on U.S. intentions, the President's admonition against "other armies and governments" becoming involved in Korea, lest the fighting "spread into a general war," may well have been interpreted as a thinly veiled threat against the PRC, upon the analogy of Malik's effort to deter further U.N. military action on August 22nd. Against the background of the Matthews and MacArthur statements and the alleged air attacks along the Yalu River, Truman's "general war" warning was susceptible of more than one interpretation, the more so since Peking had already announced its interest in the Korean conflict.

The Chinese Communist Response

Peking's overt responses to these events were diplomatic protests and militant domestic propaganda. Its covert responses may have included preparations for the military deployment actually carried out during September and October. Prior to the Inchon landing, however, the PRC did not commit itself publicly to action in Korea but couched its most bellicose messages in purely defensive terms.

On August 27th Chou En-lai formally protested the alleged attacks to Secretary of State Acheson and to U.N. headquarters. He demanded that Washington "punish" the responsible pilots and "undertake the responsibility of compensating" for all losses. Chou asked the Security Council to "condemn the United States aggression [*sic*] forces in Korea . . . and take immediate measures to bring about the complete withdrawal" of U.S. troops from Korea. On August 30th he repeated his twofold proposal to the Security Council in a cable charging further air attacks against Chinese fishing boats. The next day Malik introduced a formal resolution embodying Chou's demands. Neither Malik nor Chou, however, called for PRC representation at discussions on this matter.

Peking exhibited a curious caution in its handling of these incidents. Whereas Chou's cable of July 6th had termed the U.S. policy on Taiwan "an act of open aggression," he now described the air attacks as "a serious criminal action encroaching upon China's sovereignty." His protest to Acheson called the situation "extremely serious" but made no threats of countermeasures beyond reserving the right "of raising further demands." Furthermore, Chou's failure to demand PRC participation in Security Council discussion of his charges contrasted with his previous insistence that Peking be represented for consideration of the Korean problem.

This relatively moderate reaction contrasted even more with the militancy of Chinese Communist press treatment of the alleged air intrusions. In content and extent, this campaign is significant as the first clear mobilization of Chinese public opinion for possible military action. A wave of mass rallies throughout the country sparked an unprecedented outburst of anti-American propaganda in which war with the United States received repeated, explicit emphasis. This new emphasis was reflected in the shift in the propaganda image of U.S. imperialism from one of helplessness to one of ferocity. In July the celebrated author, Mao Tun, had scornfully depicted the U.S. as "a greedy and stupid hog, incapable of correcting its mistakes even though its snout bleeds from wounds received in Korea." [10] Now he wrote alarmingly:

This mad dog seizes Taiwan between its hind legs while with its teeth it violently bites the Korean people. Now one of its forelegs has been poked into our Northeast front. Its bloodswollen eyes cast around for something further to attack. All the world is under its threat. The American imperialist mad dog is half beaten up. Before it dies, it will go on biting and tearing.[11]

As cartoons and comment spread this image throughout the Chinese Communist press, a new note appeared in local speeches. In pledging "resistance to American aggression," speakers no longer employed the passive term *fan tui.* Now they introduced the exhortation to action, *k'ang yi,* previously used in the fighting against Japan and against the Chinese Nationalists.[12] In addition to routine pledges of increased production, individuals swore to give their lives, if need be, against American imperialism. This "voluntary mobilization" was couched in purely defensive terms, to be sure. Nowhere was military action predicated upon the need to assist the DPRK. Within this limitation, however, the possibility of war remained a central theme.

People's Liberation Army units near Peking reported "furious anger [at] the news of attacks in the Northeast by U.S. planes," while an antiaircraft gunner echoed an infantryman's statement, "We must teach them a lesson. . . . We are ready for action. We are ready to shoot down any planes that dare intrude into our territory." [13] The following statements are typical of the campaign:

American imperialists try to scare us with war. Honestly speaking we can never be scared by such a threat. . . . We, with 450 million people, are ready to deal a deadly blow to anyone who should dare to invade our territory. . . .[14]

The combatant delegates of the North Anhwei Army Area participating in the Combat Heroes and Model Workers' Meeting vehemently said that a debt of blood will be exacted from the United States murderers of peaceful Chinese citizens. . . .[15]

Li Chin-chuang, worker of the Shinchingshan Steel and Iron works, said, "If the American imperialists dare start a war of aggression against us, I shall be the first to enlist. . . ." [16]

The masses of the Chinese people are determined to fight for peace and are ready to take up arms at any time against whoever disturbs the peace and whichever imperialist provacateurs dare to violate the territorial integrity of China. . . . Mothers who want peace for the sake of their children declare their willingness to send their sons to the front if that is the best way to defend peace. . . . Officers and men of the PLA . . . say to the warmongers, "We have weapons in our hands; we love peace and do not fear war." [17]

Peking publicized the Matthews and MacArthur statements as "proof" of American aggressive intent, dismissing the White House repudiation as "a cover-up." [18] In short, the Chinese people had reason to anticipate immediate war with the United States.

The contrast between this mobilization of violent public opinion and Chou En-lai's more moderate notes to Acheson and Lake Success paralleled that between the initial alert sounded by *World Culture* on August 26th and the milder translations broadcast abroad. It would appear that Peking was anxious not to strike too bellicose a tone in its official international utterances, lest it prejudice its chance to take part in U.N. deliberations, if not as a permanent member at least on an *ad hoc* basis connected with Korean discussions. No such constraint limited its domestic communications, which now prepared the population for the contingency of war without, however, committing the government to any specific action.

Rebuff at the U.N.

If Peking still desired to keep the door open at Lake Success, it will be worth while to examine U.N. activities for their possible relevance to Peking's actions. We have noted that, despite Chou's telegrams calling for Security Council action on Taiwan (August 24th) and in spite of the alleged air intrusions (August 27th and 30th), only his initial cable of August 20th demanded PRC representation at discussions of the Korean question. The accompanying table gives the dates of Sino-Soviet actions pertaining to Chinese Communist representation on the Council during August and September.

TABLE 3

SINO-SOVIET MOVES TO OBTAIN PEOPLE'S REPUBLIC OF CHINA
REPRESENTATION IN SECURITY COUNCIL

Subject	Sino-Soviet Introduction of Item to Council	U.S.S.R. Demands PRC Representation	PRC Demands Participation	Council Votes
Korean settlement	Aug. 4 (U.S.S.R. resolution)	Aug. 4	Aug. 20	Sept. 6
U.S. in Taiwan	Aug. 24 (PRC cable)	Aug. 29	Sept. 16	Sept. 28*
U.S. air intrusions	Aug. 27 (PRC cable)	Sept. 5	Sept. 10	Sept. 11

* The initial vote on September 28th denied PRC participation. However, Yugoslavia abstained, and on September 29th announced its support for PRC participation, thereby causing a revote: 7 yeses, 3 noes, and 1 abstention.

Peking's delay in demanding participation in the discussion of matters other than Korea suggests that it did not wish to press for Security

Council invitations until the key issue, the Korean War, had been re-solved. Introduction of the Taiwan item was a purely propagandistic move, designed to increase political pressure upon the U.S. position from such likely sources as India and Yugoslavia. As for U.S. air activity in Korea, there was no prospect that the Council would "condemn" it, much less effect the "immediate withdrawal" of U.S. forces demanded by Chou's cables on the air intrusions.

Korea, however, remained a vital concern. On September 1st Jacob Malik once more urged discussions with Pyongyang and Seoul, insisting it was "essential to come to a clear understanding, as any failure to do so could only lead to harm." [19] He then called for a separate vote on the heart of his original resolution and offered a significant amendment: the proposal to invite "representatives of the Korean people, *i.e., the representatives of North and South Korea.*" The explanatory phrase here put into italics had not appeared in his August 4th resolution. It raised to the level of formal diplomacy the Soviet concept of parity between North and South Korea. Previously Malik had used such terminology only in his commentary upon the resolution. In view of the formal ties between the USSR and the DPRK, his amendment served to emphasize Moscow's apparent willingness to compromise, provided, of course, Washington would reciprocate by denying ROK jurisdiction over all Korea.

Such a compromise was not acceptable, however, and on September 2nd the Council decisively defeated Malik's separate resolution by eight votes to two. Four days later his original proposal, including the invitation to Peking, also failed, this time by eight to one. Thus ended any immediate prospect of negotiations in the Security Council. Malik's maneuvers had failed to elicit any modification in the U.S. or the U.N. position. The approaching Fifth General Assembly opened new possibilities for maneuver, but attention shifted back to the battle front as Tokyo and other points reported an impending U.N. counteroffensive.[20]

Following the Council votes, Chinese Communist domestic communications suddenly muted the war theme. From September 8th to October 14th, *Jen Min Jih Pao*'s front-page space allocated to the war seldom exceeded 25 per cent, as in the period August 16–26 before the alleged incidents. Similarly, the term *k'ang yi* virtually disappeared from Peking's propaganda, not to reappear until the outbreak of full-scale combat between Chinese and U.N. armies. After placing the populace on an alert for possible war, Chinese Communist news media suspended their attention to American imperialist threats and reverted once more to domestic issues as the focus of concern.

Peking may have been awaiting developments on the battle front and in the General Assembly before moving into the next phase of strategy. Certainly the rejection by the Security Council of Malik's resolution on September 6th ended whatever hope may have remained after the Austin speech of August 17th that diplomatic exchanges in that forum would end the conflict. All tactics, however, for deterring a U.N. advance across the parallel had not yet been exhausted. Should additional political moves succeed, there might be no need to act militarily or to implement the *World Culture* statement: "North Korea's enemy is our enemy. North Korea's defense is our defense." Should diplomacy fail, the Chinese populace had already been alerted to the possibility of war through propagandistic exploitation of the provocative developments of late August.

As in the earlier period, the shifting emphases in domestic propaganda and the contrast between domestic and international propaganda suggest that Peking remained cautious and flexible with respect to the war. While increasing its involvement steadily through successive political developments, the PRC still refrained from military participation in the war. It is probable that final plans were elaborated during late August and early September for eventual intervention, should it prove necessary. The massive redeployment of the PLA from mid-September through November can hardly have occurred without considerable advance planning. But this is to anticipate the sequence of events.

From Pusan to Pyongyang

On September 15, 1950, the U.S. X Corps landed at Inchon, the port of Seoul, and two days later General Walton Walker's Eighth Army together with ROK units opened their major counterattack out of the Pusan perimeter. Within two weeks these twin offensives joined, cut off retreat for thousands of DPRK troops with all their equipment, and drove the remaining North Korean forces across the thirty-eighth parallel. On September 29th General MacArthur ceremoniously welcomed President Rhee back to Seoul. Except for the mopping up of enemy guerrillas, the liberation of South Korea was complete.

As early as September 19th Rhee had announced his intention of pursuing North Korean troops above the parallel, regardless of U.N. action. On October 1st ROK troops implemented his announcement, while MacArthur publicly ordered Pyongyang to "forthwith lay down your arms and cease hostilities under such military supervision as I may direct." [21] One week later U.S. units crossed the parallel in force, although stiff enemy resistance slowed their advance. On October 19th the U.S. First Cavalry and ROK First divisions entered the DPRK capital of Pyongyang. Kim Il-sung's regime had escaped north to Sinuiju, on the Yalu River. The major enemy defenses had been shattered and the unification of Korea seemed at hand.

During this brief period of slightly over a month the entire course of the war had been reversed. Yet political developments during the same weeks triggered a chain of events that was to reverse the combatants' positions still another time, and in an equally short period. In the aftermath of Inchon, Peking steadily increased the signs of its interest in the fate of North Korea. Moscow made one final move to bring about political negotiations through the U.N. When Chinese and Russian maneuvers failed to halt the U.N. advance, Peking began the movement of 300,000 troops across the Yalu River.

Peking Supports Pyongyang Anew

We have already noted the sudden decline in attention accorded the war by Chinese Communist media following the final Security Council defeat of the Malik resolution on September 6th. For the first time since hostilities began, *World Culture* made no reference to the war in its international commentary.[22] In content, too, the mobilization theme disappeared from view. *Jen Min Jih Pao* dismissed the Inchon landing as a "gamble" that "was completely lost" since it had failed to trap Pyongyang's armies.[23] Showing no sign of concern, it described U.S. troops as weakened by "low fighting spirit" and "distant reinforcements." Consequently, "If the fighting lasts for a long period of time, they will surely be defeated." Although Inchon did not seem to affect this aloof posture, its aftermath spurred Chinese Communist efforts to deter the U.N. from entering the DPRK. Only then did Peking's domestic propaganda renew the war alert, and in a cautious, gradual way so as to delay final mobilization of public opinion until the die had been irrevocably cast for war.

Peking reaffirmed its support for Pyongyang in an interesting manner. On September 18th the Security Council heard General MacArthur's charge that the PRC had "furnished substantial if not decisive military assistance to North Korea by releasing a vast pool of combat-seasoned troops of Korean ethnic origin" prior to hostilities.[24] Peking had not responded publicly to the earlier statements from Austin and Truman warning it against involvement in the war. Now, however, it decided to acknowledge the MacArthur charge. On September 22nd a Ministry of Foreign Affairs spokesman admitted the troop transfers, implying that further assistance might be forthcoming:

The Chinese people scorn this accusation. They have no fear of it. Furthermore, we clearly reaffirm that we will always stand on the side of the Korean people—just as the Korean people have stood on the side of the Chinese people during the past decades—and resolutely oppose the criminal acts of American imperialist aggressors against Korea and their intrigues for enlarging the war.[25]

This was the first official PRC comment on the war issued primarily for foreign consumption since Chou En-lai's protests over the alleged border incidents of late August. In the interim Peking had withheld further expression of affinity with Pyongyang. In part this may have stemmed from a continued hope of gaining admission to the U.N. If so, such hopes ended on September 19th when the General Assembly defeated, by thirty-three votes to sixteen with ten abstentions, an Indian proposal to admit the PRC.[26] At the very time when this constraint against open support for the DPRK disappeared, an urgent need of military intervention arose as North Korean defenses crumbled before the U.N. offensives. Thus the timing and content of the September 22nd statement suggest it was intended to allay Western doubts about Chinese Communist willingness to assist in North Korea's defense.

After this official move, *Jen Min Jih Pao* renewed the war alert, although in a muted tone. Commenting upon an alleged U.S. air attack against Antung on September 22nd, the paper concluded, "There is only one explanation: the American imperialists are deciding to extend their armed aggression against China." ²⁷ No photographs accompanied reports of the incident nor did it trigger the widespread propaganda campaign of the August attacks. On the following day, however, this authoritative newspaper strengthened the alert signal in the most closely argued rationale for supporting Pyongyang that had yet appeared. In explaining the troop transfers acknowledged by the Ministry of Foreign Affairs spokesman, *Jen Min Jih Pao* declared:

We Chinese people are against the American imperialists because they are against us. They have openly become the arch enemy of the People's Republic of China by supporting the people's enemy, the Chiang Kai-shek clique, by sending a huge fleet to prevent the liberation of the Chinese territory of Taiwan, by repeated air intrusions and strafing and bombing of the Chinese people, by refusing new China a seat in the U.N., through intrigues with their satellite nations, by rearing up again a fascist power in Japan, and by rearming Japan for the purpose of expanding aggressive war. Is it not just for us to support our friend and neighbor against our enemy? The American warmongers are mistaken in thinking that their accusations and threats will intimidate the people of China.²⁸

Although not a call for immediate mobilization, this detailed defense of assistance to North Korea went beyond the earlier alert that had discussed fighting the U.S. exclusively for the defense of Chinese territory. As the situation deteriorated in Korea, Peking increased its public commitment to Pyongyang both abroad, so as to deter invasion of the DPRK, and at home, so as to prepare the populace for action should deterrence fail.

Peking Defines Its Position

Although Chinese Communist interest in Korea had been expressed officially as early as August 20th, one month had passed with no precise definition of that interest or the extent to which it might involve Peking in the war. As the question of U.N. troops crossing the thirty-eighth parallel moved to the forefront of international attention and U.N. speculation, however, the PRC moved, overtly as well as covertly, to define its position more precisely.

On September 24th Chou En-lai cabled U.N. headquarters to protest against alleged U.S. air intrusion over Antung. His wording went well beyond the accusation of "criminal action" contained in his August protests:

The case is even more serious than the strafings by the United States airplanes which occurred formerly . . . [and] exposes more clearly than ever the determination of the United States of America to extend the aggressive war against Korea, to carry out armed aggression on Taiwan, and to extend further her aggression against China.

After summarizing his past notes, Chou warned:

The flames of war being extended by the United States in the East are burning more fiercely. If the representatives of the majority of states attending the United Nations General Assembly should still be pliant to the manipulation of the United States and continue to play deaf and dumb to these aggressive crimes of the United States, they shall not escape a share in the responsibility for lighting up the war-flames in the East.[29]

In view of the forthcoming General Assembly debate on crossing of the parallel, Chou's references to "the manipulation of the United States" and "lighting up the war-flames" appeared as thinly veiled pressure designed to swing wavering delegations against a continuation of the conflict.

Covert communication made this objective more explicit. On September 25th General Nieh Jung-chen, acting Chief of Staff of the PLA, issued an indirect warning to the U.N. during an informal dinner conversation with the Indian ambassador, K. M. Panikkar. According to Panikkar's published account, Nieh said that China would not "sit back with folded hands and let the Americans come up to the [Sino-Korean] border." [30] Admitting the risk of general war, he continued, "We know what we are in for, but at all costs American aggression has to be stopped. The Americans can bomb us, they can destroy our industries, but they cannot defeat us on land. . . . They may even drop atom bombs on us. What then? They may kill a few million people. Without sacrifice a nation's independence cannot be upheld."

This was followed by still another warning in an official speech by Chou En-lai to the Central People's Government Council (CPGC). Although less specific than the Nieh remarks, it focused more directly upon the crossing of the parallel as a possible *casus belli* than did

Nieh's exclusive emphasis upon Chinese defensive concerns. Speaking on September 30th, Chou declared: "The Chinese people enthusiastically love peace, but in order to defend peace, they never have been and never will be afraid to oppose aggressive war. The Chinese people absolutely will not tolerate foreign aggression, nor will they supinely tolerate seeing their neighbors being savagely invaded by the imperialists." [31]

These words embodied the most open threat yet voiced by a PRC official of Chinese action in the event of U.N. pursuit across the parallel. Chou concluded his warning, "Whoever attempts to exclude the nearly 500 million Chinese people from the U.N. and whoever ignores and violates the interests of this one-fourth of mankind and fancies mainly to solve arbitrarily any Far Eastern problems directly concerned with China, will certainly break their skulls."

Domestic treatment of Chou's speech drew no attention to his remarks concerning "neighbors being savagely invaded by the imperialists." *Jen Min Jih Pao* merely reprinted the speech without comment, while *World Culture* quoted lengthy portions of his foreign-policy section but *omitted* the key sentences relating to Korea.[32] However, following the U.N. advance into North Korean territory on October 7th, this section of the address leaped to prominence in key Chinese Communist journals. It was quoted by both *World Culture* and *Hsüeh Hsi* (Study), the latter terming it "the most important" portion of the entire speech, "above all with respect to the Korean war." [33] This changing pattern of emphasis suggests that Chou's words were directed, in the first instance, to foreign audiences, for their possible effect upon U.S. actions in Korea and U.N. decisions at Lake Success. The warning was not intended to mobilize domestic response until its impact abroad had been determined. When the speech had failed to achieve the desired result abroad, it could still be used domestically as a call for mobilization.

On October 1st ROK units crossed the thirty-eighth parallel, and MacArthur broadcast his ultimatum ordering Pyongyang to surrender. Next day Chou En-lai formally summoned Panikkar to a dramatic midnight meeting at the Ministry of Foreign Affairs. Dismissing the ROK advance as inconsequential, Chou declared that should U.S. troops invade DPRK territory China would enter the war.[34] At last the *casus belli* was fully defined. In the next few days Washington received additional reports of Chou's warning through allied and neutral channels, and through American embassies in Moscow, Stockholm, London, and New Delhi.[35]

Peking's Warnings: How Credible?

It may be worth while to stop at this point to assess the credibility of Peking's warnings against U.N. crossing of the thirty-eighth parallel. It is not our purpose to reconstruct the situation as it confronted American intelligence analysts. Such a task would require reviewing the entire range of information then available to those responsible for evaluating Chinese Communist moves, placing this information against the background of prior alarms, and examining alternative explanations of its significance. Our sole concern at this point is the degree to which Peking believed its position sufficiently clear to decision makers in Tokyo and Washington. This is important if we are to support the hypothesis of a belated intervention decided on reluctantly as a last resort, and to reject the hypothesis of a carefully premeditated intervention designed to trap U.N. forces in North Korea. It also is relevant to interpreting subsequent Chinese Communist moves. If Peking believed its warnings to have been understood but rejected by Tokyo and Washington, U.S. and U.N. assurances about safeguarding Chinese interests while advancing to the Yalu would give no satisfaction to China.

The problem of communicating a threat is formidable, and in the context of the Korean War it was especially difficult. Peking had employed belligerent language with respect to "liberation" of Taiwan in the face of Seventh Fleet opposition, yet it had failed to make good its threat. Korea was apparently less important politically and emotionally than Taiwan, and accordingly the Chinese Communists had failed to take military action either during the six-week stalemate at Pusan or in the two weeks following the Inchon landing. Was Peking really now moving with caution but with determination, so as to "strive for the best but be prepared for the worst?" [36]

Three aspects of the Chinese warning affect its credibility. First, the content of the threat and its means of communication establish prima facie evidence of intent. Second, the available means of implementing the threat must be considered. Finally, the credibility of the threat must be weighed in terms of its rationality, juxtaposing the risks against the goals. Since in international relations the third aspect is seldom susceptible to objective evaluation by the recipient of the threat, we shall concern ourselves primarily with the first two aspects, the evidence of intent and the means of implementation, though this will not resolve completely the uncertainty of interpretation. Taking solely the evidence available up to October 7, 1950, we cannot say that there was no element of bluff in Chinese pronouncements. Nor can we conclude that Chinese Communist intervention was inevitable regardless of U.N. action. We can, however, estimate the degree to which Peking felt its deterrent posture had been sufficiently communicated and the extent to which this feeling was justifiable.

So far as formal communication was concerned, Peking's successive statements from August 20th to October 2nd steadily increased the PRC commitment to the DPRK. By the end of this period Communist China had clearly defined the *casus belli* as the entry of U.S. forces into North Korea, and its own response as military intervention on behalf of the DPRK. This much had been communicated, informally and formally, through neutral diplomatic channels. It had been indicated in official public statements, although much less explicitly, as well as in the controlled domestic press. Whereas references to the "liberation" of Taiwan had become *less* specific following the U.S. move of June 27th, the references to Korea had become *more* so. As the conditions upon which Peking predicated its entry into the war came nearer, Communist China became increasingly explicit in its communication of intent.

In the U.S., it was suggested at the time that communication through Indian channels degraded the credibility of Chinese warnings and that the latter were designed to increase neutralist pressure upon the U.S. position at the U.N.[37] However justifiable such skepticism may have seemed from the American point of view, it rested upon considerable oversimplification of the facts. True, we have already noted the softening of Communist attacks against Nehru's "neutralism" following his correspondence with Stalin and Acheson in mid-July. Yet Indian proposals at the U.N. had fallen considerably short of Malik's position, while Delhi's relations with Peking became increasingly strained as the PRC made clear its determination to "liberate" Tibet. India was espousing some policies favorable to the PRC, such as its admission to the

U.N. while differing markedly with Communist claims on the origin of aggression in Korea. Finally, Chinese Communist aspirations for Asian leadership on Asian matters made Indian channels politically preferable to more traditional agents, such as the Danish, Swedish, or Swiss representatives. India, therefore, stood as a likely link between the two blocs.

If the content and method of communication were rationally conceived, what of the available means for making good the threat of intervention? Peking had already stationed 180,000 of its best troops in Manchuria, a fact repeatedly noted in the Western press. In mid-September, massive military redeployment reinforced these troops, and the movements continued into October. These movements were not concealed from foreign diplomats in Peking, nor had Peking reason to doubt that the sudden increase in PLA concentration along the Yalu River would be detected by U.S. intelligence.[38] Given the absence of troop movement into Manchuria from July to September and the subsequent increase of forces there from 180,000 to at least 320,000 troops, the Nieh-Chou warnings were visibly strengthened by military dispositions.[39]

Whatever errors in judgment or in implementation may have accompanied Sino-Soviet strategy, it was logically conceived within the Communist frame of reference. In retrospect it appears consistent with a literal reading of the warnings issued. The signals did in fact alert U.S. officials to the possibility of Chinese Communist entry into the war. On October 9th the Joint Chiefs of Staff specifically authorized MacArthur to engage Peking's forces in Korea "as long as, in your judgment, action by forces now under your control offers a reasonable chance of success." [40] By October 2, 1950, the Chinese leadership could logically believe its position clearly understood: if U.S. forces pursued the goals enunciated by Austin and MacArthur, namely, the complete defeat of the Democratic People's Republic of Korea, Peking would resist with force.

The U.S. position seemed unequivocal. On September 30th Ambassador Austin had declared, "The opportunities for new acts of aggression should be removed. . . . The aggressor's forces should not be permitted to have refuge behind an imaginary line. . . . The artificial barrier which has divided North and South Korea has no basis for existence either in law or in reason." [41] On October 1st MacArthur's ultimatum demanding unconditional surrender of North Korean forces had opened, "The early and total defeat and complete destruction of your armed forces and war-making potential is now inevitable." [42] At this point, Moscow made its final move at the United Nations for a political settlement to end hostilities in Korea.

Moscow's Final Maneuver

On October 2nd, coincident with Chou En-lai's formal warning to Panikkar, Soviet Foreign Minister Vyshinsky introduced an omnibus resolution in the Political and Security Committee of the Fifth General Assembly. This committee already had before it an eight-nation proposal embodying the U.S. position for unifying Korea, by force if necessary, and facilitating its political and economic development under U.N. supervision.[43] Vyshinsky's counterproposal represented the most comprehensive statement of Moscow's position yet to emerge. In essence it was identical with that offered by Malik in early August. Yet Vyshinsky's greater status, the more detailed nature of his proposal, and the importance of these last hours before the crossing of the parallel give it a special importance.

Vyshinsky's resolution called for (1) an immediate cease-fire in Korea, (2) an immediate withdrawal of all foreign troops, (3) all-Korean elections to a national assembly, (4) a joint North-South Korean commission to govern in the interim with equal representation of both sides, (5) the elections to be observed by a U.N. commission with "representatives of states bordering on Korea," (6) economic assistance, and (7) admission of a reconstituted Korean government to the United Nations.

In 1948 Soviet refusal to sanction all-Korean elections had left the country divided. A concession on this point suggested a willingness to compromise, particularly since the preponderance of population lay in the south. Implementation of Soviet election agreements in East Europe, however, had proved disastrous for non-Communist parties. Any Soviet-proposed agreement on Korea was likely to contain loopholes unacceptable to the United States, but only counterproposals could test Soviet flexibility on such points. Other portions of the resolution appeared even less likely of acceptance by Washington. Considering the military situation, the Soviet demands were high: cessation of hostilities presumably at the parallel, removal of American troops before the establishment of a unified government, parity for Pyongyang and Seoul despite Seoul's larger constituency, and the admission of Peking to U.N. supervision of elections.

Yet the Soviet move was not wholly futile. On October 3rd Sir Benegal Rau proposed that the two contending resolutions be placed before a special committee that would attempt to draft a compromise proposal before moving the matter to the General Assembly on October 6th. Austin expressed his reluctant approval, but warned that this procedure would delay a solution, perhaps benefit the aggressors, and probably prove hopeless since Vyshinsky allegedly had termed the two resolutions irreconcilable. Vyshinsky immediately denied this allegation and termed the Indian move "a new situation" which deserved support as did all efforts at conciliation.[44]

On October 4th the Indian move failed, with thirty-two delegations opposed, twenty-four in favor, and three abstaining. The relatively large number of affirmative votes evidenced the widespread desire to end the conflict by a compromise. When delegations were faced with a choice between the Soviet and the U.S. positions, however, the voting was decisive. On the same day, the First Committee rejected Vyshinsky's resolution by forty-six votes to five with eight abstentions; it approved the eight-nation proposal by forty-seven to five with seven abstentions. On October 7th the General Assembly set the final seal of approval on the unification of Korea by force.

It is impossible to determine the spirit in which Vyshinsky advanced his proposal. With ROK troops already in North Korea and political pressures mounting in the U.S. for a quick victory, it seems to have been late for serious debate and negotiation, particularly in the open forum of Lake Success. Moscow may have recognized this and merely attempted to record its "peaceful" intentions for propaganda purposes.[45] The support for the Indian compromise move evidenced hope that a last-minute effort might prevent the necessity for U.N. forces to cross the thirty-eighth parallel.

Moscow could have counted on some such move, in view of Malik's experience. During the August debates in the Security Council, the British and Norwegian delegates, as well as the Indian, had indicated that restoration of the *status quo ante bellum* might open the way for discussions with Pyongyang as well as with Seoul.[46] Vyshinsky's proposal was consistent with the earlier one by Malik in its willingness to abandon the DPRK as the only legal government in Korea provided Washington did the same with the ROK. At the same time it insisted on parity between North and South Korea.

Linked with Peking's warnings that China would resist U.S. incursions into North Korea, the Vyshinsky proposal carried some weight. Neutral delegations, such as India, Yugoslavia, and Burma, opposed unifying Korea by force lest this "increase tension" and "embitter international relations" in the area.[47] Additional Asian-African opposition to the U.S. policy came in the form of abstentions.[48] Until the final balloting, Vyshinsky had reason to hope that the doubts and fears of many delegations might be sufficiently aroused to defeat the eight-nation resolution. In addition, he may have hoped to improve the political climate for Chinese Communist intervention in the event the resolution were successful. The doubts expressed during the debate by non-Communist delegates might help to justify Peking's move, at least in the eyes of the uncommitted nations.

Basically, however, Sino-Soviet strategy failed to achieve its objectives. It neither persuaded the U.N. to admit Pyongyang and Peking to negotiations based upon a cease-fire nor deterred the U.N. forces from entering North Korean territory. On October 7–8 the U.S. First Cavalry Division crossed the thirty-eighth parallel, followed immediately by the rest of the U.S. Eighth Army. On October 8th General MacArthur addressed his second ultimatum to Pyongyang, calling upon North Korea "for the last time . . . forthwith to lay down your arms and cease hostilities." [49]

Peking Reacts

The timing and nature of the Chinese Communist reaction to these U.N. developments bear out the hypothesis that the crossing of the thirty-eighth parallel was the final contingency determining Peking's entry into the war.

On the eve of the U.N. decision *Jen Min Jih Pao* offered its first anonymous military commentary since Inchon. It admitted the war was "in a new state" inasmuch as North Korea "withdrew from South Korea to consolidate its power against the American imperialists." [50] However, while portraying a massive U.N. build-up, it expressed its routine faith in Pyongyang's victory through "the long period of war of resistance." No hint of Chinese Communist intervention was forthcoming nor was any attention given Chou En-lai's public warning against "savage invasion of neighbors" in his September 30th speech. On October 9th, however, the newspaper singled out Chou's earlier statement for attention in its front-page editorial, noting, "So far as the situation is concerned with respect to China's neighbor, Korea, the Chinese people have made public their position." [51] It attacked the General Assembly resolution as proof "that the American-British aggressive bloc has precariously expanded the sphere of aggressive war in the Far East. In other words, the threat of aggression [against] the People's Republic of China is more [pronounced]. Everyone in the country should watch this development attentively."

On October 10th a Ministry of Foreign Affairs statement amplified these warnings: "Now that the American forces are attempting to cross the thirty-eighth parallel on a large scale, the Chinese people cannot stand idly by with regard to such a serious situation created by the invasion of Korea . . . and to the dangerous trend towards extending the war. The American war of invasion in Korea has been a serious menace to the security of China from its very start." [52] The Ministry's statement proceeded to alert the country for mobilization, and *Jen Min Jih Pao* reproduced this under the headline "War to China's Borders." [53] As already noted, both *World Culture* and *Study* echoed the alert at this time, keynoting their comment with Chou En-lai's statement of September 30th.[54]

Within a week, the first Chinese Communist troops crossed the Yalu River, unannounced and undetected. The first ten days of October form the closing period of one phase in Sino-Soviet strategy and the initial period of another. The political maneuvers of Peking and Moscow now gave way to military action. Peking's warning had been ignored and its challenge accepted. Attention was now to shift from the council chambers to the battle front, where the success or failure of that challenge would be decided.

VII

PEKING CROSSES
THE YALU

※

ON OCTOBER 10th the Ministry of Foreign Affairs warning against the invasion of North Korea ended verbal efforts to deter the United Nations advance. Now Peking moved to mobilize the Chinese people and to deploy its armies across the Yalu River, backing up words with action.

CHINESE COMMUNIST MOBILIZATION AND INTERVENTION IN KOREA,
OCTOBER–NOVEMBER 1950

October 14–16   "Volunteer" units of the PLA Fourth Field Army begin secret movement into Korea.

October 23   Wu Hsiu-ch'uan named PRC delegate for Security Council discussion of Taiwan, in response to Security Council invitation voted September 29.

October 26   Chinese People's Volunteers (CPV) attack ROK units at Yalu River and at points forty miles below Sino-Korean boundary.

October 28   *World Culture* revives use of term for active defense, *k'ang yi,* in introduction of Resist-America, Aid-Korea theme.

November 1   First MIG's appear along Yalu in unsuccessful attack against U.S. aircraft.

November 2	CPV attack U.S. units on western and eastern fronts.
	Chinese Communist media make first reference to organization of "volunteers."
November 4	"Democratic Parties" in PRC formally inaugurate Resist-America, Aid-Korea campaign.
November 5	U.N. Commander MacArthur notifies Lake Success of "Chinese Communist military units" in Korea.
November 7	DPRK communiqué officially acknowledges Chinese Communist "volunteers" in action since October 25.
	All Communist forces break off action at battle front.
November 11	PRC Ministry of Foreign Affairs spokesman acknowledges "volunteers" in Korea.
November 24	MacArthur announces "end the war" offensive.
	Wu Hsiu-ch'uan arrives at Lake Success.
November 26	CPV counterattack along entire Korean front and smash U.N. lines in east and west.

As this chronology suggests, the Chinese Communist intervention was initially cautious and limited. Once the Chinese had ordered their units into action, it was necessary to preserve tactical surprise, as far as this was possible after the warnings of the political phase. It was also desirable, no doubt, to conceal military movements so as to reduce the likelihood of a United States counterblow in the deployment stage and to maintain flexibility in case there were a softening of U.S. policy.[1] A certain caution and diffidence is indicated by the "volunteer" status accorded to the People's Liberation Army units in Korea, which may have stemmed from a belief that minimizing the ostensible involvement of the People's Republic of China would lessen whatever political and military penalties the intervention might bring in its wake.

Between the initial Chinese People's Volunteers' attacks of late October and the massive Chinese counteroffensive of late November there was a marked lull in the fighting, which came about through Communist initiative and disengagement. During this period more than 200,000 Chinese Communist troops entered North Korea. Not until the major engagements of November 26th was Peking fully and finally involved in what General MacArthur aptly described as "a new war." In this sense it may be said that Peking's point of no return did not come until late November. While China crossed the Yalu on October 15th, she did not cross the Rubicon until November 26th.

Mobilization: The First Stage

Prior to the initial contact between the CPV and U.N. forces, Peking succeeded in secretly deploying its armies for combat. Evidence on troop identification, training, and equipment is inconclusive with respect to the question of advance planning, but generally supports the timing of decisions suggested by our examination of previous developments. The first stage of mobilization was designed to maximize preparations for combat without jeopardizing security requirements or the flexibility of reaction to U.N. actions in Korea.

Military Moves [2]

We have already noted the series of PLA shifts which increased forces in Northeast China and in Shantung during the summer of 1950, as well as the sudden augmentation of the northeast concentration by 120,000 troops in September-October. We have seen that, following the initial redeployment of late May to mid-July, there was little change in troop dispositions until late September, when entire armies moved northward in a process which was to continue throughout the fall of 1950. Although we cannot pinpoint these movements to the day or to the precise number of troops involved, the following chart and maps offer a general picture of Chinese Communist military movements from the outbreak of war in Korea to the massive engagement of November 26, 1950.

Between mid-October and November 1, from 180,000 to 228,000 crack Fourth Field Army troops crossed into North Korea. Yet more than two-thirds of this force had been in Northeast China since July. Its failure to enter Korea until one week after U.N. units had crossed

Time	South China	East China	Honan-Hupeh	Shantung	Northeast	Korea
May to mid-June	39th, 40th	20th, 26th 27th	38th, 50th, 66th	......	Original 4th Field Army,† plus 42nd	......
Mid-June to late July	......	20th, 26th	50th, 60th	27th, 39th	42nd, 38th, 40th	......
August to mid-September	......	20th, 26th	50th, 60th	27th, 39th	42nd, 38th, 40th	......
Mid-September to October 15	......	......	......	27th, 39th, 66th, 26th	42nd, 38th, 40th, 50th, 20th †	......
October 15-30	......	......	......	26th, 27th	20th ‡	42nd, 38th, 39th, 40th, 50th, 66th
November 1-15	......	......	......	......	(‡)	42nd, 38th, 39th, 40th, 50th, 55th, 26th, 20th, 27th

* These armies varied in size at the time of initial contact with U.N. forces because of delays in deployment to the front. U.S. estimates ranged from 15,000 to 40,000 troops for each army. Subsequent POW testimony makes 40,000 more credible as far as final strength was concerned.
† No precise figures have been found for the portion of the Fourth Field Army in the northeast prior to these shifts, but most estimates agree that approximately 100,000 regular troops were in the area, in addition to the armies identified above.
‡ Advance units of other armies moved into Northeast China as reserves for later redeployment in Korea but have not been identified here to avoid confusion with the initial intervention of October–November 1950.

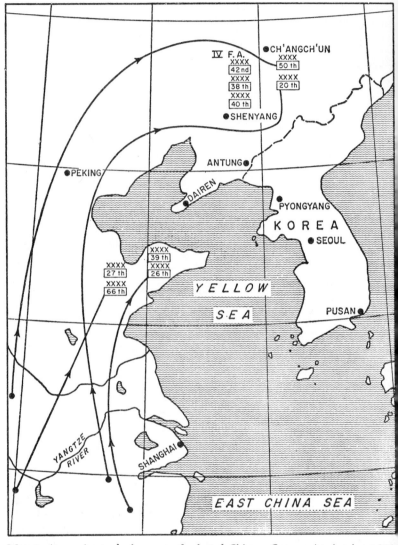

MAP 3. Approximate deployment of selected Chinese Communist Armies, 1950
Mid-September to October 15

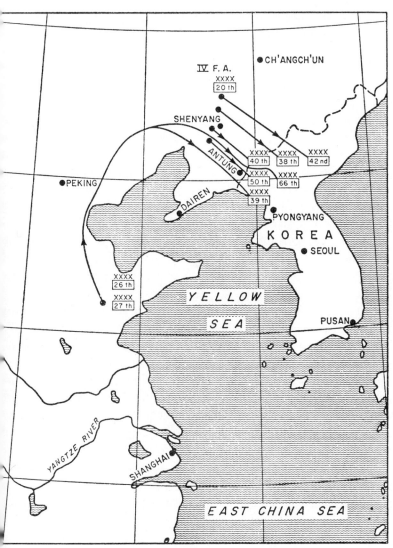

MAP 4. Approximate deployment of selected Chinese Communist Armies, 1950
October 15–30

the thirty-eighth parallel suggests, like so much other evidence, Peking's reluctance to enter the war until all political means had been exhausted.[3] One must also take into account, however, the strategic problems that faced Peking in determining to intervene.

First, of course, was the risk of a U.S. counterblow, perhaps with atomic bombs, against the Chinese mainland. We shall examine later the evidence of Chinese Communist concern with this problem as reflected in semi-official statements and domestic propaganda. It has been suggested that Peking discounted the prospects of any U.S. air attack against mainland China because of advance assurances through Soviet secret agents that high-level plans in Washington ruled out such a move.[4] No evidence has been found to support such speculation. It is unlikely that Peking would have taken so serious a step as entry into the Korean War on the basis of a foreign agent's report about American intentions, particularly in view of past reversals of U.S. policy both on Taiwan and in Korea. Even were such information in the hands of Sino-Soviet strategists, it was at most only a contributing factor in the decision to intervene, and not a determining one.

Second, Mao Tse-tung's strategic doctrine was based on superiority of numbers, large-scale mobile warfare over vast areas, and guerrilla fighting amidst a friendly populace in home territory.[5] Yet these conditions which had accounted for Mao's successes in the Chinese civil war were largely absent in Korea. So far as comparative strength was concerned, during the first half of November reinforcements swelled the CPV strength in Korea to between 270,000 and 340,000 men. However, they faced approximately 440,000 U.N. troops of vastly superior firepower. Furthermore, only in the northernmost part of Korea did the battlefield extend over a wide front in mountainous territory, suitable for surprise attack and guerrilla warfare. Much of the lower peninsula was a mere one hundred miles wide, and a mobile strategy was hampered there by U.N. coastal and air attacks. Regardless of Peking's ideological propinquity to Pyongyang, the CPV moved amidst an alien people in unfamiliar territory. Below the thirty-eighth parallel, the populace would be actively hostile.

Logistical problems posed additional obstacles. Transport lines into Korea were readily pinpointed and vulnerable to enemy air attack. The Yalu River would not freeze over sufficiently for heavy movement before November. Until then, six major bridges provided access to the battle front, the most important of which were twin 3,098-foot-long highway and railroad spans linking Antung and Sinuiju. In August U.S. aircraft had allegedly crossed the international boundary line on several occasions. The Chinese command must therefore have been apprehensive about the interdiction of its communication lines at the Yalu, which might have prevented the massing of "volunteers" during the critical build-up phase. This consideration alone must have restrained China's optimism about her military prospects in Korea.

To be sure, there were favorable factors which Peking may have considered to compensate for these negative conditions. First, Peking may have anticipated no serious resistance from the more than 200,000 Republic of Korea troops which comprised over half of the U.N. force. Initial engagements were likely to be with South Korean units moving toward the Yalu River well in advance of U.S. troops. The first Chinese Communist blow could be delivered against these isolated ROK detachments, inferior in number and far from reinforcements. Success would signal Peking's entry into the war without, however, provoking as threatening a counterblow as if the defeat were suffered primarily by U.S. forces. It would then be up to Washington to choose between continuing the offensive and going over to the defensive. Meanwhile, Chinese People's Volunteers and Democratic People's Republic of Korea armies would occupy the mountainous area bordering China. Should the bridges be cut, heavy equipment and reinforcements could cross the frozen Yalu at will after early November.

In the period between the mid-October CPV crossings of the Yalu and the great Chinese counteroffensive of November 26th, the military situation developed in a way that China could interpret as to her own advantage. A seventy-five-mile gap opened between General Walton Walker's Eighth Army on the western front and General E. M. Almond's X Corps which landed at Wonsan on the eastern front. In addition, American reliance upon motorized transport and armored units left these armies, particularly the X Corps, strung out over long, hazardous mountain roads. Not only was the U.N. force split in two, but the two parts were atomized. Small units were separated from one another by many miles, and both lateral and feeder communications were inadequate.[6] Thus the over-all CPV numerical inferiority was offset by the vulnerability of the U.N. force to local attacks by superior numbers.

Although this reconstruction of Chinese Communist estimates concerning the prospects of intervention, both before and after the Yalu crossing, is based on purely circumstantial evidence, it is borne out by the manner in which Peking entered the war, gradually and with a belated concern for the secrecy of military movements. We shall consider these movements further in examining CPV behavior after the initial contact with U.N. forces. At this point, however, we must turn to other pre-combat military preparations for whatever clues they provide to the question of Chinese Communist intervention.

Preparation for Combat

The way in which Peking prepared its troops for combat indirectly sheds light on its decision to enter the Korean War. The available evidence concerning re-equipment, training, and political indoctrination, although inconclusive, argues against the probability that Chinese military intervention had been determined upon in advance of the conditional warnings issued by Peking in late August and September.

In contrast with the sudden increases in Soviet equipment delivered to DPRK forces in the spring of 1950, just before the invasion, there is little evidence of Soviet deliveries to the PLA prior to CPV entry into North Korea. None of the Chinese armies engaged in the fighting of October-November had been trained in handling Russian weapons, and the only known piece of Soviet equipment used by them at this time was one type of submachine gun.[7] The overwhelming majority of CPV units entered Korea with the same potpourri of captured Japanese and American weapons that had served them during four years of civil war in China. So widespread was their use of American firearms seized from defeated Chinese Nationalist units, that American troops repeatedly mistook enemy for friendly fire.[8]

During the summer and fall, the detailed attention of the Peking press to the destructiveness of U.S. firepower in Korea, both on the ground and in the air, indicated a realistic appraisal at higher levels of enemy strength. In the absence of extensive deliveries of heavier Soviet artillery and antiaircraft weapons, CPV units might be expected to have undergone intensive training and maneuvers to prepare them to face opposition more formidable than they had met hitherto. Except for isolated units, however, most of the troops continued in economic reconstruction until their assignment to Korea. Additional reinforcements were hastily recruited from farms and schools, and these received little training in military tactics before entering combat.[9]

The political indoctrination of CPV units appears to have varied considerably, depending upon the caliber of officers in charge. In early October one group reportedly learned that they were to fight as "volunteers" in Korea.[10] Many of the soldiers in the initial attacks, however, did not learn of their assignment until they were approaching the Yalu River or, in some cases, until after they had actually crossed into North Korea.[11] Except for the routine application of anti-American propaganda, most troops received little indoctrination to prepare them for fighting U.S. forces in Korea.[12]

It is possible that Peking believed its own propaganda concerning the inevitable superiority of the Communist cause and the quick collapse of U.N. resistance, and therefore made no serious preparations for combat in terms of re-equipment, training, and political indoctrination.[13] In view of the long military history of virtually the entire Chinese Communist Party elite, however, this seems most unlikely. Whatever illusions may have existed in June about the American "paper tiger," the subsequent course of the war had amply demonstrated U.S. military capability. We have noted the early expectation of a "prolonged war" in the Peking press, and its sober accounts of American mobilization throughout the summer. Having experienced the results of miscalculation in June, and having been deterred from the planned invasion of Taiwan by the U.S. Seventh Fleet, it is highly improbable that Sino-Soviet strategy would have calculated upon an easy victory a few months later. Once the successes garnered through the initial impact of surprise had been realized, pursuit of U.N. forces would face the problem of logistical operations over difficult terrain against unopposed enemy air attacks of a kind which had repeatedly hampered the DPRK in its summer offensives. In short, the same factors which had confronted Pyongyang with "prolonged war" promised to pose a similar problem for Peking.[14]

If faith in easy victory cannot account for China's piecemeal preparations, the relatively short time between the decision to enter the war and the implementation of that decision may have precluded fuller preparation for combat. If the agreement to commit Chinese Communist armies was not arrived at before late August, and then predicated upon the contingency of a U.N. invasion of North Korea across the thirty-eighth parallel, logistical difficulties were bound to impede rapid, extensive re-equipping with Soviet weapons. Not only did strained transport facilities limit arms shipments from Russian depots, but the training of PLA units in the handling of Soviet weapons was handicapped by the lack of cadres capable of bridging the linguistic gap between Russians and Chinese.[15]

Similarly, warning to Chinese troops of imminent combat in Korea was apparently not authorized until U.N. forces had actually crossed the parallel, coincident with Peking's official warnings through the Ministry of Foreign Affairs spokesman and domestic elite journals against "supinely tolerating the savage invasion of neighbors." Whether for security reasons or because of the constraints imposed by the unwillingness of the regime to commit itself publicly before the determining contingency had occurred, few of the troops redeployed in late September and early October knew of their ultimate assignment. It is also possible that concern for morale may have prevented the authorities from telling the troops they were to fight U.S. forces, particularly since the prolonged fighting against Japanese and Chinese Nationalist armies had undoubtedly left the average soldier with little enthusiasm for a new war.

While positive proof is lacking, the evidence indicates that China made no early plans to commit the PLA to combat in Korea. The military movements, the equipping, training, and indoctrination of troops, diplomatic developments, and shifts in the propaganda line all combine to indicate that the initial decision to take military action, should political moves fail, was made in late August. Implementation of this decision came with the initial war alert of early September, the troop redeployment beginning in mid-September, and the formal warnings from Chou En-lai in late September and early October. Final mobilization, however, was not authorized until after the U.N. rejection of the warnings and the crossing of the parallel.

Mobilizing the Populace

As we have already noted, Chou En-lai's refusal to tolerate "the savage invasion" of China's neighbor was given public prominence by the Foreign Office statement of October 10th and by subsequent editorials in *Jen Min Jih Pao, World Culture,* and *Study.* This opened the first stage in the mobilization of the Chinese people through the public information media.[16] Its distinguishing characteristics are several. First, the war alert of early September reappeared in a massive propaganda campaign throughout China. Unlike the earlier alert, however, this new material contained frequent, explicit references to defending Korea, as well as to protecting the motherland. Second, despite the renewed militancy of public statements, no specific call for "volunteers" occurred at this time. Finally, the campaign began in the guise of "spontaneous" expressions of opinion, with no formal committee to inspire them and with little front-page attention by *Jen Min Jih Pao.* Not until late October, when the issue was joined at the battle front, did the characteristics of the campaign change. The mobilization of public opinion then entered its second stage.

On October 13th *Kung Jen Jih Pao* declared, "We cannot stand idly by when the American imperialist, a notorious enemy, is now expanding its war of aggression against our neighbor and is attempting to extend the aggressive flames to the border of the country." Professor Ch'ien Tuan-sheng, dean of the College of Social Science at Peking National University, was quoted: "Korea and our country are separated by a river. The safety of the Korean People has been threatened. It means that the safety of the Chinese people is also threatened." [17] Workers in Kwangtung swore "never to be afraid of an antiaggression war to safeguard peace" and pledged themselves to "support the statement made by the spokesman of the Foreign Ministry with actual deeds . . . ever ready to deal the American imperialists a telling blow." [18] Representatives of minority nationalities from Inner Mongolia and elsewhere issued a joint statement, warning: "By spreading the flames of aggressive war to the very borders of China, they [American imperialists] are menacing the security of the whole world, but especially of China. . . . We are determined to strengthen the National Defense Forces and to strike down any imperialist aggressor who dares to flout the will of the Chinese people." [19]

Meanwhile *Jen Min Jih Pao* paid the war scant heed, giving it only occasional front-page coverage throughout October as it had in the latter half of September. New official protests against alleged U.S. overflights of Chinese territory received only perfunctory attention.[20] Several factors may have accounted for this somewhat restrained domestic posture at the very time CPV units were crossing the Yalu. Peking may have tempered its home-front propaganda for security purposes connected with concealing its move into Korea. In addition, it may have wished to test enemy response to CPV intervention, before committing itself to total mobilization. In any event, no news of the "volunteers" appeared at this time. Indeed, none of the propaganda themes went beyond a general alert.

October closed with a significant concatenation of inflammatory messages in the three key journals, *Jen Min Jih Pao, World Culture,* and *Study.* The coincidence in timing with the initial fighting between CPV and ROK forces in Korea was in all probability not an accidental one. The belligerency of these articles, written on the eve of combat, is striking.[21] In its first editorial on the Truman statements of mid-October, which had expressly denied U.S. designs beyond Korea, *Jen Min Jih Pao* declared: "The ambitions of the U.S. imperialist bandits will not be satisfied with the attack on Korea. Truman will certainly extend his aggressive war to the borders of China . . . following in the footsteps of the Japanese predecessors who also began with aggression against Korea and then the Northeast and the interior of China. But this aggression will not be tolerated by the Chinese people." [22]

Study echoed this alarm, noting, "The war in Korea has now entered a new phase. . . . Their [the U.S. imperialists'] position . . . gravely threatens the security of our fatherland. China and Korea are separated by one river, with the two countries having over 1,000 li of common front." [23] In addition to this defensive theme, there was new emphasis on neighborly obligations which were said to impel Chinese action, since the Korean people "took an active part in China's revolutions and did not hesitate to shed their blood and sacrifice themselves for our cause."

The most complete statement of the intensified war alert came from *World Culture*. Just as this journal had made the initial prophecy of a "prolonged war" and had been the first to declare, "North Korea's defense is our defense," so now, once again, it signaled a new turn of policy. In its editorial call for "resistance against the American imperialist aggressors," it reintroduced the key term *k'ang yi*. This term, connoting active defense, had not been evident since the campaign of early September. Now it became the hallmark of the formal Resist-America Aid-Korea movement which lasted from November 1950 to the armistice of July 1953. Its appearance at this time, after the first CPV fighting had occurred in Korea but before Peking or Pyongyang had officially announced the "volunteer" movement, marked the transition from partial to full mobilization of public opinion in the People's Republic of China. The editorial in which it appeared merits quotation:

Can the Chinese people be unconcerned with the barbarous aggression against our neighbor, Korea, or with the threat to our national defense line in the Northeast, or with the repeated violations of our territory, our territorial waters, and air? No, we definitely cannot be unconcerned! It is very clear now that American imperialism is following the beaten path of Japanese imperialism—the wishful thinking of annexing Korea, and then from there invading our Northeast, then North China, East China, and finally the whole of Asia and adjacent areas. . . .

We definitely will not beg for [peace] from the aggressor. . . . Neither are we afraid of the aggressor. The American aggressor is not in the least stronger than the fascist Japanese of yesterday, while the Chinese people are more united and stronger than ever before. . . .

The Chinese people will not tolerate a repetition of the history of 45 years ago. Therefore we must be on the same front as the Korean people to oppose and to end the American imperialist aggression. . . . Rise up in the struggle against the American imperialist aggressors, to aid our heroic Korean brethren, and to defend peace in the Far East.[24]

It is interesting to note that assistance to Korea was still justified by its relevance for China's defense. On occasion, it was presented as repayment for past services rendered by the Korean people. Rarely, however, was it recommended on the basis of proletarian internationalism and socialist solidarity.

For a fuller understanding of the Chinese intervention, we must now examine the second stage of the general mobilization for war that began in late October.

Mobilization: The Second Stage

Between October 26th and November 7th the CPV engaged U.N. forces, both South Korean and American, along a wide front extending from coast to coast. Through surprise and local superiority in numbers, Chinese Communist units defeated their ROK opponents and forced a general withdrawal of Eighth Army lines. On November 5th MacArthur notified Lake Success that Chinese prisoners of war had revealed "Chinese Communist military units deployed for action against the forces of the United Command." Two days later North Korea officially acknowledged that Chinese "volunteers" had been fighting with DPRK units since October 25th. At the same time, all Communist forces suddenly broke contact with U.N. units along the entire battle line. During the following lull, however, Peking continued to send troops across the Yalu River and moved its domestic propaganda campaign into high gear to mobilize "volunteers" for fighting in Korea.

CPV-U.N. Engagements

Following the capture of Pyongyang on October 19th, U.N. forces advanced rapidly in an attempt to overrun remnant DPRK units and to end the war before winter hit the mountainous area adjoining China. On the west coast, General Walker's Eighth Army, including British and Turkish troops and flanked by four ROK divisions, crossed the Ch'ongch'on River and advanced toward the temporary DPRK capital of Sinuiju. It encountered stiffening enemy resistance approximately forty miles below the Yalu. On the east coast, General Almond's X Corps had landed at Wonsan and Iwon, and had joined ROK detachments moving up the coast. Its forces advanced inland toward the Changjin Reservoir and probed north toward the Yalu. Between the two main U.N. armies, ROK detachments advanced toward the Sino-Korean border. There was no continuous defense line and little direct communication linking the two field headquarters.[25]

On October 26th the first U.N. troops reached the Yalu River. At the border village of Chosan, near the Suiho hydroelectric basin, a battalion of the Seventh Regiment, Sixth ROK Division, looked across into China, well in advance of its parent unit to the south. That night Chinese Communist troops surrounded the battalion and decimated it in an ambush. On October 27th, while this action was still in progress, CPV attacks hit the main body of the Sixth ROK Division, with its companion Seventh and Eighth divisions which extended along the flank of the Eighth Army. As South Korean forces fought their way back to Unsan, forty-five miles below the border, they encountered new ambushes by CPV troops who had infiltrated behind their lines.

On November 1st the U.S. First Cavalry Division rushed reinforcements to the beleaguered ROK troops, only to find itself under surprise CPV attack. Heavy fighting continued for two days with growing losses on the American side. Suddenly the Communist attacks ended, and Chinese forces melted back into the hills whence they had come. Nevertheless, General Walker pulled back the entire Eighth Army line, together with the badly mauled ROK divisions, and established defensive positions along the Ch'ongch'on River. Advance units of the U.S. Twenty-fourth Division, already within fifteen miles of the Yalu, retreated fifty miles down the west coast. The initial battle between American and Chinese troops had ended in victory for the Communist side, its first since the Inchon landing and the Pusan breakout of mid-September.

Meanwhile similar action flared up on the east coast. On the day of the Yalu River ambush, the Twenty-sixth Regiment, Third ROK Division, ran into CPV fire near the Changjin Reservoir, seventy-five miles below the border and an equal distance from the engagements on the west coast. On November 2nd the U.S. Seventh Marine Regiment arrived to relieve the ROK troops, and fought a five-day battle with the 124th Chinese Communist Forces Division south of Chinhung-ni. By November 7th Communist casualties forced this division to withdraw, and the engagement ended in victory for the U.N. forces.[26]

At this point the entire front became quiet. No Communist attacks occurred for two weeks, nor did reconnaissance uncover enemy positions along the prospective line of U.N. advance. Was Peking prepared to give only token resistance in North Korea? Interrogation of two dozen Chinese prisoners of war, captured before November 5th, indicated that at least five regular divisions, estimated at 10,000 men each, had crossed the Yalu.[27] Another 200,000 troops were thought to be concentrated at bridgeheads within two nights' march of the front.[28] Actually, as we have seen, more than 180,000 "volunteers" had already entered Korea by this time, and at least 90,000 more were scheduled to join them within three weeks. Given this impressive force and the signal victories attending surprise attacks in October, why did Peking not commit its full strength to an immediate all-out offensive against the disrupted U.N. defenses?

It is possible that delay was caused by the need for a greater concentration of force than was available when the initial engagements occurred. There are, however, two other possible explanations. First, the pause in the Communist attacks may have been due to the kind of military considerations that are spelled out in Mao Tse-tung's classic study, *On the Protracted War*. Second, political considerations may have dictated a limited blow followed by a suspension of activity, in order to test and examine the U.N. response to Chinese Communist intervention. These two explanations are not mutually exclusive, but must be reviewed in more detail to determine their compatibility with other evidence on the motivations behind Peking's entry into the war at this time.

Mao's Strategic Design

Although *On the Protracted War* was written during the Japanese invasion of 1938, the volume was republished in China in 1951, implying that its doctrine was still accepted by the Chinese when the Korean War began. The following excerpts highlight the correlation between the book's contents and CPV strategic behavior during October-November 1950: [29]

The strategy should be that of employing our main forces in a mobile warfare, over an extended, shifting and indefinite front: a strategy depending for success on a high degree of mobility, and featured by swift attack and withdrawal, swift concentration and dispersal. [p. 163]

Adherents of the theory of a quick victory are wrong. They either completely neglect the contrast between strength and weakness and notice only the other contrasts, or they exaggerate China's advantage out of all true proportion and beyond recognition, or with overweening confidence, take the relative strength at one time and one place for that in the whole situation. . . . At any rate, they lack the courage to admit the fact that the enemy is strong while we are weak. [p. 179]

Since the war is a protracted one and the final victory will be China's, we can reasonably imagine that this protracted war will pass through the following three stages. The first stage is one of the enemy's strategic offensive and our strategic defensive. [p. 183]

At the end of the first stage, owing to the insufficiency in his own troops and our firm resistance, the enemy will be forced to fix a point as the terminus of his strategic offensive; halting his strategic offensive on reaching the terminus, he will then enter the stage of retaining the occupied territories. [p. 185]

Because the enemy force, though small, is strong (in equipment and the training of officers and men) while our own force, though big, is weak (only in equipment and the training of officers and men but not in morale), we should, in campaign and battle operations, not only employ a big force to attack from an exterior line a small force on the interior line, but also adopt the aim of quick decision. To achieve quick decision we should generally attack, not an enemy force holding a position, but one on the move. We should have concentrated, beforehand [and] under cover, a big force along the route through which the enemy is sure to pass, suddenly descend on him while he is moving, encircle and attack him before he knows what is happening, and conclude the fighting with all speed. If the battle is well fought, we may annihilate the entire enemy force or the greater part or a part of it. Even if the battle is not well fought, we may still inflict heavy casualties. [p. 209]

We say that it is easy to attack an enemy on the move precisely because he is then not on the alert, that is, he is inadvertent. These two things—creating illusions for the enemy and springing surprise attacks on him—are used to make the enemy face the uncertainties of war while securing for ourselves the greatest possible certainty of gaining superiority, initiative, and victory. [p. 217]

We have always advocated the policy of "luring the enemy to penetrate deep" precisely because this is the most effective military policy for a weak army in strategic defense against a strong army. [p. 224]

These excerpts, omitting references applying only to the Sino-Japanese War, offer an image of combat which parallels the early Chinese tactics in Korea.³⁰ The Chinese Communist press hinted at the parallel. The term "prolonged war" appeared intermittently throughout the summer of 1950. Even as the "volunteers" staged their initial attacks on U.N. positions, a *World Culture* writer observed that, "The rugged mountains of North Korea are an ideal graveyard for the imperialist invaders." ³¹ After describing the advantages for guerrilla warfare now that U.S. troops were advancing inland, he quoted Secretary of Defense George Marshall, "The greatest danger today is lack of reserves in trained manpower." At least in this stage of the war, Mao's strategic doctrine would appear to have been applicable.

Yet this strategic approach was to lose its validity as the Chinese troops moved south. The narrowing of the peninsula below the Sinanju-Hungnam line precluded any real prospect of mobility, while U.S. air and naval superiority further threatened to limit CPV operations. Does this mean that *On the Protracted War* misled CPV strategists? ³² Or was it seen as operative only for the first stage of hostilities? A third alternative deserves statement, although it cannot be explored without access to materials beyond our reach. Did Peking anticipate a prolonged war in the northern portions of Korea where the strategy would remain operative, and did the precipitate U.N. withdrawal of December throw its calculations awry? We do not know the answers, although Chinese Communist propaganda explicitly warned the populace to expect a "prolonged struggle" in Korea. Since *On the Protracted War*'s first appearance in 1938, however, atomic weapons had entered the picture. To what extent did the atomic bomb affect the calculations of Sino-Soviet strategists in the fall of 1950?

The Atomic Bomb: "A Paper Tiger"

In attempting to reconstruct elite estimates on the consequences of entering the Korean War, we have no direct evidence bearing upon the problem of a U.S. nuclear counterstrike. The Chinese leaders must surely have weighed the probability of an atomic attack, its probable military impact, the accumulative impact of several such attacks upon the economic and political system, and the willingness as well as the capability of Soviet retaliatory power to counter U.S. nuclear blows. In the absence of direct evidence, however, we must infer from scattered, tangential materials the most plausible reconstruction of Chinese Communist thinking on the subject.

That the elite anticipated some risk of U.S. air attack is indicated by the construction of air-raid shelters in Mukden and by air-raid drills in key cities throughout Northeast China.[33] In addition, the sudden appearance of MIG fighters along the Yalu River in late October may have been a defensive precaution to interdict bombers en route to military staging areas and industrial centers in Manchuria. On November 1st six to nine MIG's attacked U.S. aircraft along the Yalu River.[34] Throughout the remainder of the month MIG sorties engaged American fighters near the Sino-Korean border.[35] The Russian jets stayed well behind the battle front, and no identification of enemy pilots was possible. However, their skill in maneuver argued against their being Chinese, in terms of the known capabilities of PLA pilots.

We know that the nuclear risk was at least present in the minds of military men in Peking, since General Nieh discussed the matter in September with Ambassador Panikkar.[36] As we shall see from our next review of Chinese Communist propaganda, the regime also expressed awareness of public concern in this area. It issued explicit reassurances in early November on the improbability of a U.S. atomic attack, its impact should it occur, and the probable Soviet response. All of this permits us to conclude that Chinese Communist intervention was decided upon with at least some realization that it might trigger U.S. retaliation through nuclear as well as non-nuclear air attack.

What consequences were anticipated should a U.S. nuclear blow result? Again, we do not know, but several points lead us to suspect that the consequences were not expected to be catastrophic. First, the published remarks, albeit scanty, of Chinese Communist leaders depreciated the strategic significance of atomic bombs. In August 1946 Mao Tse-tung remarked to an American journalist: "The atom bomb is a paper tiger with which the U.S. reactionaries try to terrify the people. It looks terrible, but in fact is not. Of course, the atom bomb is a weapon of mass destruction, but the outcome of war is decided by the people, not by one or two new weapons."[37] It is true that four years had elapsed since Mao spoke these words, but during this time there was no public modification of this disparaging estimate of nuclear power, at least in discussions between Chinese Communist leaders and outsiders. Nieh, in talking with Panikkar, admitted that atomic attacks might kill "a few million people," but added, "After all, China lives on the farms. What can atom bombs do there?" [38] On the one hand, Nieh's reference to the possible casualties seemed to overstate the case. On the other hand, his dismissal of the consequences was not addressed specifically to the impact upon China's ability to fight in Korea but rather to the likelihood of the U.S. defeating the People's Republic of China on her own ground.

It may be that Soviet strategic estimates led the Chinese Communist analysts to recognize the possibility of a U.S. atomic attack but to underestimate its consequences. If the Chinese Communists relied upon Soviet military publications for information on this matter, they were poorly served. Down to 1950, apparently, little if anything came from this source on the strategic import of nuclear warfare.[39] Chinese strategists may have been informed by their Soviet counterparts that the U.S. supply of atomic bombs was small and the delivery capability weak, making improbable the employment of nuclear power against the Chinese mainland.[40] Soviet development of an atomic bomb in 1949 may have served as some reassurance either that the U.S. could be deterred from an atomic attack by threat of retaliation, or that a U.S. nuclear blow would actually trigger a Soviet nuclear counterblow. Both hypothetical situations were projected in domestic propaganda, as we shall see shortly. We have no information concerning high-level exchanges which may have occurred between Chinese and Soviet planners on this particular aspect of the problem. It is significant, however, that U.S. possession of the atomic bomb does not seem to have compelled reassessment of Mao's strategic doctrine, although the latter was developed in the pre-nuclear age. This does not mean that the Chinese Communist military intervention was undertaken in complete disregard of the possible consequences of a U.S. nuclear strike, but rather that the Chinese accepted a calculated risk, which they felt to be justified by the overriding considerations favoring intervention.

Political Considerations

So long as the U.S. response to Chinese Communist intervention remained uncertain, prudence argued for a cautious approach, lest the enemy be impelled to attack the mainland, perhaps employing his atomic capability. As Mao had warned in 1948:

We oppose overestimating the strength of the enemy. . . . But in every particular situation, every specific struggle (no matter whether military, political, economic, or ideological struggle), we must not despise the enemy. On the contrary, we should take the enemy seriously, concentrate all our efforts on fighting, and thus we can win victory.[41]

The chronology is suggestive. On November 5th General MacArthur dispatched a "special report" to the United Nations, in which he detailed instances of Chinese Communist belligerency in the form of antiaircraft fire across the Yalu, MIG attacks over the border, and CPV units in Korea identified by prisoners of war.[42] On November 7th the official DPRK communiqué announced that "volunteer units formed by the Chinese people participated in operations along with the People's Armed Forces, under the unified command of the General Headquarters . . . [and] mounted fierce counteroffensives on the west front on October 25." [43] At this point CPV attacks ceased, and a lull settled over the battle front.

Disengagement provided Peking with an opportunity to assess the U.S. and U.N. reaction to its intervention, to prepare against counterblows, and to step up mobilization should the need remain and the risks be tolerable. By labeling its armies "volunteers" and by limiting the initial engagements, Peking may have hoped to minimize the U.S. response and to remain free for political maneuver should the response exceed expectations or should it meet Sino-Soviet goals of compromise.

On November 11th a Ministry of Foreign Affairs spokesman replied to the MacArthur report. He admitted that "the Chinese people" were fighting in Korea, but denied official responsibility for this. His argument merits quotation at length for its relevance to China's problem of limiting the U.S. response:

This reasonable expression of the Chinese people's will to assist Korea and resist American aggression is not without precedent in the history of the world, and no one can object to it. As is well known, in the 18th century, the progressive people of France, inspired and led by Lafayette, assisted the American people in their war of independence by similar voluntary action. Before the Second World War, the democratic people of all countries of the world, including the British and American people, also assisted the Spanish people by similar voluntary action in the Spanish civil war against Franco. All these have been acknowledged throughout the world as just actions. . . . Since the expression of the Chinese people's will . . . is so reasonable, so just, so righteous, magnanimous, and so flawless, the People's Government of China sees no reason to prevent their voluntary departure for Korea.[44]

Throughout the Spanish civil war, the Non-Intervention Committee, composed chiefly of West European nations, had recognized the fiction of "volunteers" from Germany, Italy, and the Soviet Union. China's contention that her forces in Korea were "volunteers" was not without precedent, and Peking might hope that the analogy with the Spanish civil war would permit a general acceptance of that contention. This device could not be relied upon to deter U.S. military action, but it might discourage or weaken the efforts of America's allies. The "volunteer" approach, the limited initial attack, and the subsequent disengagement, suggest that China intervened in Korea with due consideration of the risks and a determination to minimize them. All the way through, of course, Peking also derived some comfort from the deterrent effect of the Sino-Soviet mutual defense treaty.

If the lull in the ground fighting was intended to test the American response to Chinese intervention, that response was not long in appearing. Until this time the Manchurian sanctuary had been scrupulously observed, and U.S. aircraft had refrained from attacking the Yalu River bridges even at their terminal points in Korea. On November 6–7 MacArthur requested, and the Joint Chiefs of Staff approved, the amending of these restrictions so as to permit attacks on the Korean side of the river.[45] Implementation of this directive gave Peking evidence of the precise degree to which Washington was prepared to modify its strategy in the face of CPV intervention. On the one hand, the U.S. would assume an increased risk of accidental overflight in order to attack entry routes into Korea. On the other hand, it was willing to jeopardize the success of the missions, including the safety of its pilots and planes, rather than attack MIG bases and antiaircraft positions on the Chinese side from which defensive fire protected the crossing points. Hence the waiting period may have served to moderate Peking's fears concerning its sanctuary in the rear. In addition, it may have served as a test of Peking's hopes that the battle front would enter, in accordance with Mao's strategic doctrine, a "second stage" that would find the U.N. stabilizing its defensive positions along an extended line in North Korea. This would permit a war of attrition close to China's base of supply while ensuring a territorial basis for continuing the official DPRK regime. Thus both political and strategic considerations may have induced Peking to suspend its offensives against the U.N. lines in November.

Mobilization of the Populace

During this period Chinese Communist communications on the home front dropped the constraints that had characterized the first stage of mobilization. On October 26th the Chinese People's Committee in Defense of World Peace and Against American Aggression was formed in Peking to spearhead the mass propaganda campaign which was to last for the duration of the war.[46] The next day *Jen Min Jih Pao* carried a front-page headline, "American Troops Invading Korea Approach Our Borders." In less than a week every major city in China held public meetings at which thousands pledged to defend the fatherland amidst the "spontaneous demands of volunteers anxious to fight the American imperialists in Korea." On November 2nd the Peking press made its first reference to such "volunteers," although a subsequent DPRK communiqué acknowledged their presence at the front since October 25th.[47]

At this point all communications media turned to the "Resist-America" theme, with its attendant call for combat in Korea. Despite the battle-front lull, *Jen Min Jih Pao* saturated its pages with war propaganda in its most discursive treatment of the conflict since June 25th. The staggering volume of "Resist-America Aid-Korea" material warrants a separate study in itself.[48] Our principal concern, however, is to determine whether this propaganda reflected the expectations, if not the aims, of the Chinese leaders at the time of the intervention.

Unfortunately, the clues in communications media to the goals and expectations of Peking with respect to military action in Korea are highly ambiguous. Indeed, they are notable more for what they leave unsaid than for what they say. Thus the initial *Jen Min Jih Pao* editorial following CPV action in Korea declared: "The voluntary aid of Chinese patriots . . . will bring the possibility of turning the tide of war, annihilating and repulsing the unconsolidated American troops, and forcing the aggressors to accept a just and peaceful solution of the Korean question." [49] This seemed to argue for a limited use of force to accomplish what political maneuvers had failed to accomplish, namely, a negotiated end to the war along some unspecified line of compromise. Nothing in the article posited the total destruction of U.N. authority in Korea as the goal of CPV intervention.

Once again it was *World Culture* that provided the most sober estimate of future events. Two articles in successive issues probed the possible consequences of Chinese "volunteer" action. The first, probably written prior to the official DPRK acknowledgment of "volunteer" action, predicted:

There are two possibilities. . . . One is that the American imperialists will be forced off the Korean peninsula. . . . The second is that after U.S. troops suffer defeat, they [will] continue to increase reinforcements, ceaselessly expending men and material, becoming mired ever deeper and more helplessly. . . . This way American imperialism will have no troops to spare for attacking Indo-China or other places and cannot increase troops in Europe. Its satellites will complain, the anti-war spirit of the U.S. people will increase, and this will prevent the imperialists from starting a large war.[50]

This was a curious article in the context of mass mobilization. It foresaw the possibility of a "prolonged war," yet its rationale for accepting such a war nowhere touched upon China's immediate interests. Indeed its reference to Europe reflected primarily Soviet interests that were to be served by tying down U.S. forces in Korea. At the very least, the article would seem to have tempered rather than aroused enthusiasm for "volunteering."

One week later a different *World Culture* analyst detailed a wider range of possible consequences from Chinese Communist military action in Korea:

It is possible that American imperialists will not dare to carry on all-out war against China, but rather will limit the war to Korea itself, only fighting those Chinese who take part in the Korean war as volunteers. [In this case] the war might go on for a very long time. . . . The Korean people might drive the American imperialists from Korea. . . . The U.S. imperialist troops, after several defeats, might withdraw.

The second possibility is that the Americans might . . . ignite World War III.[51]

The possibility of general war was now explicitly envisaged, albeit with the expressed reassurance of ultimate victory because of Soviet strengths and U.S. weaknesses. The alternative outcome, a "very long war" limited to Korea, was depicted as a "victory" since it would deny the U.S. possession of all Korea and constitute a drain on American resources. The writer explicitly warned that decisive victory might not be attainable "through a knockout blow," thereby raising the prospect of stalemate at the battle front.

So sober a view of future possibilities was perhaps merely preventive medicine to forestall any setbacks in domestic morale that might follow from reverses at the front. Given the previous role of *World Culture,* however, in signaling significant policy developments, it would appear that these estimates reflected at least some of the thinking at higher levels. It is impossible to determine how widely such views may have prevailed within the elite, but taken together with Chinese Communist military and political behavior as a whole, they appear to reflect the genuine doubts and uncertainties of the leaders in determining to intervene.

In this regard, it is significant that throughout its propaganda of November 1950 Peking insisted that the war was likely to be a long one. The guiding directive for the campaign declared: "The patriotic movement of Resist the U.S., Aid Korea, Protect Our Homes, and Defend Our Country, is possessed of a comparatively prolonged nature . . . to last and wax stronger with time." [52] *Jen Min Jih Pao* warned: "The imperialists have only begun to be battered and they will continue to carry out atrocities. Therefore we must continue to conduct firm counterattacks against them. . . . Forward! March on, under the enemy gunfire and bombs, to final victory!" [53] On the eve of General MacArthur's "win the war" offensive, *Current Affairs Journal* noted: "The enemy has not yet been dealt decisive blows and the American aggressors are prepared for war on a still bigger scale."[54]

This journalistic restraint does not prove conclusively that the goals of intervention were limited or that the elite believed decisive victory to be only a remote possibility.[55] It does suggest, however, Peking's unwillingness to encourage hopes for a quick or total victory. It contrasts markedly with the image of an intervention lightly undertaken in expectation of quick victory, the image which might emerge from a study of equipping, training, and indoctrination alone. In short, hortatory as the appeal to the public was, it nevertheless retained the element of restraint and caution that had marked Peking's more authoritative comment on the Korean War from its inception five months previously.

In addition to conceding the possibility of a prolonged war, Chinese Communist propaganda dealt with the prospect of atomic attacks against the civilian populace.[56] Apart from anti-atomic bomb material connected with the so-called Stockholm Peace Appeal, a new approach to the nuclear threat appeared at the time of the war alert of late October and early November.[57] A basic directive for "Resist America" propaganda outlined themes to reassure audiences both about the probability of atomic warfare and about the effects of atomic bombs should they be used.[58] "The atomic bomb is now no longer monopolized by the U.S. The Soviet Union has it too. If the U.S. dares to use the atomic bombs, she naturally will get retaliation, and deservedly." On the other hand, the directive continued:

Its military effectiveness, at most, is in large-scale bombing. . . . The atomic bomb itself cannot be the decisive factor in a war. . . . It cannot be employed on the battlefield to destroy directly the fighting power of the opposing army, in order not to annihilate the users themselves. It can only be used against a big and concentrated object like a big armament industry center or huge concentration of troops. Therefore, the more extensive the opponents' territory is and the more scattered the opponents' population is, the less effective will the atom bomb be.

Jen Min Jih Pao provided graphic eye-witness accounts of the Hiroshima bombing in which survivors denied rumors that sterility was an aftereffect and detailed measures for protection against atomic blasts.[59]

Editorials inveighed against fear of the bomb as a military weapon. While this might have reflected the regime's anxiety over public concern about the bomb, rather than its own expectations of atomic attack, it is interesting that Peking did not argue that such an eventuality was out of the question. Its references to Soviet atomic capability, for instance, implied that the latter might deter a U.S. atomic attack but nowhere stated it would guarantee immunity against the threat.[60] In short, the regime appears intentionally to have left open the possibility of a U.S. atomic counterblow to its move into Korea.

To conclude, the first three weeks of November saw Chinese Communist propaganda mobilizing the populace for a prolonged war in Korea. Both the intensity of the campaign and its specific content left little doubt as to the seriousness of the undertaking. Amidst the exhortations to "volunteer" were relatively frank statements of the uncertainties ahead, including the possibilities of atomic attack against China and of World War III. While a quick, total victory in Korea was occasionally envisaged, it received little stress. Seldom was the goal of combat defined beyond the general statement of "achieving a just peace." If the rulers of China entertained a more optimistic or ambitious estimate of the future, they did not reveal it at this time.

Diplomatic Hiatus

It would appear that China considered the die was cast when U.N. troops crossed the thirty-eighth parallel, and that she then abandoned diplomacy pending a decision on the battle front. It may be more than a coincidence that the Chinese Communist invasion of Tibet began simultaneously with final U.N. approval of crossing the parallel. The Tibet campaign immediately offended India, which had been important in pleading Peking's cause at Lake Success. Furthermore, the two-month lapse between the Security Council invitation of September 29th and the arrival of Peking's delegate to discuss the Taiwan question on November 24th cannot be wholly attributed to circumstances beyond Peking's control. In part, at least, it suggested a disregard for diplomatic exchanges until military moves had improved the Communist situation in Korea.

Tibet and India

We have seen how Sino-Soviet analyses of Indian foreign policy underwent marked modifications during the first months of the Korean War. Beginning with Nehru's attempt to mediate the dispute in early July, Delhi's moves were welcomed, though not uniformly, by the Chinese Communist press and by Soviet diplomats at the U.N.[61] In September Indian efforts to win PRC admission to the General Assembly were applauded in Peking. *World Culture* even erroneously identified separate Russian and Indian resolutions on the matter as a joint "Indian-Soviet move." [62] Both Nehru in New Delhi and Rau at Lake Success repeatedly stated their support for the initial U.N. resolutions of June 25th and 27th, but Indian disapproval of Sino-Soviet action in Korea was omitted from the Chinese press.[63]

It seems likely that the Communist evaluation of Indian motives changed once, if not several times, during these developments. Initially, both Peking and Moscow may well have believed their public descriptions of Nehru as "a tool of imperialism." His divergences from American policy, however, suggested that India might be exploited, at least tactically, to divide "the imperialist camp." By September the Chinese had progressed to the point of utilizing Panikkar to communicate Chinese Communist warnings against crossing of the thirty-eighth parallel.

Peking as well as Moscow, however, undoubtedly remained fully aware of the differences between the Indian position and that of the Communist bloc, particularly on the critical question of Korea. Whatever shift in tactics was justified by the opportunity to exploit Indian leverage within the U.N., no fundamental change appeared at this time in the Communist appraisal of so-called "third force" countries. Soviet spokesmen made no concessions to Indian proposals at Lake Success. In Peking, activation of the long-heralded "liberation of Tibet" signaled Chinese unwillingness to modify basic policies for the sake of friendly relations with Delhi.

It is the timing rather than the details of the Tibetan invasion that concern our inquiry. Since October 1949 Peking had proclaimed its intention to "liberate" the area, while Delhi had voiced willingness to recognize Chinese suzerainty together with hope of maintaining Indian trade and pilgrimage privileges there.[64] Just as the PRC had found it possible to postpone the Taiwan operation, so too it could have delayed indefinitely the occupation of Tibet.[65] However, on October 7, 1950, PLA troops began their march into Tibet.[66] On the same day the General Assembly passed its resolution approving the U.N. advance into North Korea.

Although rumors of the PLA invasion circulated for several weeks thereafter, Ambassador Panikkar received no response to his inquiries in Peking.[67] Finally, on October 24th, Chinese Communist broadcasts officially confirmed the move into Tibet. A rapid exchange of sharp notes immediately ensued between Peking and New Delhi. Indian wishes for a peaceful settlement of Sino-Tibetan relations were rebuffed as "affected by foreign influences hostile to China and Tibet." [68] Chamdo had fallen to the PLA on October 19th with little struggle, and Chinese troops appeared to be advancing cautiously against scattered opposition. *Jen Min Jih Pao* featured the "liberation struggle" intermittently throughout November.[69] On November 16th Peking closed its correspondence with Delhi on a more positive note, stressing Sino-Indian "friendship" but still maintaining that "outside obstruction" and "foreign forces and influences" had operated both in India and Tibet to impede a settlement.

Whatever specific motivations may have prompted the Tibetan move at this time, Peking cannot have been unaware of its probable impact abroad. The Indian memorandum of October 21st specifically pointed out

that a military action at the present time against Tibet will give those countries in the world which are unfriendly to China a handle for anti-Chinese propaganda at a crucial and delicate juncture in international affairs. . . . Opinion in the United Nations has been steadily veering around to the admission of China into that organization before the close of the present session. . . . Military action on the eve of a decision by the Assembly will have serious consequences and will give powerful support to those who are opposed to the admission of the People's Government of China . . . to mispresent China's peaceful aims.

Only after receipt of this memorandum did Peking publicly verify the "liberation."

The Chinese Communist response to this note was unequivocal. "The problem of Tibet and the problem of the participation of the People's Republic of China in the United Nations are two entirely unrelated problems. If those countries hostile to China attempt to utilize as an excuse the fact that the Central People's Government of the People's Republic of China is exercising its sovereign rights in its territory Tibet, and threaten to obstruct the participation of the People's Republic of China in the United Nations organization, it is then but another demonstration of the unfriendly and hostile attitude of such countries toward China." [70] Had Peking written off the U.N. as a determining factor in formulating policy?

Invitation, Acceptance, and Delay

Some answers to the above question are suggested by the chronology of developments that followed the Security Council resolution of September 29th:

CHRONOLOGY OF DEVELOPMENTS CONCERNING PEOPLE'S REPUBLIC
OF CHINA PARTICPATION IN SECURITY COUNCIL
DISCUSSIONS ON TAIWAN

September 29   Security Council passes resolution inviting PRC participation in discussion of Taiwan question on November 15.

October 2   Security Council invitation officially dispatched from Lake Success.

Jen Min Jih Pao first reports invitation, without comment.

October 8   *World Culture* terms invitation a "victory" for the PRC.

October 23   PRC officially notifies Lake Success of acceptance.

November 10   Malik informs Security Council that U.S. authorities in Prague had not issued visas to PRC representatives up to November 7. "Had the instructions to issue the visas been given in time, I believe that the representatives of the PRC might well have been here by now." Chou En-lai cables to Trygve Lie that delegation will arrive "about" November 18.

November 13 Wu Hsiu-ch'uan leaves Peking, heading PRC delegation.

November 16 U.S. transportation officials learn PRC delegation scheduled to arrive November 24.

November 18 PRC delegation arrives in Prague.

November 24 Wu Hsiu-ch'uan arrives in New York, confers with Lie.

Malik demands, allegedly at Chinese insistence, immediate Security Council meeting next day.[71]

Why did Peking wait almost one month before formally accepting the invitation? Why did the PRC delegation take ten days to travel from China to Lake Success? It is possible that considerations of national prestige argued against showing undue haste. Not only was the invitation connected with the issue of Taiwan, which was much less urgent than the Korea problem, but the issuance of an invitation after weeks of delays, debate, and rebuffs to Chinese participation on other matters and in other U.N. organs made it far less a recognition of Peking's sovereign right than the grudging offer of a limited privilege.[72]

However, more than "face" appears to have conditioned Chinese Communist behavior in this instance. The main problem was Korea. When the invitation was issued, the U.N. action on the thirty-eighth parallel had yet to be determined. Once determined, the Sino-Soviet response had to be implemented. The initial skirmishes between CPV and U.N. detachments, moreover, did not decide the outcome of Chinese military participation in the war. Under such uncertain circumstances it may have been deemed prudent to abstain from direct participation in U.N. debate until PRC representation could be effected in a posture of maximum strength. Soviet diplomacy and Chinese threats had failed to modify U.N. policies. Only a change in the balance of forces demonstrated on the battlefield would warrant a return to the public forum. Diplomatic activity was suspended and, at the same time, Chinese forces in Korea undertook to disengage tactically.

Chinese behavior in this period suggests that the desire for admission to the U.N. was so much less urgent than the factors determining intervention in Korea that all the efforts made at Lake Success to proffer representation as an inducement to China to refrain from crossing the Yalu or entering Tibet were a waste of time. Several points support this hypothesis. First, the debate preceding the Security Council invitation both implicitly and explicitly had linked the invitation with Chinese non-involvement in Korea.[73] One week previously the General Assembly had appointed a seven-man committee to study and make recommendations on the problem of Chinese representation. Press speculation interpreted this as a move to postpone further discussion of the matter until termination of the Korean conflict could facilitate its consideration in a less hostile atmosphere.[74]

Peking had ample time to weigh its prospects for U.N. admission and for the subsequent acquisition of Taiwan against the consequences of intervention in Korea. Even after committing itself militarily, the PRC had further opportunity to reconsider. Following the special MacArthur report of November 5th concerning CPV entry into the war, the Security Council voted on November 8th to invite PRC participation in discussions of the special report. This time no delay was specified, and the invitation was to be acted upon as soon as possible. On November 10th, no reply having come from Peking, Sir Benegal Rau cautioned that "reasonable time" must be given for the Chinese response, since "My government considers that the situation in Korea is so dangerous and so explosive that the great need of the hour is to lessen tension and remove fear." Rau was seconded by the French and British, who urged that Chinese interests in Korea, including power from the hydroelectric installations, be guaranteed if Chinese forces would withdraw. A six-nation draft resolution introduced at this time specifically offered "to hold the Chinese frontier with Korea inviolate and fully to protect legitimate Chinese and Korean interests in the frontier zone" and authorized a U.N. commission to negotiate "problems relating to conditions on the Korean front in which States or authorities on the other side of the frontier have an interest." It warned, however, of "the grave danger which continued intervention by Chinese forces in Korea would entail for maintenance of such policies."[75]

Peking had now won the right to participate in Security Council discussions on Korea, as well as on Taiwan. Although the invitation was technically limited to issues raised in MacArthur's special report on CPV intervention, the draft resolution explicitly recognized the PRC as an interested party to be represented at Lake Success provided, however, that Peking withdraw all Chinese forces from Korea.

On November 11th Chou En-lai cabled his refusal of this second invitation. He repudiated the MacArthur report as "not only one-sided and malicious, but also unlawful," since it came from the U.N. Command "engendered illegally by the Security Council under the manipulation of the United States during the absence of the permanent members, the Soviet Union and the People's Republic of China." [76] Instead, Chou proposed that the PRC delegate combine talks on Taiwan with "discussion of the question of armed intervention in Korea by the United States government." On the same day Peking officially acknowledged the presence of its "volunteers" in Korea and countered MacArthur's report with a detailed listing of alleged U.S. air violations over Chinese territory,[77] thus underscoring Chinese unwillingness to attempt diplomatic maneuvers at Lake Success at this time.

The new harshness with which Chinese Communist media treated the U.N. confirmed that Peking now accorded the world organization a less important place in its plans. On November 18th *World Culture* belittled the U.N. in blunt language:

American imperialists threaten that if China does not stop helping Korea, not only America will be China's enemy but the entire United Nations will be the enemy. The Chinese people do not fear this threat. If the United Nations is used by the U.S. as its tool of aggression, the United Nations is not then the instrument of the peoples of the world for peace. The United Nations loses its strength in becoming an agressive instrument of the American imperialists and their satellites. Without the participation of the People's Republic of China, the United Nations is nothing more than a name.[78]

Speaking the same day at the Second World Congress of Defenders of Peace in Warsaw, Kuo Mo-jo, head of the PRC delegation, unleashed a bitter attack against the U.N.:

Controlling the United Nations, the U.S.A. has converted it into its domain and is utilizing the U.N. to make its criminal actions. . . . The

American imperialists desecrate the U.N. By their criminally aggressive actions in Korea, they have turned the U.N. flag into a shameful rag. . . . The United Nations . . . has now become a screen behind which the aggressors violate peace. The U.N. Charter has become just so much paper.[79]

Although Kuo postulated the usual conditions for "freeing the U.N. from the domination of American imperialists," the main tenor of his remarks left little prospect that Wu Hsiu-ch'uan's arrival would usher in serious diplomatic negotiations at Lake Success.

In sum, Peking's flouting of Indian sensitivities about Tibet, its delay in implementing the Security Council invitation of September 29th, and its public condemnation of the United Nations emphasized the shift from diplomatic to military means in its approach to the Korean problem. The goals of Chinese policy in Korea, however, may not have been so rigidly defined or so certain of attainment as to permit complete reliance upon military means. In each of the above instances, Peking maintained minimal relations as a basis for renewed diplomatic activity, should this prove desirable. The cardinal fact, however, is that in November 1950 the People's Republic of China maximized its mobilization for a major, prolonged military struggle in Korea.

The present examination of Chinese intervention and the events leading up to it has been confined deliberately to the situation as it must have confronted the Chinese leaders in the summer and fall of 1950. This limitation, it is hoped, has facilitated the exposition without distorting the evidence or the conclusions.

Following the massive CPV counteroffensive in late November, the rapid retreat of U.N. forces to a line south of Seoul confronted Peking with a situation that appears to have exceeded its most confident expectations. Its diplomatic behavior under these propitious circumstances demands separate examination to avoid obscuring the motivations that prompted the initial intervention. Between November 26 and December 31, 1950, battle-front developments did in fact signal, as MacArthur said, "a new war," not only for Washington but for Peking as well. It is on the eve of those developments that the inquiry may fittingly come to an end.

VIII

MOTIVATIONS
BEHIND INTERVENTION

※

HAVING REVIEWED Chinese Communist diplomatic, military, and propaganda patterns relating to the Korean War, we may now re-examine the hypotheses advanced in explanation of Peking's interven-tion in that war. In the absence of more direct evidence bearing on key Sino-Soviet decisions, it is impossible to prove or disprove the validity of the various hypotheses. However, we may assess their plausibility on the basis of specific inferences and generalizations derived from the evidence in the foregoing chapters.

Basic to such evaluation is an assumption of rational decision making in Peking. This posits decisions as resulting from a logical assessment of desired goals and available means and as being implemented in a manner calculated to make the gains outweigh the costs. The actual decisions made may be inferred from negative as well as positive evi-dence, providing our assumption is valid. To take a negative example first, it was widely believed in Western circles that a determining factor in Chinese Communist concern over North Korea was the reliance of Manchurian industry upon power supplies across the border as well as along the Yalu River. This belief prompted explicit reassurances from Western spokesmen, both in Washington and at Lake Success, concern-ing "China's legitimate interests" near the frontier. Yet we have seen that Peking ignored this issue completely in its domestic as well as its foreign communications. The absence of propaganda about the pro-tection of the hydroelectric installations, despite the need to maximize popular response to mobilization of "volunteers," suggests that this consideration played little if any role in motivating Chinese Communist intervention.

Another instance illustrates the use of positive evidence. Some observers thought that Peking could not tolerate the presence of hostile forces on the Yalu River, within striking distance of the valuable industrial base in Northeast China. Delegates at Lake Success suggested a buffer area, together with international guarantees against border violations. Yet Peking apparently accepted as calculated risk the possibility of American atomic bombing of its cities, including those in the Northeast. General Nieh's remarks to Ambassador Panikkar, shelter construction in Mukden, and domestic propaganda on the consequences of atomic attack support this view, which suggests that the security of Manchurian industry was not a primary factor in determining intervention.

Russian Considerations

First, we shall consider the possibility that Soviet policy dictated Chinese Communist participation in the Korean War. Not only is this the most simple explanation but, if credible, it raises important implications for subsequent Sino-Soviet relations. Unfortunately, there is no firm evidence to support or counter such an explanation. To be sure, the image of Chinese Communist intervention resulting solely from Russian directives and against Chinese preferences is compatible both with Peking's behavior and with its dependence upon Moscow. However, China may have interpreted her own interests in such a way as to make Russian dictation unnecessary. In this case, Soviet influence may have been a contributing, rather than a determining, factor in the Chinese decision to enter the war.

As a Determining Factor

The least complicated explanation of Chinese intervention sees it as a reluctant response to Russian directives. No evidence has been uncovered which substantially supports or refutes this hypothesis. The explanation is consistent with Peking's unenthusiastic and pessimistic comment on the war in July, with its definition of the United States threat in purely defensive terms related to China's own interests in September, and with its delay in committing military forces to combat in Korea until the last stage of the Democratic People's Republic of Korea collapse in October.

In view of Peking's reliance upon Moscow for basic military and economic assistance, the hypothesis is plausible enough. On Taiwan, Mao Tse-tung faced a rival regime openly supported by the most powerful country in the Pacific area. The Sino-Soviet alliance offered him some assurance in case of a U.S. attack, but this depended primarily upon Stalin's willingness to assume the responsibility for China's defense. Furthermore, only Soviet Russia stood as a ready source of credit, equipment, and technical assistance vital to rebuilding China's shattered economy.

Finally, Peking's entry into the war jeopardized some of China's interests to a considerable degree. North and Northeast China could be devastated by U.S. air power. American retaliation might take the form of returning Nationalist forces to the mainland through scattered landings and airdrops which could establish contact with pockets of continuing anti-Communist resistance. Even should the fighting remain confined to Korea, it would tax Chinese resources, already drained by more than a decade of foreign invasion and civil war. Intervention in Korea would delay admission of the People's Republic of China to the United Nations and the simultaneous expulsion of Chiang Kai-shek's rival representatives. Not only would commitment in Korea prolong Peking's absence from this world forum, but its military requirements might force the Taiwan invasion to be postponed indefinitely.

These are persuasive considerations on behalf of the thesis that Moscow forced Peking to enter the war against its will. They presume, however, that no Chinese interests, independently perceived by the Chinese Communist Party elite, reinforced Russian policy considerations.

As a Contributing Factor

This approach depicts Moscow as influencing Peking's decision but not dictating it. It does not deny the objective factors that left Mao dependent upon Stalin for essential military and economic support. In addition, Peking had to rely upon Moscow to a considerable degree both to define the situation vis-à-vis the United States and to provide the diplomatic and military means of coping with that situation, whether in the Far East or in the United Nations. The inexperience and weakness of the new regime left no escape from this outside advice and support.

This alternative hypothesis shifts the emphasis from coercive to voluntary aspects of Chinese Communist relations with the Russian elite. The subjective element in the Communist component of policy predisposed Mao and his associates to rely upon "friendly" Soviet views of the world and to reject alternative explanations, whether "unreliable" Indian or "hostile" American, as inimical to CCP interests.

If Peking regarded the war as vital to its own interests, as well as to those of the Soviet Union, its entry into the war must have been far less dangerous to Sino-Soviet harmony than if the Soviet Union had coerced China against the will of her leaders. To be sure, we have no firsthand information on the exchanges that undoubtedly occurred between the two capitals in the summer of 1950, and therefore we cannot say what degree of harmony then existed between Moscow and Peking. However, we have ample material on the way in which Peking justified its behavior, and from this we may go further toward estimating the likelihood that Chinese interests were indeed directly involved, and hence that China entered the war of her own free will.

Chinese Communist Interest in the War

There are two levels of analysis at which we can assess Peking's behavior. First, we can examine the explicit goals of intervention as defined in the elite's domestic and foreign communications. To a considerable degree these were rationalizations for public consumption, but they may have included genuine goals of policy. Moreover, Peking may not have been immune to its own propaganda, particularly when many external developments could be interpreted as confirming its own assertions of "imperialist aggression." Second, we can consider the implicit, unstated goals which followed logically from declared objectives but whose outlines remained blurred or concealed. In part, inferences must be made not only from the avowed goals but from the frame of reference within which those goals emerged. In moving from explicit to implicit goals, the treatment unfortunately must be highly schematic and the conclusions tentative.

There is no certainty as to the degree to which the Chinese Communist leadership consciously defined its entire range of goals, much less the extent to which it affixed priorities among objectives. Furthermore, for analytical purposes, we must separate interrelated goals. As a final caution, it should be remembered that this reconstruction of the considerations that may have influenced the initial intervention applies only to the period down to late November 1950. The subsequent course of events on the battlefield may well have altered Chinese goals and expectations.

A "Just" Peace in Korea

To what degree was Peking motivated by its avowed concern for a "just solution" to the Korean conflict? Down to August 1950, relations between the PRC and the DPRK had been conspicuous by their absence. Before the mobilization of late October, little in domestic Chinese Communist propaganda implied responsibility for the outcome of the war. No Chinese troops assisted Pyongyang during the slowing of North Korean offensives in August and the rapid U.N. counteroffensives in September and early October. Not until Kim Il-sung's regime stood with its back to the Yalu did China salvage DPRK fortunes. Neither before nor during the first three months of war did the degree of interest in Pyongyang evinced by Peking warrant acceptance at face value of its concern for a "just" peace, based upon the *status quo ante bellum*.

This is not to say that the Chinese Communist leadership was prepared to accept with equanimity the total defeat of North Korea. As a minimal goal, intervention must have been intended to preserve an entity identifiable as the DPRK, and to prevent unification of all Korea under U.N. supervision. The late date of Chinese Communist entry into the war suggests that it was the political importance of the North Korean government, rather than its territorial integrity, that was at stake. Although intervention was officially predicated upon U.N. crossing of the thirty-eighth parallel, no Chinese People's Volunteers and Democratic People's Republic of Korea defense lines were established during the August-October period, not even to protect Pyongyang. To

Peking, a "just" Korean peace was not an end in itself but rather a means toward fulfilling other related goals of policy.

U.S.-Japanese Relations

One of those goals was reversal of the existing course of U.S.-Japanese relations. Peking's propaganda repeatedly drew attention to the "rearming" of Japan manifested in plans for "police" and "self-defense" forces. It attacked the "use" of Japanese personnel and resources in the Korean War. It cited the "historic path of [Japanese] aggression" against China, which lay through Korea and Manchuria. Finally, it accused the United States of seeking permanent bases in Japan through a separate peace treaty that would exclude the legitimate wartime allies Russia and China.[1]

These expressed fears appeared justified as American efforts to arrange a Japanese peace treaty, with or without the Soviet Union but on U.S. terms, accelerated in the fall of 1950. It is unlikely that Communist analysts appreciated the degree to which this development was a function of the "self-fulfilling prophecy." Washington's increased concern for the entire area, following the North Korean attack, prompted intensified American activity on the question of Japan. Communist aggressiveness had sparked a defensive reaction that both Peking and Moscow probably viewed as a previous plan of offensive design. This Communist analysis may have been reinforced by the coincidence that the final stages of the U.N. offensive in North Korea occurred just as the U.S. made a fresh *démarche* on behalf of a treaty highly favorable to American interests.[2]

Seen in this light, a total U.N. victory in Korea would facilitate a U.S.-Japan-Korea alignment. Northeast Asia would be dominated by an anti-Communist coalition. Peking's passivity in the face of American challenges on its very borders might encourage this coalition to greater ventures. A Chinese Communist show of force, however, might at least remind wavering elements in Japan of a powerful neighbor close at hand. At the most, a smashing of the U.N. offensive in Korea might swing Japan onto a new course of prudent neutrality which would stall further American advances and enable indigenous "friendly" forces to strengthen their hold at the polls and in the trade unions. Thus Korea, as in the past, was less important in itself than for its relationship to adjoining countries.

Peking's propagandistic references to historical precedent may have reflected a genuine awareness of Chinese, as distinguished from Communist, interests. Both China's experience of conquest by Japan and CCP assumptions about conflict with imperialism provided ample cause for concern, without the additional prodding from Moscow that undoubtedly occurred. Although the Japan problem received less attention in Peking's propaganda on the war than did other matters, it would appear to have held fairly high priority among the factors favoring intervention.

China's Role in Asia

Another theme of Chinese Communist propaganda linked the U.S. moves in Korea and Taiwan with "attacks against the national liberation movements in the Philippines, Viet-Nam, Malaya, Indonesia, etc." To what extent was the desire to promote Communist revolutions in Asia a motive for crossing the Yalu? Was Peking fearful that an American success in Korea would encourage Washington to similar "intervention" in Indo-China and elsewhere?

On balance, the answer would appear to be negative. If Mao moved slowly to risk his newly established regime to assist Kim Il-sung, it seems unlikely that he was any more willing to fight for the sake of Ho Chi-minh's struggling revolt. The elimination of the DPRK would alter the *status quo,* liquidating an established Communist regime. The insurrections of Southeast Asia had suffered setbacks before and were likely to experience further defeats before their final victory. What would be an irreversible blow in Korea might be merely an increase of "difficulties to be overcome" in the Philippines or Indo-China. Moreover, the U.S. occupation of Japan provided a ready sanctuary for operations in Korea. No such opportunity arose in Southeast Asia where American "intervention" might prove less successful against guerrillas in the jungles of Indo-China and Malaya.

While Mao may not have been unduly concerned over the impact of North Korean defeat upon the revolutionary movement in Southeast Asia, he may have felt Chinese Communist prestige in the area to be directly affected. Mao had offered his militant strategy of the Chinese civil war as a model for Communist parties elsewhere. This had revived the traditional image of China as a leading power in the area. Further Peking had declared that "no Asian problem can be settled without the participation of the Chinese people." For three decades Mao and his followers had struggled to win this place in the world. Was success to be immediately overshadowed by an unchallenged imperialist victory? Would not acquiescence before the American penetration of Taiwan and Korea bring into question the future role of Mao as both an Asian and a Communist leader? Various clues indicate that these considerations were a contributing, albeit minor, factor in the decision on Korea.

Vulnerability and Insecurity

Finally, Peking faced a combination of threats both inside and outside China. Initially, China's internal weaknesses cautioned against action in Korea. In the later stages of the U.N. advance, however, they may have loomed as an impelling reason to engage the enemy across the Yalu before he capitalized upon the opportunities lying inside China herself.

There is no question but that the new elite faced a host of actual and potential enemies at home. Large areas remained threatened by anti-Communist opposition, including remnant Kuomintang forces, traditional secret societies, non-Chinese peoples, and mountain bandits. Fresh recruits came to these groups as the landlords fled before the advancing movement of land reform, and through the resistance of Kazakh, Mongol, Hui, and Tibetan in defense of nomadic and religious interests. Branded as "counter-revolution" by the Chinese Communists, armed resistance within China provided an opening wedge for "imperialist agents" and "Kuomintang spies" to transform localized insurrection into regional revolt. In western and southern China, from Sinkiang-Kansu through Szechwan-Sikang down to Yünnan and Kwangtung, Chinese Communist power was too recently and too insecurely established to dismiss this as an empty threat.

True, commitment in Korea would take some People's Liberation Army forces away from "pacification" duties and might exacerbate domestic dissatisfactions by further straining the economy. Yet it would provide a pretext for more ruthless suppression of an opposition that could be denounced with more excuse as unpatriotic or traitorous.

Peking may have feared that, if it passively accepted the U.S. victory in Korea, MacArthur and Chiang would be encouraged to engage in new attacks on the Chinese mainland and raise fresh hopes for the internal opposition. In the minds of the Chinese leaders, xenophobia, assumptions about the inevitability of conflict, limited information, and acceptance of their own propaganda all contributed to a highly hostile and suspicious view of the non-Communist world in general and of the United States in particular. Much that occurred during the first months of the Korean War reinforced that view. General MacArthur's visit to Taiwan, his statements to the Veterans of Foreign Wars and to newsman in Tokyo, Secretary Matthews' call for "preventive war," and the more belligerent demands of American congressmen, news commentators, and "authoritative spokesmen" all won attention in the Peking press as "proof" of the "aggressive plans masked by the Austin-Acheson-Truman gang." Because some of the most bellicose statements emanated from Tokyo, where the direction of U.S. military power in Asia appeared to center, the cumulative anxieties of China's leaders may well have become focused in their image of an aggressive General MacArthur.

In sum, it was not the particular problems of safeguarding electric-power supplies in North Korea or the industrial base in Manchuria that aroused Peking to military action. Instead, the final step seems to have been prompted in part by general concern over the range of opportunities within China that might be exploited by a determined, powerful enemy on China's doorstep. At the least, a military response might deter the enemy from further adventures. At the most, it might succeed in inflicting sufficient damage to force the enemy to compromise his objectives and to accede to some of Peking's demands. Contrary to some belief, the Chinese Communist leadership did not enter the Korean War either full of self-assertive confidence or for primarily expansionist goals.

It is difficult to assess the exact importance of the interaction between objective vulnerabilities and subjective anxieties. By placing this interaction last in our review of Chinese Communist considerations, we suggest both its elusiveness and its lesser role. On the one hand, intervention in Korea, at least at the conscious level of decision making, need not be explained solely in this light. On the other hand, it may have colored CCP judgment at key points in the crisis, and may help to explain Peking's rejection of political reassurances and gestures of good will from American, British, Indian, and other U.N. spokesmen.

From this amalgam of likely Chinese Communist interests as viewed from Peking, it would seem that a Soviet *diktat* was not needed to bring the PRC into the war. There may have been differences between the two allies as to the timing and extent of the move. Closer study of Soviet materials may throw light on this question. There undoubtedly were questions of mutual responsibility, some of which may have been resolved to the dissatisfaction of one or both partners. Presumably the imbalance of bargaining power in negotiating over Korea worked to China's disadvantage. But the final decision to fight appears to have been basically a Chinese decision, conditioned by Russian advice and encouraged by Russian support.

We have suggested that several motives prompted intervention in the Korean War. We have further indicated the limited, flexible construct of minimal goals attending that intervention. In particular, we have stressed the political importance of intervention in relation to its expected effect on U.S.-Japanese relations, China's role in Asia, and the security of the regime against subversion or attack from domestic anti-Communist groups assisted by American or Nationalist forces, or both. These findings throw fresh light on the Communist withdrawal from the battle front in the period, November 6–26.

The CPV Disengagement Reconsidered

Earlier, we suggested that this disengagement was consistent with Mao's strategic doctrine and that it may be explained, also, as a pause designed to test the U.S. response to Chinese intervention. Although both explanations remain plausible, especially in combination, we must seriously ask ourselves whether China would have abandoned her offensive of late November if the U.N. forces had remained stationary or had withdrawn. To put the question another way, would the securing of a narrow territorial base for the DPRK have met the minimal goals of Chinese policy? In the absence of an official public commitment to any particular objective, such as restoration of the *status quo ante bellum* or the complete expulsion of U.N. authority from all Korea, Peking would not have lost face by safeguarding DPRK authority in only part of its former territory. At the same time, it would have proved its willingness to accept costs and risks for objectives common to both partners in the Sino-Soviet alliance. The rigors of winter, already evident in the North Korean mountains, might prompt Washington to modify its goals so as to effect a mutually satisfactory compromise. Such a compromise would result from Chinese rather than Russian or North Korean action, thus advancing the stature of the new regime both in the eyes of its own people and in the eyes of fellow Asians. Moreover, the evidence indicates that Sino-Soviet strategy down to November 1950 remained sufficiently defensive and flexible to make possible a hit-and-run attack. The Chinese armies were inadequately equipped and provisioned for sustained combat and inadequately clothed for below-zero temperatures. Captured CPV documents revealed the extent to which these inadequacies prevented the pursuit and annihilation of U.N. forces trapped in the November 27th counteroffensive:

A shortage of transportation and escort personnel makes it impossible to accomplish the mission of supplying the troops. As a result, our soldiers frequently starve. . . . They were unable to maintain the physical strength for combat; the wounded personnel could not be evacuated. . . . The fire power of our entire army was basically inadequate. When we used our guns there were no shells and sometimes the shells were duds.[3]

When all this has been said, however, it remains true that the scope of Chinese Communist troop deployment and the content of Chinese domestic propaganda showed a readiness to risk prolonged war if the initial attack failed to achieve minimal goals. Prisoners of war reported their objectives to include destruction of the U.N. armies in North Korea and the recapture of key points well behind existing U.N. lines.[4] Although these points *were* retaken by the CPV, it was not because the U.N. armies defending them were destroyed but because they were redeployed south of the thirty-eighth parallel, in effect outrunning Communist forces.

Thus an apparent contradiction existed between the capability of the CPV and the mission assigned them. Are we to assume that the U.N.

offensive of November 24–26 interrupted Chinese efforts to remedy their logistical deficiencies? Was the Chinese mission publicized in maximal terms for the sake of troop morale but defined more narrowly in private? Would a U.N. withdrawal to a defensible line across the neck of the peninsula have led to further Communist offensives or merely to probing efforts? Alternatively, would a U.N. air strike across the Yalu River against CPV staging areas have prompted Peking to abandon intervention? How would Russian responsibility under the Sino-Soviet treaty of alliance have been defined in this latter instance?

These questions cannot be answered adequately on the basis of evidence at hand. It is difficult enough to establish what took place in the summer and fall of 1950, without speculating about Chinese actions in supposititious situations. Tentative answers may be inferred from the evidence presented above, but interesting as such speculation might be, it lies outside the framework of our inquiry.

IX

IN RETROSPECT

※

Consequences of Chinese Intervention

OUR STORY would be incomplete were it to end abruptly on November 27, 1950, with the massive engagement between the Chinese Communist and United Nations armies. Without carrying our analysis of Sino-Soviet strategy beyond this point, it may still be helpful to summarize the immediate military and political consequences of Peking's intervention in the war. Finally, we should look briefly at the events of 1950 in relation to the general problem of limited war.

Military Aftermath

The U.N. "home-by-Christmas" offensive of November 24–26 quickly reversed direction with the Chinese People's Volunteers and the Democratic People's Republic of Korea counteroffensive of November 27–29.

On the western front, collapse of the Republic of Korea II Corps resistance exposed the right flank of the United States Eighth Army, imperiling all non-Communist forces in the area. In the east, CPV interdiction of the single supply line connecting the First Marine Division at the Changjin Reservoir with its supply bases at Hamhung and Hungnam threatened to trap 20,000 American and Korean troops in a frozen valley of death. Thickening ice on the Yalu River obviated dependence on the shattered bridges and facilitated a constant build-up of Peking's Third and Fourth Field armies, operating on the west and east fronts respectively. Long winter nights further aided the movement of manpower and material, which remained concealed during daytime U.N. air attacks.

Faced with annihilation under the weight of continued offensives by perhaps all of the 400,000 People's Liberation Army troops known to be in Manchuria, and compelled to restrict air operations to attacks on Korean territory with non-nuclear weapons, the U.N. command executed a rapid retrograde movement. One week after the CPV counterattack, the center of the U.N. line had fallen back fifty miles. On December 5th the U.S. Eighth Army abandoned Pyongyang. Ten days later General Almond's troops halted below the thirty-eighth parallel, completing a defensive perimeter north and east of Seoul. Virtually no major engagements occurred on this front during the entire month. Possession of motorized transport together with a punishing naval and air bombardment of Communist routes of advance permitted the entire U.N. force in the west to outrun the enemy and to reach a line permitting a firm defensive stand.

On the eastern front, different circumstances dictated different tactics, but the end result was the same. The First Marine Division, virtually surrounded sixty miles from its main supply base, had to fight a running battle along the entire line of retreat.[1] Though suffering 4,395 casualties in battle and 7,338 from other causes, mostly frostbite, the division sufficiently mauled attacking CPV units to prevent further enemy offensives against the evacuation point of Hungnam.[2] From December 11th to 24th, a massive amphibious operation moved 105,000 military personnel, 91,000 Korean refugees, 17,500 vehicles, and 350,000 measurement tons of cargo out of Hungnam. The U.N. forces on the east coast thus survived to fight another day.

Exactly six months after the North Korean invasion, the defenders of South Korea were back where they started. But the thirty-eighth parallel had no military significance and could hardly become the locus of a prolonged defense. In January 1951 fresh Communist offensives compelled the U.N. forces to undertake phased withdrawals to a line running from a point seventy miles below the parallel in the west to a point forty-five miles above it in the east. Once again Seoul was abandoned to the enemy, this time after "scorched earth" tactics that destroyed the few major buildings remaining from its previous seizure and liberation.

As Communist supply lines lengthened, U.N. lines shortened. This, together with a U.N. monopoly of the air over most of North Korea, reimposed the conditions that had resulted in stalemate, although along a more southerly line of battle, in 1950. Communist superiority in manpower was matched by U.N. superiority in firepower. Moreover, heavy U.N. air attacks on Communist supply lines crippled the build-up in North Korea, while in South Korea, except for isolated guerrillas, no enemy attacks hampered the flow of supplies from rear to front. In the spring of 1951, slow grinding offensives by both sides exacted large losses, particularly from the Communist armies, but failed to move the front more than one hundred miles. The net gains fell to the U.N., which by June held a line on the west coast slightly below the thirty-eighth parallel, near Kaesong. In the center, U.N. troops crossed the parallel some twenty miles, to Ch'orwon. From there the line turned east in an approximately straight line until, near the coast, it suddenly veered northward to terminate forty-five miles inside DPRK territory.

At this juncture, the Soviet delegate to the Security Council, Jacob Malik, made a radio address in which he proposed cease-fire talks between the belligerents in Korea. During the subsequent two years, the battle front remained inactive except for probing and patrolling. Attention switched to the seemingly interminable discussions at Kaesong and later at Panmunjom. Not until the last days of May 1953 did Communist offensives resume the level of intensity evident in early 1951. The results were some small but strategic gains in territory for the Communists and heavy casualties for the U.N. forces, chiefly the ROK troops. Basically, however, the armistice line agreed to on July 19, 1953, approximated the battle front as it was on June 24th, 1951, when Malik made the initial proposal for cease-fire talks.

In sum, Chinese Communist intervention succeeded in thwarting the declared U.N. objective of unifying Korea and in ousting U.N. forces from almost all of the Democratic People's Republic of Korea. It failed to accomplish any of the military objectives of the initial North Korean invasion, since the Communists were forced to accept U.N. possession of a more defensible line than the thirty-eighth parallel. The political consequences of the intervention, however, were of broader import than the military ones.

Political Aftermath

One major political consequence of Peking's entry into the Korean War was the undisputed establishment of "new China" as a force to be reckoned with in Asia. Whatever might have been the merits or demerits of hotly debated alternative U.N. strategies for countering Chinese Communist intervention, the outcome of events proved to all Asia, if not to all the world, that the government of Mao Tse-tung was both willing and able to defend its interests against direct U.S. opposition. Peking's failure to "liberate Taiwan" detracted from, but did not nullify, this image of Communist China. It is difficult to think of any single course of action that could have so enhanced the stature of the new regime as did intervention in Korea. Had China acquiesced in the unification of Korea under U.N. auspices, with the consequent elimination of the DPRK, her standing as a power would have suffered as much as it was in fact strengthened by her resistance.

This is not to say that the People's Republic of China was universally admired because of its action in Korea, but rather that its power won respect, and in some instances, fear. Given the political objectives attending the North Korean attack as well as the Chinese intervention, particularly with respect to Japan and South Asia, China's belligerence proved of mixed value. On the one hand, it strengthened the morale of Communist parties and induced some non-Communists to move cautiously, lest they become the target of Chinese power. Conciliation of China was deemed necessary to avoid further tension in Asia. On the other hand, Peking's behavior alerted many Asians to the threat posed by Communist China. It disabused many of their beliefs that the new regime was more Chinese than Communist. For others it spurred greater determination to counter Communist activity, both at home and abroad.

A second consequence of intervention was its impact upon subsequent Chinese Communist foreign policies. The events of 1950 removed whatever doubts the Chinese Communist Party might still have entertained that America remained its chief enemy. In so far as it identified the U.N. with the U.S., Peking may well have written off membership in the international organization as of marginal utility. A priori assumptions about the basic conflict between capitalism and socialism were "proved" correct, for Mao Tse-tung and his followers, by American activities in Asia.

Less certain is the impact of the Chinese intervention upon Sino-Soviet relations. The research for this study has not disclosed likely sources of tension in the alliance among the decisions which led to intervention. This does not prove that none existed, although it lessens the probability. Of one effect upon the alliance, however, there is no doubt. Soviet military assistance to China after the latter's entry into the war completely re-equipped the PLA and provided Peking with a first-line jet air force second to none in Asia, except that of the United States. This tangible benefit, added to the deterrent effect of the alliance upon U.S. strategy during the war, justified Mao's policy of "leaning to one side."

The behavior of India during the summer and fall of 1950 appears to have modified Chinese Communist assumptions concerning the rigid demarcation of the world into two camps. Peking's propaganda and diplomacy vis-à-vis New Delhi changed as Nehru's statements and Rau's activity at Lake Success markedly diverged from "Anglo-American imperialism." No basic change, however, occurred in Chinese Communist suspicion of non-Communist governments, and the calculated flouting of Indian sensitivity in the invasion of Tibet demonstrated the narrow limits within which Peking's attitude shifted at this time. It seems likely that the post-Stalin changes in Sino-Soviet strategy toward the uncommitted Afro-Asian nations germinated in Peking's dealings with these countries during the Korean War.

The political effects of Chinese Communist intervention were particularly strong in the United States where shock at having misjudged Peking's intentions was mixed with frustration at having to suffer setbacks because of military and political limitations on action. From 1950 to 1952 a so-called "Great Debate" racked U.S. politics. Ostensibly focused on strategy, it ranged over domestic, foreign, and military policies to an extent without parallel in twentieth century America. The political rumblings of August 1950 over strategy in the Korean War grew to near-earthquake proportions in the spring of 1951 when President Truman removed General MacArthur from his command for repeatedly and publicly challenging the national policy of the United States. The resulting congressional furor led to a six-week investigation in which every important American figure associated with Far Eastern policy and Korean War strategy, except President Truman, gave testimony, most of which was made public. The controversy carried over to the 1952 presidential campaign where candidate Eisenhower's pledge to "go to Korea and see for myself" played a dramatic, albeit marginal, role in winning the election.

The impassioned debate over responsibility for the U.N. setback at the hands of the Chinese Communists diverted attention from the lessons the events of 1950 taught concerning limited war in the nuclear age. A serious problem in the conduct of such war is the hazard of miscalculation, where failure to analyze the enemy's intentions and to anticipate his response to alternative courses of action may raise the level of violence to thermonuclear proportions. Such failure may stem from many sources, including the inadequacies of strategic intelligence, the complexities of decision-making machinery, and the enemy's irrational behavior. But our study suggests an additional focus of attention; namely, the role of communication among belligerents, be they active, proxy, or prospective participants in the war. Inadequate communication, or the failure to convey accurately to an opponent one's intentions and one's probable responses, played a pivotal role between August and October 1950 in precipitating war between CPV and U.N. forces. Such communication is, of course, a two-party process; both sender and receiver influence its outcome. This study has concentrated on Communist behavior and therefore derives its picture of events primarily from the actions and reactions of one side. Nevertheless, the conclusions of this study do have some value in the general context of interbelligerent communication.

Communication Among Nations in Limited War

In the Korean War, certain aspects of communication among the interested governments were peculiar to that war. Normally, prior to hostilities, major states enjoy direct relations through diplomatic channels. The absence of U.S. recognition of the People's Republic of China placed an added burden upon communication between Peking and Washington. It is not unusual, however, for states with mutually accredited diplomatic representatives to address one another by indirection through public speeches, inspired newspaper reports, and even through third parties. Therefore the absence of direct channels of communication between Peking and Washington need not invalidate the clues afforded by this study to the role of communication as one source of miscalculation in limited war.

Subjective Limitations

One obstacle to successful communication, particularly between Communist and non-Communist regimes, is the difficulty each side has in projecting itself into the frame of reference within which the other operates. Yet this is necessary if one is to understand the opponent's interpretation of one's own signals, as well as the motives behind his.

This study has attempted to view events from the perspective of Peking, which ascribed motivations and patterns of decision making to "Wall Street warmongers" and "Anglo-American imperialists" and in other ways departed sharply from reality. Peking ignored the pluralistic political process in the West and failed to differentiate between the true locus of power in Washington and the confusion of voices on both sides of the Pacific Ocean. Utterances by "authoritative spokesmen" in Tokyo were given equal weight (if not greater) with statements from Secretary Acheson and President Truman. *Ad hoc* American decisions on Korea and Taiwan were interpreted as the outcome of carefully designed schemes for "aggression" in Asia. Failure to comprehend the frame of reference within which Washington reacted led Peking to miscalculate the effect of communications designed to deter the U.S., and to exaggerate the threat posed by actual U.S. intentions.

This was not a unilateral phenomenon. American communications for Chinese Communist consumption were inadequately adapted to the CCP frame of reference. To be sure, hindsight facilitates the reconstruction of Peking's perspective to a degree that was impossible during the actual course of events. Yet a similar if less conclusive exercise, carried out in 1950, might have alerted U.S. officials to the pitfalls of dealing with the new regime as if it were more Chinese than Communist.[3] Judgments in Washington reflected a belief in basic conflicts within the Communist world that, if properly exploited, would inhibit Peking's actions in Korea. One such conflict was seen in a supposed clash between "innately Chinese" qualities and "alien Communism." This theory comfortingly left intact the presumed bonds of "friendship" between "the Chinese and American peoples." Another clash was seen in Peking-Moscow relations, where "Chinese national interests" were thought to conflict with "Russian domination." This, it was said, would keep Mao from pulling Stalin's chestnuts out of the fire. Such assumptions consistently attributed to the Chinese Communists a benevolence they were far from feeling. Hence American "assurances" to Peking were never enough to support the aims of U.S. policy.

The problem is complicated further by the differing audiences to which different communications were addressed. Thus the Chinese Communists uniformly interpreted the remarks of Ambassador Austin as responding to statements from his Soviet counterpart, Jacob Malik. In actuality, Austin was speaking primarily for domestic consumption at one point, to American allies at another, and to uncommitted delegations at a third. To take only one instance, in early September the Austin-Truman statements expressing anxiety over possible Chinese Communist involvement in the war had the purpose of influencing U.N. members to oppose PRC admission to the international organization. In Peking, however, such remarks were taken at face value. When this interpretation was buttressed by MacArthur's communiqué concerning military co-operation between the PRC and DPRK before the North Korean invasion, Peking responded with a warning that such co-operation would continue. The warning, however, failed to achieve its aim of heightening U.S. anxiety on this point, since such anxiety did not underlie the Austin-Truman-MacArthur statements.

A third problem is communication over highly sensitive matters such as terminating hostilities or deterring enemy action. In August 1950, Soviet strategy faced a dilemma. How was the Soviet Union to signal willingness to compromise DPRK objectives in the war without admitting Soviet responsibility for DPRK action? More serious, how might the enemy interpret this signal? At that moment, North Korean armies were hammering at shrinking U.N. lines. Was it wise to concede hard-fought gains in advance of the U.N. counteroffensive? Or would it be too late to stop the U.N. armies once they had tasted the fruits of victory? These problems placed special burdens upon those who framed Malik's message at Lake Success.

The American position was also difficult. It was decided to unite Korea by force while avoiding an expansion of the conflict to Korea's neighbors. How would this affect "legitimate Chinese interests"? If the Chinese were tempted to intervene, how could they be deterred from actually doing so? The solution was a policy of reassurance coupled with a demonstration of firmness and force. Administration spokesmen emphasized the former while MacArthur stressed the latter. The advance to the Yalu River was to have been so conducted as to convince Peking of U.N. determination without alarming the Chinese as to U.N. intentions. In some quarters it was feared that any compromise in this policy would prompt Peking to the same miscalculation of U.S. intentions that had invited the initial North Korean invasion. The uncompromising stand of the United States, of course, had exactly the opposite effect from the one intended. It neither reassured nor deterred the PRC.

Objective Limitations

In retrospect, both sides ran afoul of the political hazards inherent in public communication. In open diplomacy, political prestige limits the choice of action to what seems popularly acceptable. It was impossible for Malik to formulate his statements more explicitly in the world forum of the Security Council. It was only slightly more feasible for U.S. policy to reverse course in response to publicly delivered threats of Chinese Communist intervention. This is simply to say that the success of the Malik proposal and of the Chinese threat to intervene was in part dependent upon international communications that, in fact, failed to work because of the constraints of publicity.

Korean developments were affected in other ways by the absence of direct relations between Peking and Washington. On the one side, Chinese Communist calculations depended primarily upon Soviet interpretations of American and U.N. intentions. This introduced a Soviet bias into the information available to decision makers in Peking. On the other side, American knowledge of Chinese Communist views came, to a considerable degree, through Indian channels. For a number of reasons, this made such information difficult and, for some officials, impossible to evaluate. Hence Chinese calculations exaggerated the threat posed by American policy, while American calculations downgraded the seriousness of Chinese concern. An "entirely new war" resulted. These objective limitations compounded subjective elements in the communications process. Removal of the former would still have left the latter as basic obstacles to a mutual comprehension of enemy intentions and reactions.

The subjective obstacles to communications cannot be wholly eliminated, for they are rooted in the beliefs and the environment of men who decide policy. Their impact may be lessened, however, through persistent efforts to understand their role in shaping the perspective of both communicator and recipient. It would be misleading to single out any factor as determining the collision between Chinese and United Nations armies in 1950. Nevertheless the Korean War provides an instructive warning concerning the dangers of failure in communications in a limited-war situation.

It is tempting to conclude an inquiry into the origins of a particular war with a judgment as to its inevitability, or alternatively to conclude that it need never have occurred. With hindsight, it is possible to juxtapose human attitudes and actions so as to demonstrate some sort of predetermined outcome, just as it is possible to postulate alternative attitudes and actions that might have altered the final situation.

The Korean War lends itself to such efforts, as indeed do all other wars in history. Yet the temptation must be resisted, for it would vitiate the purpose of this study. We have probed the possible patterns of Chinese Communist calculations for insight into the rationale underlying Peking's entry into the Korean War. That rationale has emerged as a compound of considerations which were historically derived from China's development or ideologically posited in the Communist credo. Only future historians with access to archives of the People's Republic of China can attest the validity of this analysis. Until then we must suspend final judgment and make the most of the materials at hand to derive insights concerning Communist China's strategy and tactics.

NOTES

※

PREFACE

1. My understanding of this broader problem was stimulated and enhanced by discussions wiith Alexander George and with Thomas C. Schelling.

I. THE FRAMEWORK OF POLICY

1. For example, Chiang Kai-shek defined as "lost territories" vast areas well beyond China's twentieth century borders, basing his claim both on precedent and on population pressure. "In regard to the living space essential for the nation's existence, the territory of the Chinese state is determined by the requirements for national survival and by the limits of Chinese cultural bonds. Thus, in the territory of China a hundred years ago, comprising more than ten million square kilometers, there was not a single district that was not essential to the survival of the Chinese nation, and none that was not permeated by our culture. . . . Not until all lost territories have been recovered can we relax our efforts to wipe out this humiliation and save ourselves from destruction." Chiang Kai-shek, *China's Destiny*, Roy Publishers, New York, 1947, p. 34. A Chinese textbook published under Chiang's rule identified more than one million square miles of "lost territories." Hou Ming-chiu, Chen Erh-shiu, and Lu Chen, *General Geography of China* (in Chinese), 1946, as cited in George B. Cressey, *Land of the 500 Million*, McGraw-Hill, New York, 1955, p. 39.

2. Edgar Snow, *Red Star Over China*, Random House, New York, 1944, p. 96. Copyright 1937, 1938 by Edgar Snow. Reprinted by permission of Random House, Inc.

3. When Mao spoke, Outer Mongolia had existed as a self-proclaimed independent republic for fifteen years. Sinkiang, the largest Mohemmedan area in China, was under *de facto* Soviet domination with only nominal *de jure* Chinese authority in the province. Tibet remained a highly autonomous buffer between China and India. In 1944 Mao restated his conviction that Outer Mongolia would federate with China if given a free choice. Guenther Stein, *The Challenge of Red China*, McGraw-Hill, New York, 1945, p. 443.

4. Theodore Shabad, *China's Changing Map*, Frederick A. Praeger, New York, 1956, p. 4.

5. Chiang Kai-shek, *op. cit.*, p. 78, attributes the chaotic years of interregnum following collapse of the Manchu Dynasty to "secret activities of the Imperialists . . . the chief cause of civil wars among the warlords." The empire's

disintegration he blames on so-called "unequal treaties" which "completely destroyed our nationhood, and our sense of honor and shame was lost. . . . The traditional structure of the family, the village, and the community was disrupted. The virtue of mutual help was replaced by competition and jealousy. Public planning was neglected and no one took an interest in public affairs;" *ibid.*, pp. 79 and 88.

6. K'o Pai-nien, "Hsin-min chu-yi te wai-chiao cheng-tse" (The Foreign Policy of the New People's Democracy), *Hsüeh Hsi* (Study), Vol. I, No. 2, Oct. 1949, pp. 13–15. K'o later became ambassador to Romania.

7. Hu Sheng, *Ti-kuo chu-i i Chung-kuo cheng-chih* (Imperialism and Chinese Politics), Peking, 1949. An English edition in 1955 revised much of the book, but left intact its criticism of czarist policy, despite Soviet attacks in the interim; see Allen S. Whiting, "Rewriting Modern History in Communist China: A Review Article," *Far Eastern Survey*, Vol. XXIV, No. 11, Nov. 1955.

8. For a survey of these criticisms, see Allen S. Whiting, "Communist China and 'Big Brother,'" *ibid.*, Vol. XXIV, No. 10, Oct. 1955.

9. Mao Tse-tung, "On Coalition Government," *Selected Works of Mao Tse-tung* (hereafter cited as *Selected Works*), Vol. IV, New York, International Publishers, 1956, pp. 310–311; delivered to the Seventh National Congress of the Chinese Communist Party, April 24, 1945.

10. *Central China Post* (Hankow), Nov. 25, 1931, quoted in O. Edmund Clubb, "Chinese Communist Strategy in Foreign Relations," *Annals of the American Academy of Political and Social Science*, Vol. CCLXXVII, Sept. 1951, p. 156.

11. Mao Tse-tung, "Analysis of the Classes in Chinese Society" (March 1926), *Selected Works*, Vol. I, pp. 14–15.

12. "On New Democracy" (Jan. 1940), *ibid.*, Vol. III, p. 125.

13. *On Internationalism and Nationalism*, 2nd ed., Peking, 1952, pp. 26–27.

14. Mao Tse-tung, "On New Democracy," *op. cit.*, p. 124.

15. Mao Tse-tung, "On People's Democratic Dictatorship," July 1, 1949, as translated in C. Brandt, B. Schwartz, and J. K. Fairbank, *A Documentary History of Chinese Communism*, Harvard University Press, Cambridge, 1952, pp. 449 ff. For a parallel, though less adequate, translation, see *Mao Tse-tung on People's Democratic Dictatorship*, 3rd ed., Foreign Languages Press, Peking, 1950.

16. Mao Tse-tung, *On Contradiction*, written August 1937, published with "certain additions, deletions, and revisions, [by] the author," Peking, 1952, p. 38.

17. Mao Tse-tung, "On Policy" (Dec. 25, 1940), *Selected Works*, Vol. III, p. 218.

18. Robert C. North and I. de S. Pool, *Kuomintang and Chinese Communist Elites*, Stanford University Press, Stanford, Calif., 1952, pp. 51 ff.

19. Chang Kuo-t'ao, in an interview with the author in Hong Kong, 1955, recalled that CCP members seldom discussed foreign affairs not directly related to China, and avoided critical examination of Soviet politics. Chang ranked high in the CCP Politburo prior to his expulsion in 1938.

20. Michael Lindsay, *China and the Cold War*, Melbourne, Austral., 1955, p. 172. Lindsay acted as a wartime adviser to the CCP.

21. E. Snow, *op. cit.,* pp. 76–77. Snow generously describes Mao as "surprisingly well-informed on current world politics." This appears to refer to interest rather than information, for Mao did echo the diversity of Comintern comment on subjects ranging from fascism and the Spanish civil war to the New Deal and problems confronting Negroes and Indians in the United States. Indicative of his information level, however, was his statement, "There are countries permanently under the menace of aggressive powers, such as Siam, the Philippines, Central American countries, Canada, India, Australia, Dutch Indies, etc.—all more or less under the threat of Japan. We consider them our friends." *Ibid.,* p. 87. This indiscriminate lumping together of all countries bordering the Pacific Ocean as "under the threat of Japan" had little basis in reality.

22. Mao Tse-tung, "On New Democracy," Bombay, India, in *The Strategy and Tactics of World Communism,* Supplement III, C.: *Communism in China,* House Committee on Foreign Affairs, Washington, 1949, p. 81. This statement was omitted from Peking's official English edition, which was identical in other respects; see Mao Tse-tung, *Selected Works,* Vol. III, pp. 106–157.

23. Lu Ting-yi, "Explanation of Several Basic Questions Concerning the Postwar International Situation," *Emancipation Daily* (Yenan), Jan. 4–5, 1947, in *United States Relations with China,* Department of State, Washington, 1949, pp. 710–719. Anna Louise Strong, "The Thought of Mao Tse-tung," *Amerasia,* Vol. XI, No. 6, June 1947, p. 173, attributes the statement to Mao Tse-tung on the basis of interviews in Yenan during the summer of 1946.

24. Mao Tse-tung, "How Yu Kung Removed the Mountains" (June 11, 1945, concluding speech at the Seventh National Congress of the CCP), *Selected Works,* IV, p. 318.

25. Mao Tse-tung, "On the Danger of the Hurley Policy" (July 12, 1945), *ibid.,* pp. 328–329. Michael Lindsay, *op. cit.,* pp. 165–166, attempts to view U.S. moves from Yenan's standpoint. Lindsay cites instances which increased CCP suspicions of Washington motives. His charges include American failure to implement agreements for co-operation with Yenan on matters of communications and military affairs, Ambassador Hurley's repudiation of promises given in November 1944 to seek KMT-CCP unity, and American toleration of Japanese troops serving with KMT forces despite Washington's avowed obligation to evacuate the defeated enemy from all China. In addition, Lindsay notes allegations of United Nations Relief and Rehabilitation Administration (UNRRA) discrimination against Communist-held areas as adding to experiences which reinforced CCP assumptions of imperialist, i.e., American, hostility.

26. Allen S. Whiting, "The New Chinese Communist," *World Politics,* Vol. VII, No. 4, July 1955, p. 601. This information was obtained from interviews with former CCP members among the 14,000 Chinese prisoners of war who refused repatriation in the Korean War. Party cadres also explained Soviet factory removals as designed to keep productive plants from Nationalist control for return to Communist use at a later time. Michael Lindsay, *op. cit.,* pp. 12–14, recounts a talk in 1949 with "a theorist of the CCP" who challenged his eyewitness account of postwar Soviet troop misbehavior in Berlin: "But Mr. Lindsay, if you had read Marx, Engels, and Lenin you would know that these stories

cannot be true as it is theoretically impossible for the representatives of a socialist power to behave in such a way."

27. Mao Tse-tung, Aug. 11, 1949, commentary for Hsinhua News Agency "On the White Paper," reprinted in *Imperialism and All Reactionaries Are Paper Tigers* ("Enlarged Edition"), Foreign Languages Press, Peking, 1958, pp. 12–13.

II. PROBLEMS AND POLICIES

1. Cheng Lien-tun, "None Shall Starve," *People's China,* Vol. I, No. 4, Feb. 16, 1950, p. 21.

2. Tien Huo-nung, "China's Agriculture in Speedy Rehabilitation," *ibid.,* Feb. 1, 1950, pp. 7 ff. The rest of the paragraph draws on this article.

3. Ch'en Yün, Vice Premier of the Government Administrative Council (GAC) and Chairman of the Committee of Financial and Economic Affairs, "The Problem of Commodity Prices and the Issuance of Government Bonds," report to the fourth meeting of the Central People's Government Council (CPGC) of the PRC, Dec. 2, 1949, in *New China's Economic Achievements, 1949–1952,* Peking, 1952, pp. 33–35.

4. Po I-po, Vice Chairman of the Committee of Financial and Economic Affairs of the GAC, "The Draft Budget for 1950," report to the fourth meeting of the CPGC of the PRC, Dec. 2, 1949, in *ibid.,* pp. 39 ff. Po noted that in addition to the category "Military Expenditure," ". . . items under Administrative Expenditure like locally raised funds in support of the war front and initial expenditures for military control in newly Liberated Areas, or transportation expenditure which falls under the category of financial expenditures, are really in fact expenditures for the war."

5. Mao Tse-tung, "Turn to Production," Dec. 5, 1949, in H. Arthur Steiner, *Maoism: A Sourcebook,* University of California at Los Angeles, 1952, mimeo., pp. 131–132.

6. Mao Tse-tung to the seventh session of the CPGC, April 13, 1950, quoted in an editorial, "New China Has Conquered Inflation," *People's China,* Vol. I, No. 10, May 16, 1950, p. 4. *Ibid.,* p. 17, Chen Tan, in "The People's Army Turns to Production," remarks, "With the liberation of Taiwan and Tibet all the PLA's five million men can join the all-out assault on the production front."

7. Liu Shao-ch'i, May 1, 1950, in *Hsin Hua Yüeh Pao,* Vol. II, No. 1, pp. 5–10.

8. Ke Chia-lung, "Manchuria's Economic Victories," *People's China,* Vol. I, No. 11, June 1, 1950, p. 8.

9. *Kansu Jih Pao,* March 17, 1950, in *Hsin Hu Yüeh Pao,* Vol. II, No. 1, p. 20.

10. Mao Tse-tung, "Report to the Party Plenum," *People's China,* Vol. II, No. 1, July 1, 1950, pp. 4–6, given June 6 to third plenary session of the Seventh Central Committee of the CCP. Six years later Liu Shao-ch'i remarked to the Eighth CCP Congress: "One important way of increasing our funds for construction is to economize more on military and administration expenditures. The Central Committee of the Party had already decided on this policy in 1950.

But it was not carried out earlier because of the outbreak of the war to resist U.S. aggression and aid Korea." *Eighth National Congress of the Communist Party of China,* Peking, 1956, Vol. I, pp. 47–48.

11. Wu Yuan-li, *An Economic Survey of Communist China,* Bookman Associates, New York, 1955, pp. 415 ff.

12. *Ad hoc* evidence that involvement in the Korean War was not anticipated by Peking's economic planners came in 1953 when Minister of Finance Po I-po claimed that budgeted military appropriations for 1950 of 23.2 trillion Jen Min Piao (JMP) compared with actual expenditures of 28.3 trillion JMP, although the projected Taiwan invasion never occurred; the large underestimate in the budget would appear to indicate that the Korean expenditures were unexpected. Po I-po, "Report on the 1953 State Budget of the People's Republic of China," supplement to *People's China,* March 16, 1953, quoted in W. W. Rostow, *The Prospects for Communist China,* Wiley & Sons, New York, 1954, p. 232.

13. Hsü Tsai-tan, "Northeast China Sets the Pace," *People's China,* Vol. I, No. 7, April 1, 1950, pp. 8 ff.

14. Ke Chia-lung, *loc. cit.*

15. Tsai Ying-p'ing, "The Road to Final Victory," *People's China,* Vol. I, No. 4, Feb. 16, 1950, p. 27, offers estimates of the total amount captured in the civil war, without indicating condition of equipment or its subsequent disposition in combat. This includes 52,051 pieces of artillery; 297,740 machine guns; 2,612,126 small arms; 598 tanks; 378 armored vehicles; 492,799,000 rounds of ammunition; and 5,183,390 shells.

16. *Changsha Hsin Hunan Pao,* Aug. 1, 1957, in *Survey of the China Mainland Press* (hereafter cited as *SCMP*), No. 1619, American Consulate General, Hong Kong. This historical review, "Eight Years of the Chinese People's Liberation Army in Hunan," came from the headquarters and the political department of the Hunan Military District Commission, PLA. It summarized the campaign thus: "Bandits and irregularly armed bands, totalling over 250,000 men, were destroyed or regrouped; over 142,600 pieces of firearms of all descriptions were seized, including over 2,600 light or heavy machine-guns and over 600 large or small cannon."

17. See Lo Jui-ching's report of Oct. 1, 1950, summarizing armed opposition in southwestern areas, Kwangsi, Jehol, Liaotung, and Kirin, as quoted in Shih Ch'eng-shih, *People's Resistance in Mainland China, 1950–1955,* Union Research Institute, Hong Kong, 1956, pp. 1–2.

18. General Su Yü, "Liberation of Taiwan in Sight," *People's China,* Vol. I, No. 4, Feb. 16, 1950, p. 89. According to an editorial note, General Su "ranks among the top military strategists in the PLA, is Vice-Commander of the Third Field Army." The speech was made in Shanghai.

19. Frank A. Kierman, Jr., *The Fluke That Saved Formosa,* Communist Bloc Program, China Project, B/54–3, Center for International Studies, M.I.T., June 1, 1954. Kierman reports casualties "in the tens of thousands."

20. *People's China,* Vol. I, No. 10, May 16, 1950, p. 22.

21. *Jen Min Jih Pao,* April 21, 1950, and May 21, 1950, reprinted in *Hsin Hua Yüeh Pao,* Vol. II, No. 1, p. 14, and No. 2, p. 249. A misprint may have

occurred in the earlier editorial asserting "The Fourth Field Army must prepare for the liberation of Taiwan." All other Chinese references, including those in *Jen Min Jih Pao,* refer to the Third Field Army as assigned this task.

22. *New York Times,* Jan. 6, 1950; the statement was made on Jan. 5. For a review of additional statements from U.S. officials indicating abandonment of commitment to Chiang and to the defense of Taiwan, see John W. Spanier, *The Truman-MacArthur Controversy and the Korean War,* Harvard University Press, Cambridge, Mass., 1959, pp. 51–57. In particular, Acheson's comments upon the Truman statement and the leaking from General MacArthur's headquarters in Tokyo of a State Department "information directive" anticipating the fall of Taiwan indicated the lack of American willingness to defend the island against Communist Chinese attack.

23. *New York Times,* April 30, 1950, and July 2, 1950. Louis Johnson, then Secretary of Defense, later testified that between June 10 and 24, 1950, "the troops opposite Formosa had been increased from more than 40,000 to about 156,000." *Military Situation in the Far East, Hearings Before the Committee on Armed Services and the Committee on Foreign Relations,* United States Senate, 82nd Cong., 1st Sess., Washington, D.C., 1951, p. 2621. For a more detailed description of the build-up with slightly larger figures, see Captain Walter Karig, USNR, Commander Malcolm W. Cagle, USN, and Lieutenant-Commander Frank A. Manson, USN, *Battle Report: The War in Korea* ("prepared from official sources"), Rinehart and Company, Inc., New York, 1952, p. 41.

24. Cheng Lien-tun, "The PLA in Production," *People's China,* Vol. II, No. 3, Aug. 1, 1950, p. 10. Cheng gives the time required for this move as "over one month," and describes the economic assignments in detail.

25. *Chinese Communist Forces (CCF) Army Histories,* Dec. 1, 1954, Order of Battle Branch, Office of the Assistant Chief of Staff, G-2, Eighth U.S. Army. These histories checked contemporary intelligence estimates against later interrogations of Chinese prisoners of war. While lacking precise numbers on unit strength, they provide an internally consistent account of troop movements in 1950–1951 that permits rough estimates on the forces in different areas of China.

26. *The Common Program and Other Documents of the First Plenary Session of the Chinese People's Political Consultative Conference,* Peking, 1950.

27. Michael Lindsay, *China and the Cold War,* pp. 12–14.

28. O. Edmund Clubb, "Chinese Communist Strategy in Foreign Relations," *Annals of the American Academy of Political and Social Science,* Vol. CCLXXVII, Sept. 1951, p. 158.

29. *Hsin Hua Yüeh Pao,* Vol. I, No. 2, p. 340, and Vol. I, No. 4, p. 841.

30. *Pravda,* Jan. 2, 1950; also translated in *Current Digest of the Soviet Press* (hereafter cited as *CDSP*), Vol. II, No. 2, p. 23.

31. For the text of the 1945 Treaty of Friendship and Alliance, see *United States Relations with China,* Department of State, Washington, D.C., 1949, pp. 585–587. The text of the 1950 Treaty of Friendship, Alliance and Mutual Assistance is in *People's China,* Vol. I, No. 5, March 1, 1950, pp. 25–26.

32. See the speech by Chou En-lai, Feb. 15, 1950, and New China News Agency editorial comment of Feb. 15, 1950, in *People's China,* Vol. I, No. 5, March 1, 1950, pp. 28–32.

33. For a defense of the Soviet position in Port Arthur and Dairen against charges of an "unequal" treaty, see Chao Yi-ya, "Kuo-chi chu-i hsüeh-hsi t'i-kan" (Study Principles of Internationalism), *Hsüeh Hsi* (Study), Vol. I, No. 4, Dec. 1949, pp. 7–9. For references to unidentified sources of criticism against Soviet policy, see Ch'ien Chün-jui, "Kuo-chi chu-yi te chu-yao piao-chih tuei Ssu-lien ti you-yi" (The Hallmark of Internationalism: Friendship toward the Soviet Union), *ibid.*, pp. 4–6; Liang Ch'un-fu, *Hsin-Chung-kuo ti wai-chiao* (New China's Foreign Relations), Canton, Jan. 1950; Hu Hua, *New Period of Sino-Soviet Friendship and Cooperation* (in Chinese), Tientsin, Feb. 1950. This appears to have been the cause for organizing the Sino-Soviet Friendship Association in October 1949. It quickly mushroomed throughout China, claiming a membership of millions. It was particularly active during the following five years in propagandizing the alliance through publications, films, cultural exchanges, etc. Not until 1957 was a parallel organization formed in the Soviet Union.

34. These supplementary agreements were not signed until March 27, 1950, but undoubtedly were discussed during the Mao-Stalin conference. Full texts were not published.

35. *Jen Min Jih Pao*, April 5, 1950, defended the joint-stock companies, quoting Lenin and citing Soviet practice during the New Economic Policy for precedent. By implication, similar concessions were possible for capitalist countries: "Under proper conditions this is permissible in principle, not only with the Soviet Union but with other People's Democracies and with certain capitalist countries." It is doubtful this represented serious expectations. More likely it was a propagandistic response to domestic criticism of the agreements. For reference to such criticism, see Ti Ch'ao-pai, "The Meaning and Method of Sino-Soviet Economic Co-operation" (in Chinese), *ibid.*, April 21, 1950: "Some persons ask: Sinkiang is our territory. Isn't it disadvantageous for us if the Soviet Union gets half the production for helping exploit its resources? . . . If capitalists demand the same kind of co-operation, can we agree? . . . Why not have this co-operation in the heart of our industrial areas? Why only in faroff Sinkiang?"

36. Mao had earlier defended "leaning to one side" in the following terms: "At present the rulers in Britain and the United States are still imperialists. Would they extend aid to a people's state? . . . Suppose these countries would be willing in the future to lend us money on terms of mutual benefit, what would be the reason for it? It would be because the capitalists of these countries want to make money and the bankers want to earn interest to relieve their own crisis; that would be no aid to the Chinese people"; Mao Tse-tung, "On the People's Democratic Dictatorship" (July 1, 1949), in Conrad Brandt, *et al.*, *A Documentary History of Chinese Communism*, pp. 455–456.

37. Even had other loans been available to compete with the Soviet offer, a precise estimate of the benefit derived from the agreement would call for more data on the specific terms of trade, the manner of readjusting to annual fluctuations in delivery and payment, and the complicated problem of weighing the Soviet need for Chinese products in the light of alternative sources and of allocation of Soviet resources. Discussion of the size of the loan depends upon an understanding of the problem of repayment. Such considerations go beyond the scope of the present discussion.

38. A Soviet paraphrase of the trade agreements indicated very favorable terms for Russian representatives, who were to enjoy all diplomatic privileges as well as extraterritoriality for the offices of their missions; A. S. Korolenko, *Torgovliye Dogovory i Soglasheniya SSSR s Inostrannyme Gosudarstvami* (Trade Treaties and Agreements of the USSR with Foreign States), Moscow, 1953. No limit was placed on the number of persons who might enjoy such privileges in China. Other countries conceded such privileges to only one to three Soviet trade officials. These included Belgium, Sweden, Great Britain, Denmark, Iran, Turkey, France, Switzerland, Italy, and Finland, as well as Bulgaria, Czechoslovakia, Hungary, and Romania. Only the German Democratic Republic, the Democratic People's Republic of Korea, and Poland gave unlimited access to privileges as did China. Korolenko also noted that the agreements specified "in clear and categorical language that 'Both governments shall ensure the delivery of commodities in accordance with the contingencies appended to the agreement.' "

39. On Oct. 12, 1954, a communiqué climaxing the visit of N. S. Khrushchev and N. A. Bulganin to Peking announced that all Sino-Soviet joint-stock companies would be dissolved on Dec. 31, 1954. Transfer of shares to Chinese title was announced Jan. 1, 1955, with compensation of unspecified amounts to be paid out of future production of the companies. This came twenty-five years earlier than specified in the 1950 agreements, although the latter stipulated that the transfer was to be without compensation. The Khrushchev-Bulganin mission also agreed to additional loans for China.

40. Liu Shao-ch'i, vice president of the World Federation of Trade Unions and honorary president of the All-China Federation of Labor to the Trade Union Conference of Asian and Australasian Countries, Nov. 16, 1949, as broadcast by NCNA, Peking, Nov. 23, 1949.

41. In August 1946, Liu Shao-ch'i told an American correspondent: "Mao Tse-tung has created a Chinese or Asiatic form of Marxism. His great accomplishment has been to change Marxism from its European to its Asiatic form. He is the first who has succeeded in doing so." Anna Louise Strong, *Dawn Out of China*, People's Publishing House, Bombay, 1948, p. 29. For detailed examination of the so-called "Maoist strategy" and its implementation in India, see John H. Kautsky, *Moscow and the Communist Party of India*, John Wiley & Sons, Inc., New York, 1956.

42. Kautsky, *op cit.*, traces the differing Soviet views in detail during 1947–1949. Strong, in an interview with the author, told of Soviet opposition to her manuscript on Mao and his theories, possibly the cause of her expulsion from the Soviet Union in 1947.

43. In addition to Kautsky, see also Ruth T. McVey, *The Calcutta Conference and the Southeast Asian Uprisings,* Interim Reports Series, Modern Indonesia Project, Southeast Asia Program, Cornell University, Ithaca, New York, 1958.

44. For pre-recognition criticism of Nehru, see attacks upon his Tibetan views, NCNA, Sept. 2, 1949; *Jen Min Jih Pao*, Sept. 7, and NCNA of Sept. 8, 1949, reprinted in *Hsin Hua Yüeh Pao*, Vol. I, No. 1.

45. Huang Ts'ao-liang, *Chan-hou shih-chieh hsin-hsing-shih* (New Aspects of the Postwar World), Shanghai, April 1950, pp. 63 ff.

46. *Jen Min Jih Pao* editorial for Anti-Colonialism Day, in *People's China,* Vol. I, No. 4, Feb. 16, 1950, p. 3.

47. Chou En-lai, *ibid.,* Vol. I, No. 7, April 1, 1950, p. 5. For a similar attack against "the so-called independence of the Philippines and Burma, the dominion status of India and Pakistan and the so-called republican government of the Hatta block in Indonesia," see Teng Ying-chao, speaking in Peking to the International Women's Democratic Federation, NCNA, Dec. 12, 1949, in *The Hate America Campaign in Communist China,* Washington, n.d., p. 5.

48. Huang Ts'ao-liang, *op cit.*

III. RUSSIA, CHINA, AND THE KOREAN WAR

1. For an authoritative comment on this aspect, see George F. Kennan, "What Should We Do About Russia?" *U.S. News & World Report,* June 29, 1956, p. 74. Alice Langley Hsieh contributed materially to the Japanese portion of the analysis.

2. In 1896 Li Hung-chang signed a treaty of alliance in St. Petersburg, providing for mutual assistance against Japan and precluding a separate peace treaty in case of war. In 1937 Chiang Kai-shek's representatives concluded a treaty of non-aggression with the Soviet Union that was immediately followed by Russian military assistance against the Japanese invasion.

3. For a detailed examination of the transition in United States occupation policy, see Baron E. J. Lewe van Aduard, *Japan from Surrender to Peace,* Martinus Nijhoff, The Hague, 1953.

4. Article 9 read, in part, "Land, sea, and air forces, as well as other war potential, will never be maintained." Harold S. Quigley and John Turner, *The New Japan: Government and Politics,* University of Minnesota Press, Minneapolis, 1956, p. 408. For details on American initiative in drafting the constitution, and particularly the role of General Douglas A. MacArthur in drawing up this particular provision, see Robert E. Ward, "The Constitution and Current Japanese Politics," *Far Eastern Survey,* Vol. XXV, No. 4, April 1956.

5. In addition to this clause from the preamble of the 1950 Sino-Soviet treaty and the operative articles of mutual assistance cited above in Chap. II, see the NCNA editorial, Feb. 15, 1950, in *People's China,* Vol. I, No. 5, March 1, 1950, pp. 30–32, and *Pravda,* Feb. 16, 1950, in *CDSP,* Vol. II, No. 8, April 8, 1950, pp. 17–18. See also *Izvestiia,* Feb. 12, 1950, on U.S. "plans" to "revive" Japanese militarism, and *Pravda,* Feb. 15, 1950, on alleged U.S. plans to "reorganize" the Japanese police into an armed force of 500,000 troops, both in *ibid.,* pp. 19–20.

6. The militant policy was initiated in a Cominform journal article, *For a Lasting Peace, For a People's Democracy,* Jan. 6, 1950; the *Jen Min Jih Pao* article is reprinted in *People's China,* Vol. 1, No. 5, Feb. 1, 1950, pp. 11–12.

7. One year later, General George Marshall recalled: "We had almost nothing in the summer of 1950 in the way of available troops in this country [the U.S.] other than one airborne division, the eighty-second, and a part of a Marine division. . . . We had literally almost no military forces outside of our Navy

and outside of an effective but not too large Air Force, except the occupation garrisons and, as we know, even in Japan they were only at about 60 per cent strength"; United States Congress (82nd Cong., 1st Sess.), Senate Committee on Armed Services and Committee on Foreign Relations, *Hearings on the Military Situation in the Far East,* Washington, 1951, Vol. I, pp. 352, 382. For an excellent summary of these political and military aspects of U.S. policy during 1948–1949, see John W. Spanier, *The Truman-MacArthur Controversy and the Korean War,* pp. 16–23.

8. Spanier, *op. cit.,* p. 17, from *New York Times,* March 2, 1949.

9. Dean G. Acheson, "Crisis in Asia," *Department of State Bulletin,* Jan. 23, 1950, p. 115. For Soviet attention to Acheson's speech, see *CDSP,* Vol. II, Nos. 7–8, 1950. Although Soviet comment in *Pravda* and *Izvestiia* did not touch on the implications of his remarks so far as Korea was concerned, there is no reason to presume these remarks went unnoticed in Moscow.

10. It is possible that U.N. action was so little feared that it was deemed preferable to maintain Malik's boycott rather than jeopardize surprise in Korea by returning him to the Council without a plausible excuse. Alternatively, Soviet anxiety to avoid implication in the North Korean move may have argued against exposing Malik to the spotlight at Lake Success. Whatever the reason, Malik's absence proved to be a blunder in Soviet planning.

11. For background on postwar Soviet-Korean relations, see Max Beloff, *Soviet Policy in the Far East, 1944–1951,* Oxford University Press, London, 1953, pp. 169–183; also Wilbert B. Dubin, "The Political Evolution of the Pyongyang Government," *Pacific Affairs,* Vol. XXIII, No. 4, Dec. 1950, pp. 381–392.

12. The transfer of the Koreans will be examined in more detail in the following section on Sino-Korean relations.

13. In addition to newspaper accounts, information on DPRK affairs was gained through interviews with prisoners of war and documents captured by U.N. forces in Pyongyang.

14. "Diplomatic Relations of Communist China," No. 440, American Consulate General, Hong Kong (hereafter cited as *CB*).

15. United States Department of Defense, Release No. 465–54, May 15, 1954.

IV. PEKING'S REACTIONS: JUNE–JULY

1. The following analysis is based upon examination of the authoritative Peking daily newspaper *Jen Min Jih Pao,* from June 27, 1950, to Nov. 20, 1950. Quantitatively, the proportion of space afforded the Korean War, Taiwan, and the United Nations was measured in each issue on pages one and four, normally the location of international news. Related items on other pages usually appeared as part of major propaganda campaigns or as a carryover of long speeches, and were included in the final tabulation. A comparison with the word-count of *Pravda* on these matters, as reported in *CDSP,* showed marked discrepancies of emphasis, indicating the *Jen Min Jih Pao* treatment was not merely reflecting a Russian line. Qualitative analysis then sifted the newspaper accounts, according

greater weight to original Chinese comment and New China News Agency (NCNA) reports than to reprinted TASS dispatches. Similarly, more importance was given to editorial and analytical comment than to reprinted speeches by Jacob Malik at the U.N. or Kim Il-sung in Pyongyang. Finally, the relationship between the mass propaganda campaigns on the inner pages, such as the Stockholm Peace Appeal, and the selected items on pages one and four was examined both in the Korean-Taiwan context and in that of domestic developments in mainland China.

2. *Chin Pu Jih Pao,* June 26, 1950. The headline is translated in Wen-hui C. Chen, *Chinese Communist Anti-Americanism and the Resist-America Aid-Korea Campaign,* Human Resources Research Institute Research Memorandum No. 36, Lackland Air Force Base, Texas, May 1955, p. 10. The citation incorrectly refers to the later title of this newspaper, *Ta Kung Pao.*

3. Chang Ming-Yang, "The Korean People's Just War for Unifying the Fatherland and Independence" (in Chinese), *Shih Chieh Chih Shih* (hereafter cited as *World Culture*), Vol. XXII, No. 1, July 7, 1950. His references indicate the article was written before the Truman announcement of June 30 committed U.S. ground forces to action.

4. These reports, in the *New York Times, U.S. News & World Report,* and *Time,* presumably supplemented Communist intelligence information concerning U.S. troop movements. *Time,* in particular, accurately reported developments and plans of MacArthur's headquarters in Tokyo throughout the summer and fall of 1950.

5. The obverse of *Jen Min Jih Pao's* pessimism was reflected in General Mac-Arthur's communiqué of July 19, declaring, "With the deployment in Korea of major elements of the Eighth Army now accomplished, the first phase of the campaign has ended and with it the chance for victory by the North Korean forces." *Department of State Bulletin,* July 31, 1950.

6. *World Culture,* Vol. XXII, No. 5, Aug. 5, 1950. This editorial was probably written in the last week of July, coincident with the *Jen Min Jih Pao* commentary of July 27 quoted above.

7. For a detailed analysis of the "three-phase" strategy attributed to General MacArthur, including delaying action, perimeter build-up, and counterattack, see *Time,* July 24, 1950, p. 20.

8. Radio Peking, Chinese International Service in Mandarin, July 17, 1950.

9. Radio Peking, Aug. 1, 1950.

10. Liu Ning-i, Vice Chairman of the Chinese Committee To Protect World Peace, in *Jen Min Jih Pao,* July 21, 1950.

11. *People's China,* Vol. II, No. 2, July 16, 1950, p. 4, statement released on June 28. President Truman's announcement occurred at midnight, June 27, Peking time, and probably reached the capital early on June 28. The specific hour at which Chou En-lai's statement was released is not known.

12. *Ibid.,* p. 27.

13. One reflection of this two-sided treatment of the U.N. was the usage of quotation marks in the Chinese Communist press when referring to "United Nations" actions in Korea. The invidious punctuation was not consistently used in this context, but its complete absence from other items concerning the U.N.

suggests the uncertainty of Chinese Communist attitudes toward the international organization.

14. K. M. Panikkar, *In Two Chinas,* Allen & Unwin, London, 1950, p. 103. See also Nehru's press conference of July 7, 1950, positing "the admission of the People's Government of China in the Security Council and the return of the U.S.S.R." as "necessary conditions . . . to bring the Korean conflict to a prompt and peaceful conclusion"; J. C. Kundra, *Indian Foreign Policy, 1947– 1954,* J. B. Wolters, Gronigen, Holland, 1955, p. 130.

15. Huang Ts'ao-liang, *Chan-hou shih-chieh hsin-hsing-shih* (New Aspects of the Postwar World), Shanghai, April 1950, and B. Berzhkov, "Foreign Policy Maneuvers of Indian Reaction," *New Times,* No. 22, May 31, 1950.

16. On May 5, 1950, Prime Minister Nehru termed "unwise and harmful" the exclusion of "any independent country from the United Nations"; *Jawaharlal Nehru's Speeches, 1949–1953,* Ministry of Information and Broadcasting, Government of India, 1954, p. 132.

17. Statement of Indian Government, June 30, 1950, in K. P. Karunakaran, *India in World Affairs, February 1950–December 1953,* Oxford University Press, London, 1958, p. 102.

18. J. C. Kundra, *op. cit.,* p. 130.

19. *Jen Min Jih Pao,* July 24, 1950.

20. *Ibid.*

21. *New York Times,* July 15, 1950, in a dispatch from New Delhi.

22. *Jen Min Jih Pao,* July 11 and 15, 1950. The manifesto is included in a compendium, *Wei-ta ti k'ang-Mei yuan-Ch'ao yün-tung* (The Great Resist-America Aid-Korea Movement), Peking, 1954, p. 7. A substantive change in the later campaign, noted above, differentiates this manifesto from the bulk of the material in the compendium. The campaign of July 17–24, 1950, had carryover propaganda effects extending well into August. Its purpose will be examined in more detail in the following chapter, reviewing events of August.

23. *World Culture,* Vol. XXII, No. 1, July 7, 1950, unsigned questions-and-answers section, p. 23; also Yeh Mang, "The Criminal Act of American Imperialist Aggression in Taiwan" (in Chinese), *ibid,* pp. 11–12.

24. Radio Peking to overseas Chinese press, July 20, 1950, quoting General Ch'en Yi's speech of July 16, 1950.

25. CCF Army Histories, *loc. cit.*

26. Roy L. Appleman, *The Korean War: From the Naktong to the Yalu,* in the series *The U.S. Army in Conflict with the Communist Powers,* Department of Defense, Washington, D.C., manuscript scheduled for publication. Appleman notes that three Chinese divisions marched 286 miles in 16–19 days from Antung, on the Yalu River. At this rate, advance units could have reached the Taejon-Taegu area four weeks after crossing the Yalu.

27. Karig *et al., op. cit.,* report a marked diminution of PLA strength opposite Taiwan as early as July 10, 1950.

V. August: Military and Diplomatic Stalemate

1. This account relies largely on *Korea—1950*, Department of the Army, Washington, D.C., 1952, pp. 77–82.

2. Commentaries appeared on July 3, 13, 27, Aug. 13 and 30.

3. In Nov. 1950, an authoritative Chinese Communist commentary divided the summer into two periods. "From June 25 to the beginning of August" was the time of "successful counterattacks" against alleged ROK invasion. "From the beginning of August to the middle of September" the war found both sides in "a stalemate position." See *Shih Shih Shou T'ze* (Current Affairs Journal), Nov. 22, 1950, translated in *SCMP*, No. 16, Nov. 24–25, 1950.

4. "As the result of Malik's return to the Council and his assumption of the post of President, the whole of August was spent in procedural disputes and tangles." Leland M. Goodrich, *Korea: A Study of U.S. Policy in the United Nations*, Council on Foreign Relations, New York, 1956, p. 123.

5. I am indebted to Nathan Leites for this description of a characteristic in Stalinist foreign policy, particularly evident in Malik's behavior: see N. Leites, *A Study of Bolshevism*, The RAND Corporation, Report R-239, 1953; also published by The Free Press, Glencoe, Ill., 1953, pp. 34–42.

6. *United Nations, Security Council, Official Records* (hereafter cited as *UNSC*), Fifth Year, 487th meeting, Aug. 14, 1950, No. 29, p. 9.

7. W. Phillips Davison, *The Berlin Blockade*, The RAND Corporation, Report R-302, 1958; also published by Princeton University Press, Princeton, N.J., 1958, pp. 254 ff.

8. Upon assuming the Presidency on Aug. 1, Malik immediately ruled Tsiang "illegal" as the representative of China. When the ruling was challenged, Malik was supported by only India and Yugoslavia. On Aug. 3, he proposed an agenda placing the Chinese representation issue before Korea. Only India approved this move. He then tried to insert it elsewhere on the agenda but failed to acquire the necessary seven votes for procedural matters, although he was supported by India, Norway, Yugoslavia, and the United Kingdom. Malik insulted Tsiang during the rest of the month but attempted no further rulings of this sort.

9. *Jen Min Jih Pao*, Aug. 7, 1950. Malik's speech was carried at length on Aug. 6.

10. *UNSC*, 483rd meeting, Aug. 4, 1950, No. 25, p. 14.

11. *UNSC*, 484th meeting, Aug. 8, 1950, No. 26, p. 9.

12. See U.N. General Assembly resolutions of Dec. 12, 1948, and Oct. 21, 1949, in L. Goodrich, *op. cit.*, pp. 218–221; also U.N. Security Council resolutions of June 25, 27, and July 7, 1950, *ibid.*, pp. 221–223.

13. On June 27, 1950, U.S. Ambassador Alan Kirk conveyed an *aide-mémoire* to Deputy Minister of Foreign Affairs Andrei A. Gromyko, asking that, "in view of the universally known fact of the close relations between The Union of Soviet Socialist Republics and the North Korean regime," Moscow "disavow responsibility" for the attack and "use its influence" to force a North Korean withdrawal. Gromyko's reply of June 29 rejected all points raised in the U.S. note. See *Department of State Bulletin*, Vol. XXIII, No. 575, July 10, 1950, pp. 47–48, for the official press release of June 29, 1950, containing a paraphrase of the U.S.

note and full text of the U.S.S.R. reply. The full text of both messages may be found in *The Soviet Union and the Korean Question,* Soviet News, London, 1950, pp. 91–92.

14. On July 4, 1950, Gromyko had issued a formal statement stressing the "internal struggle" of the Korean peoples and comparing the conflict with the American Civil War wherein Great Britain "intervened" on the side of the Confederacy. He noted that, while the U.N. had no authority "when it is a matter of internal conflict between two groups of one State, . . . if the Security Council valued the cause of peace, it should have attempted to reconcile the fighting sides in Korea"; *The Soviet Union and the Korean Question,* pp. 93–99. Gromyko's statement provided a precedent for the Malik proposal of Aug. 4. However, unlike the Malik proposal, Gromyko contrasted "the Korean People's Democratic Republic" with "the South Korean authorities." Further, Gromyko implied that the time for bringing the two sides together at the Council table had passed, whereas Malik's proposal was offered in a context of imminent discussion and possible favorable action by the Council.

15. Jacob Malik and Alex Bebler, the Yugoslav delegate, did not attend on Aug. 9 but were present at the other two meetings

16. On Aug. 11 Sir Gladwyn Jebb insisted that North Korean forces "should go back whence they came," at which time Pyongyang's representative might be invited to the Council. On Aug. 17 Arne Sunde of Norway seconded Jebb's remarks.

17. Based on an authoritative account of the informal meeting of Security Council members.

18. *UNSC,* 495th meeting, Sept. 1, 1950, No. 36, p. 6.

19. *Ibid.,* 484th meeting, Aug. 10, 1950, No. 27.

20. *Ibid.,* 488th meeting, Aug. 17, 1950, No. 30.

21. Radio Peking, in English, Aug. 21, 1950.

22. *UNSC,* 489th meeting, Aug. 22, No. 31.

23. See Chap. IV above.

24. *Jen Min Jih Pao,* July 29, 1950, listed twenty-eight slogans to keynote Aug. 1 celebrations. Korean references did not appear until items numbered twenty-one to twenty-three, well after slogans on Taiwan and Tibet. *Ibid.,* July 27, 1950, explicitly differentiated responsibilities: "We must liberate Taiwan, just as you [Koreans] must liberate Korea." For additional statements of this sort see Radio Peking, New China News Agency, July 21, 1950, statement of Liu Ning-i; also *Jen Min Jih Pao,* July 24, 1950, interview with Liu Ling-yuan.

25. Radio Peking in English, Aug. 15, 1950. No PLA officers were reported in this mission.

26. *Jen Min Jih Pao,* Aug. 15, 1950.

27. Radio Pyongyang, Aug. 16, 1950. The broadcast noted, "We have received many messages from the Chinese people and troops, encouraging our liberation work."

28. *Ibid.,* Aug. 15, 1950. The announcer declared, "Had it not been for the Soviet people there would not have been any August 15 liberation. With Soviet assistance democratic reforms were enforced in the Northern Half. Our might is derived from the democratic base constructed in the Northern Half."

29. This refers to the campaign as conducted through mid-August. Significant changes in its content during the last week of August and in September will be noted in the next chapter.

30. Liao Kai-lung, "Kuan-yü chan-cheng yi h'o-p'ing wen-t'i" (Problems of War and Peace), *Hsüeh Hsi,* Vol. II, No. 11, Aug. 16, 1950, pp. 17–22. The article was written on Aug. 1, 1950.

31. For earlier references to dissenting views of the Korean War, see *Jen Min Jih Pao,* July 26, 1950: "Some people ask: But if the puppet Syngman Rhee provoked this war, why has he suffered such a great defeat? This is because the reactionary cliques basically miscalculate the people's strength in their schemes . . . just as Chiang Kai-shek four years ago attacked the people's liberation areas in self-deception."

32. *Changsha Hsin Hunan Pao,* Aug. 1, 1957, in *SCMP,* No. 1619. See also Lo Jui-ching's report of Oct. 1, 1950, on resistance in Southwest and Northwest China, quoted in Shih Ch'eng-shih, *People's Resistance in Mainland China, 1950–1955,* pp. 1–2.

33. *World Culture,* Vol. XXII, No. 8, Aug. 26, 1950. This article was probably written while Chou En-lai's cable of Aug. 20 was in preparation.

34. *Ibid.,* compared with Radio Peking, NCNA in English Morse to North America, Aug. 26, 1950.

35. Radio Peking in English Morse to North America, Aug. 26, 1950.

36. On Aug. 14, *Time* claimed that MacArthur's trip to Taiwan was made without advance knowledge in Washington. This appears to have been incorrect, but may not have been so known to Peking at the time. For a different version of this trip, and for confirmation of other items, see Harry S Truman, *Memoirs,* Doubleday & Co. Inc., Garden City, N.Y., 1956, Vol. II, pp. 347–335. Additional reports, paralleling those in *Time,* appeared concurrently in *U.S. News & World Report* and the *New York Times.*

37. Reports from Taipei told of an alleged visit by Foreign Minister V. M. Molotov to Peking in early August. From Hong Kong, Agence France Presse correspondent Pierre Brisard dismissed the report about Molotov as "a fiction of Nationalist propaganda from Taipei" but referred to "three-way conferences in Manchuria" among high Soviet, Chinese, and Korean figures.

38. Department of Defense release, Dec. 15, 1954: "In August 1950 . . . a Kremlin directive providing for this [Chinese] intervention was transmitted to Peiping from Moscow by Lt. General Kuzma Derevyanko. On 14 August the Chinese Communist Party Central Committee approved the Kremlin action. . . . The stipulations of the Sino-Soviet agreement . . . covered various responsibilities and allocations for military (ground and air) operations, logistics, propaganda and agitation (external and internal), international Communist solidarity, and subsidiary military actions."

39. *Ibid.,* p. 4, claims: "In late August and early September service elements and communication units began moving into Korea for rear echelon (communication zone) functions." No support for this statement has been found in other intelligence materials, including POW interrogations. Detailed examination of Chinese Communist troop movements across the Yalu will be found below, Chap. VII.

VI. THE UNITED NATIONS CROSSES THE PARALLEL

1. *Time,* Sept. 4, 1950, p. 12. Matthews had voiced similar ideas two days earlier in Omaha, Neb. *Time* paraphrased his Omaha remarks: "Why wait to be bombed? Why not strike the first blow?"

2. MacArthur's statement was sent to the Veterans of Foreign Wars, convening in Chicago (text in *New York Times,* Aug. 29, 1950). He attacked opponents of the defense of Taiwan as advocating "appeasement and defeatism." *U.S. News & World Report* commented: "The MacArthur outline of defense strategy virtually commits U.S. to keep Communists away from the island—permanently."

3. *Time,* Sept. 11, 1950, p. 22. This account claimed Anderson lectured "on the advisability of launching an A-bomb attack on Russia." His own words were reported: "We're at war, damn it. I don't advocate preventive war. I advocate the shedding of illusions. Give me the order to do it and I can break up Russia's five A-bomb nests in a week."

4. Hanson Baldwin, in *New York Times,* Sept. 1, 1950, claimed Matthews' speech had been a "trial balloon," endorsed by Johnson, "who has been selling the same doctrine of preventive war in private conversations around Washington."

5. For typical comment of this sort, see *U.S. News & World Report,* Sept. 22, 1950, pp. 4, 14–15, 32–35.

6. Chou En-lai's protests to Secretary of State Acheson and to the U.N., both of Aug. 27, 1950, are in *People's China,* Vol. II, No. 6, Sept. 16, 1950, pp. 26–27.

7. Chou En-lai to the United Nations, Aug. 30, 1950, in *ibid.,* p. 27.

8. Message to Veterans of Foreign Wars, *New York Times,* Aug. 29, 1950.

9. Harry S Truman, *Memoirs,* II, 359.

10. *Jen Min Jih Pao,* July 28, 1950, Radio Peking in English Morse to North America, July 28, 1950.

11. *Jen Min Jih Pao,* Aug. 30, 1950, Radio Peking in English to North America, Aug. 30, 1950. The same program quoted Kuo Mo-jo: "The United States aggressors are simply hordes of inhuman beasts. Their atrocities virtually eclipse those of the Japanese imperialists and the Nazis." Another writer, T'ing Ling, warned: "Now American planes have made their appearance over our territory. This is not accidental, but a part of the American imperialistic policy. . . . China will rise up in unity . . . and, together with the rest of the world, will smash the aggressive plots."

12. *Jen Min Jih Pao,* Aug. 27, 1950, introduced the term *k'ang yi* in a small item on Korea and Taiwan. It became prominent, however, on Sept. 1 when the newspaper featured it in reports of mass meetings in protest against the air intrusions.

13. Radio Peking in English to North America, Aug. 30, 1950. Throughout this period, the statements appearing in foreign-language broadcasts paralleled those in domestic broadcasts and newspapers.

14. East China Regional Service on Sept. 3, 1950, speech of Shen Ti-hua, deputy mayor of Shanghai.

15. *Ibid.*
16. Radio Peking in English to North America, Sept. 8, 1950.
17. Radio Peking in English Morse to North America, Sept. 10, 1950.
18. *Jen Min Jih Pao,* Sept. 1, 1950.
19. *UNSC,* 495th meeting, Sept. 1, 1950, No. 36, p. 6.
20. Malcolm W. Cagle, Commander, USN, and Frank A. Manson, Commander, USN, in *The Sea War in Korea,* U.S. Naval Institute, Annapolis, Md., 1957, discuss the lack of secrecy surrounding U.N. preparations in Japan, pp. 80–81. The imminent invasion was dubbed "Operation Common Knowledge" in Tokyo, and a U.S. Army prosecutor later charged a suspect North Korean-Japanese spy ring with possessing invasion plans one week before the landing. While the exact destination of the assault force may not have been determined by the enemy, it seems certain that a counteroffensive combined with an amphibious landing was expected in late September or early October.
21. *Hearings Before the Committee on Armed Services and the Committee on Foreign Relations,* United States Senate, 82nd Cong., Washington, 1951 (hereafter cited as *Military Situation in the Far East*), p. 3482.
22. *World Culture,* Sept. 16, 1950.
23. *Jen Min Jih Pao,* Sept. 19, 1950, International Service in Thai.
24. Fourth Report of U.N. commander, Sept. 17, 1950, in *Military Situation in the Far East,* pp. 3401–3402.
25. Radio Peking in English Morse to North America, Sept. 22, 1950.
26. The MacArthur charges against Peking may have been designed to reduce PRC acceptability to the General Assembly, in addition to whatever concern they may have reflected among American officials over the prospect of Chinese Communist involvement in the war. In early August, Averill Harriman conferred with MacArthur at Truman's request, emphasizing "the importance of getting evidence on the participation of the Chinese Communists in supporting the North Korean attack and present operations. There will be considerable support in [favor of] seating the Chinese Communists at the next meeting of the Assembly. I explained that if we could obtain real evidence of direct support for the North Koreans, this might be the reason by which we could prevent the seating of the Communists on the moral issue involved." See Truman, *op. cit.,* II, 352.

The MacArthur report delivered Sept. 18 covered the period of hostilities immediately following the Harriman visit. It noted: "To date, there has been no confirmation of direct or overt Chinese Communist participation in the Korean conflict," but provided sufficient information on pre-hostilities co-operation to strengthen the U.S. position against the Indian resolution that was defeated Sept. 19. MacArthur did not return to the theme of PRC involvement in the war until his report of Nov. 5, 1950.

27. *Jen Min Jih Pao,* Sept. 24, 1950.
28. *Ibid.,* Sept. 25, 1950.
29. Radio Shanghai in English, Sept. 24, 1950.
30. K. M. Panikkar, *In Two Chinas,* p. 108.
31. *People's China,* Vol. II, No. 8, Oct. 16, 1950, p. 9. Chou's warning came after a lengthy critique of U.S. policy: "Throughout the Chinese People's War

of Liberation, the U.S. government has sided with the enemy of the Chinese people assisting the KMT reactionaries with all its might in their attacks on the Chinese people. The enmity that the U.S. government harbours towards the Chinese people has increased since the founding of the People's Republic of China. . . . The U.S. stubbornly obstructs the representatives of the PRC from attending the United Nations . . . debars the Chinese representatives from attending the Allied Council for Japan and plots . . . a peace treaty with Japan, in order to re-arm Japan and retain America's occupation troops and military bases in Japan. . . . On the pretext of the situation in Korea, [the U.S.] dispatched its naval and air forces to invade the Taiwan Province of China. . . . Time after time, it sent its air force . . . to intrude into the air over the Liaotung Province of China, strafing and bombing, and sent its naval forces . . . to bombard Chinese merchant shipping on the high seas.

"By these frenzied and violent acts of imperialist aggression, the U.S. government has displayed itself as the most dangerous foe to the PRC. The U.S. aggressive forces have invaded China's borders and may at any time expand their aggression. MacArthur, commander-in-chief of American aggression against Taiwan and Korea, has long ago disclosed the aggressive designs of the U.S. government and is continuing to invent new excuses for extending its aggression. . . ."

32. *Jen Min Jih Pao,* Oct. 1, and *World Culture,* Oct. 8, 1950; the latter article was probably written on Oct. 3 or 4.

33. *World Culture,* Oct. 14, 1950, and *Study,* Oct. 16, 1950; both articles were probably written on Oct. 9 or 10.

34. Panikkar, *op. cit.,* p. 110. "He was emphatic: 'The South Koreans did not matter but American intrusion into North Korea would encounter Chinese resistance.' "

35. Truman, *op. cit.,* II, 362; also Cagle and Manson, *op. cit.,* p. 11.

36. Ch'en Yün, "Report on the Financial and Economic Situation," *The First Five Years of Victory,* Peking, no date, pp. 25–35; delivered to the CPGC Sept. 29–30, 1950. The quotation came immediately after a favorable prognosis of fiscal and economic developments for 1951, clouded by "the threat of a new war provoked by the American imperialists."

37. For an authoritative summary of this view, see Truman, *op. cit.,* II, 362.

38. Panikkar, *op. cit.,* p. 107, notes that after Inchon, "There were rumors of large-scale troop movements from the Peking area to the north and a western Military Attaché told me that he had information that a continuous stream of troop trains was passing Tientsin." Panikkar's secretary observed unusual security precautions attending large troop movements through Peking on Oct. 2, the night of Chou's formal warning.

39. *CCF Army Histories, loc. cit.* Roy L. Appleman, *The Korean War,* reports estimates of nine PLA armies in Manchuria as of Oct. 14 with 400,000 troops near border crossing points as of Oct. 20, 1950.

40. JCS dispatch 93709, Oct. 9, 1950, in Cagle and Manson, *op. cit.,* p. 116. These orders covered "open or covert employment anywhere in Korea of major Chinese Communist units." This changed JCS dispatch 92801, Sept. 27, 1950, authorizing action north of the thirty-eighth parallel "provided . . . there has

been no entry into North Korea by major Soviet or Chinese Communist forces, no announcement of intended entry, nor a threat to counter our operations militarily in North Korea"; *ibid.*, p. 116. Between the two dates the JCS apparently decided to accept Chou's warning of Oct. 2 at face value, to authorize U.S. resistance to any Chinese troops which entered North Korea, and to leave the extent of the resistance to MacArthur's discretion.

Military Situation in the Far East offers testimony on estimates of Chinese Communist capability and intentions prior to the Yalu crossing; see General Omar Bradley, Chairman of JCS, in II, 758–759; General J. Lawton Collins, Chief of Staff, U.S. Army in II, 1234; General Hoyt S. Vandenberg, Chief of Staff U.S. Air Force in II, 1463–1464; Secretary of State Dean Acheson in III, 1832–1835 and 2100–2101; both the Acheson testimony and Truman, *op. cit.*, II, 366, give General Douglas MacArthur's views as presented to Truman on Oct. 14–15, 1950, at the Wake Island Conference. According to notes taken at the time, MacArthur said, "We are no longer fearful of their [the Chinese Communists] intervention. . . . The Chinese have 300,000 men in Manchuria. Of these probably not more than 100,000 to 125,000 are distributed along the Yalu River. Only 50,000 to 60,000 could be gotten across the Yalu River. They have no air force. Now that we have bases for our Air Force in Korea, if the Chinese tried to get down to Pyongyang, there would the greatest slaughter."

Two questions were confused throughout this testimony: first, whether the PRC would intervene in the war, and second, what impact such intervention would have upon the war. Some persons believed the probable impact so weak as to make intervention incredible. Others believed the intervention so unlikely they downgraded the possible impact. However, the assumptions behind judgments remained implicit in many cases, making it difficult to pinpoint the sources of miscalculation.

41. Leland M. Goodrich, *Korea*, pp. 130–131.

42. *Military Situation in the Far East*, p. 3482.

43. This resolution was sponsored by Australia, Brazil, Cuba, the Netherlands, Norway, Pakistan, the Philippines, and the United Kingdom, but was largely drafted by the American delegation; Goodrich, *op. cit.*, p. 129. Vyshinsky presented his proposal on behalf of the Soviet Union, Poland, Czechoslovakia, Byelorussia, and the Ukraine.

44. See United Nations, General Assembly, *Official Records: Fifth Session, First Committee.*

45. Vyshinsky's tone contrasted sharply with that of Malik previously, as noted by *Time*, Oct. 2, 1950, which termed Vyshinsky "relatively mellow," and noted that his attacks on U.S. policy appeared "less vitriolic than usual." Such "Russian cordiality impressed a few reporters" although *Time* found "no evidence whatsoever of a real change in Soviet policy." The *New York Times* was among those "impressed" with the change in Soviet demeanor at Lake Success.

46. See Chap. V, p. 135, above.

47. Sir Benegal Rau declared: "We cannot help thinking that it would impair faith in the U.N. if we were even to appear to authorize the unification of Korea by the use of force against North Korea, after we had resisted the attempt of North Korea to unify the country by force against South Korea. The result

may be to intensify the North Korean opposition and to increase the tension in that part of the world," *New York Times,* Oct. 4, 1950. For a similar statement from the Yugoslav delegate, see Goodrich, *op. cit.,* p. 131.

48. In both the First Committee and the General Assembly voting, abstentions on the eight-power resolution included Egypt, India, Lebanon, Saudi Arabia, Syria, Yemen, and Yugoslavia. Indonesia did not participate in the voting. Afghanistan abstained on the Soviet resolution but not on the eight-power proposal.

49. *New York Times,* Oct. 9, 1950.

50. *Jen Min Jih Pao,* Oct. 8, 1950; the article was probably written Oct. 7, Peking time, or approximately forty-eight hours before the General Assembly resolution.

51. *Ibid.,* Oct. 9, 1950.

52. Radio Peking, Chinese International Service in English, Oct. 11, 1950.

53. *Jen Min Jih Pao,* Oct. 11, 1950.

54. *World Culture,* Oct. 14, 1950, and *Study,* Oct. 16, 1950; both articles were probably written on Oct. 9 and 10.

VII. PEKING CROSSES THE YALU

1. I am indebted to Alexander George for this aspect of my analysis.

2. This section traces Chinese Communist military movements from several sources, including *CCF Army Histories, loc. cit.;* Roy L. Appleman, *The Korean War;* Major James F. Schnable, *The Korean Conflict: Policy, Planning and Direction;* and Lynn Montross and Captain Nicholas A. Canzona, USMC, *U.S. Marine Operations in Korea, 1950–53,* Vol. III, *The Chosin Reservoir Campaign,* Historical Branch, G-3, Headquarters U.S. Marine Corps, Washington, 1957. The figures in this section are compiled from various estimates in these sources, and any discrepancies arise from disagreement as to the strength of CPV units. Appleman reports U.S. Army G-2 estimates that CPV divisions were at roughly two-thirds of full strength. Estimates are indicated throughout the chapter in the form of minimum-maximum figures. For the lowest estimate of troop strength, see Robert B. Rigg, *Red China's Fighting Hordes,* Military Service Publications Co., Harrisburg, Pa., 1951, which gives divisional strength as 7,000, with 15,000 to 22,000 troops to each army.

A summary of the reorganization of PLA armies in 1948–1949, with unit breakdown but without statistical estimates, may be found in *China: An Area Manual,* ORO-T 229, Operations Research Office, Johns Hopkins University, Chevy Chase, Md., 1954, pp. 132–133.

3. The best evidence available to the author places the first crossing of the Yalu by Chinese Communist troops between Oct. 14–16. An earlier time is given by a Department of Defense Release, Dec. 15, 1954, according to which "advance elements, supply and communication units" from the Fourth Field Army entered North Korea in mid-August. Examination of the report upon which this release was based makes questionable its reliability. No confirmation for this date has been found in other intelligence materials or in subsequent prisoner-

of-war testimony. This same report apparently was the basis for the Pan-Asian News Agency dispatch from Hong Kong, Nov. 16, 1950.

For other dates approximating the mid-October timing, see Appleman, *op. cit.*, quoting a North Korean civilian employee of the Pyongyang Traffic Department, who claimed "a continuous flow of Chinese through Manpojin from October 12, 1950." S. L. A. Marshall, *The River and the Gauntlet*, Morrow and Co., New York, 1953, p. 14, places the initial CPV entry into North Korea at Oct. 14. According to General E. M. Almond (ret.), "What Happened in Korea When the Chinese Marched In," *U.S. News & World Report*, Feb. 13, 1953, the first CPV prisoners of war were captured Oct. 26 and gave Oct. 16 as their date of entry into Korea. This is corroborated by *CCF Army Histories*.

4. Major General Courtney Whitney, *MacArthur: His Rendezvous with History*, Knopf, Inc., New York, 1956, p. 392. The agent allegedly was Donald MacLean, a British foreign service officer who had access to secret documents in Washington. MacLean later disappeared in the Soviet bloc.

5. Mao Tse-tung, *On the Protracted War*, from *Selected Works*, Vol. II. These lectures, delivered in June 1938, received recurrent attention during the subsequent two decades as a classic exposition of Mao's strategic doctrine.

6. For a detailed account of the problems of U.S. reconnaissance, intelligence evaluation at the front, and communication to command units, see Marshall, *op. cit.*

7. *CCF Army Histories* identifies the 26th and 27th armies as training with Soviet weapons in Shantung during July and August. Neither unit arrived in Manchuria until late November, however, missing the initial engagements. Marshall, *op. cit.*, p. 174, identifies the submachine gun as the only Soviet equipment encountered in the initial CPV attacks.

8. See Marshall, *op. cit.*

9. *Ibid.*, pp. 25–50, gives battle-front impressions of the inadequately trained infantry masses committed to action in October-November, who were unfamiliar even with grenade usage. However, Marshall did note skilled crews handling machine guns and mortars.

10. According to prisoners of war from the 39th Army, Fourth Field Army, they completed "three months of military and political training around the seventh or eighth of October" with requests for " 'volunteers' for the Korean war." In the 38th Army, "at the time when the Americans pursued the North Koreans into North Korea, 'we had a staff meeting almost every day in Manchuria. Do we join the Korean battle or don't we? About thirty per cent of us denied it.' "

11. The author interviewed many prisoners of war later in Taiwan who spoke of the *ad hoc* nature of recruitment and training for combat in Korea.

12. Once in Korea, however, indoctrination for combat included comprehensive briefings at lower levels on U.N. troop dispositions and on Communist battle plans. Such practices confused American intelligence officers questioning prisoners of war who offered detailed descriptions of CPV strategy and tactics. So incredible was this behavior that G-2 dismissed the information as a "plant." Subsequent events, however, showed the testimony to be accurate in every detail.

See, for instance, Cagle and Manson, *The Sea War in Korea,* p. 168; and Marshall, *op. cit.,* pp. 7–8.

13. Prisoner-of-war interrogations revealed early troop indoctrination along these lines. Less explicit assertions of Communist superiority and inevitable victory came in domestic media, as will be seen below. Such comment appeared primarily in low-level propaganda, however, and contrasted with more sober analysis in more responsible media.

14. According to one prisoner-of-war report, some officers declared at the outset of the CPV intervention that U.S. forces would be expelled from Korea and Chinese troops returned home within three months. This appears to have been propaganda for morale purposes and not to have reflected expectations at the highest level. Although the events in December may have encouraged such thinking, it should be noted that two developments which could hardly have been counted upon in mid-October facilitated the Chinese advance. First, between the initial CPV attacks of Oct. 26 and the major engagement of Nov. 26, the U.N. forces remained divided and took few precautionary measures against a massive CPV intervention, relying on faulty intelligence estimates and incorrect judgments of enemy response. Second, the U.N. reaction, at least at the battle front, to the major engagements of Nov. 26-Dec. 2 was a precipitate withdrawal from all North Korea, with no effort to establish an interim defense line across the peninsula. Marshall, *op. cit.,* pp. 174 ff., notes the short rations of CPV forces, the inadequate transport, and the serious logistical problems which precluded sustained offensives of more than a week.

15. When these obstacles were overcome later in the war, a steady increase in the amount of Soviet equipment was noted in Korea.

16. Although North Korean propaganda falls outside our central focus, it is interesting to note the simultaneous change in Pyongyang's treatment of Chinese assistance. Previously, infrequent passing references to PRC support had contrasted with fulsome praise for Soviet aid. On Oct. 11 Radio Pyongyang shifted emphasis, reviewing Chinese material and moral assistance and, after quoting Chou's statement of Sept. 30, declaring, "The tie uniting the Korean people and the Chinese people is strong and lasting. . . . They fought together against their common enemy, the Japanese imperialists. For the past half century and after the defeat of the Japanese imperialists by the great Soviet Armed Forces in 1945, the Korean and Chinese peoples found themselves fighting a new common enemy, the American imperialists. . . . However today, there exists stronger and closer friendship and unity than ever before between the Korean people and the Chinese people in the face of aggression by their common enemy. There is little doubt that this unity against the common enemy will crush any viciously ambitious attempt of the American imperialists. . . . The Korean people must fight to the last and crush the enemy. To do so we must further strengthen our friendship and unity with the Chinese people. Then we shall finally emerge victorious in this war against the common enemy, the American imperialists." The stress upon the "common enemy" has not been found in previous statements from Pyongyang.

17. Both statements may be found in Chinese Communist broadcasts of Oct. 14, 1950.

18. Radio Wuhan, South and Central Regional Service in Mandarin, Oct. 15, 1950.

19. Radio Peking, NCNA, in English Morse to North America, Oct. 19, 1950. Similar statements from Uighurs in Sinkiang and Tibetans in Kansu were carried by Radio Peking, Chinese International Service in Cantonese, Oct. 24, 1950.

20. On Oct. 18, 1950, Chou En-lai protested to Lake Success against alleged U.S. overflights of Oct. 13 and 14, charging reconnaissance but no attacks against Chinese territory. Chou repeated his earlier demands for Security Council action to "stop the action of extending aggression . . . and bring about the prompt withdrawal of the United States aggression forces from Korea, so that the issue may not assume more serious proportions." Chou's second protest, on Oct. 26, 1950, charged additional overflights "between October 13 and 25" but gave no details.

21. The first action between ROK and Chinese Communist units occurred Oct. 26, 1950. The statements in *World Culture* and *Study* were probably printed on Oct. 24–25.

22. *Jen Min Jih Pao,* Oct. 29, 1950, reported by NCNA, Peking, Oct. 31, 1950, in *SCMP,* No. 1, American Consulate General, Hong Kong.

23. *Study,* Nov. 1, 1950, reported by NCNA, Peking, Oct. 27, 1950, in *SCMP,* No. 1.

24. Radio Peking in English Morse to North America, Oct. 29, 1950, from *World Culture,* Vol. XXII, No. 17, Oct. 28, 1950, p. 1. This translation has been checked with the Chinese-language original.

25. This account of the October-November fighting draws upon Appleman, *op. cit.;* Schnable, *op. cit.;* Marshall, *op. cit.; Korea, 1950;* Cagle and Manson, *op. cit.;* and Rutherford M. Poats, *Decision in Korea,* The McBride Co., New York, 1954.

26. This was corroborated by subsequent prisoner-of-war testimony; see *CCF Army Histories.*

27. Appleman, *op. cit.,* and Almond, *op. cit.* Although the prisoners of war used unfamiliar unit designations as "volunteers," G-2 readily ascertained the original PLA designations in most cases, but unit strength remained unknown.

28. *Ibid.* G-2 underestimated enemy strength, in part because of CPV camouflage, concealment in villages, and night movement. Scattered reports of Chinese Communists in North Korean uniforms in Cagle and Manson, *op. cit.,* and Marshall, *op. cit.,* appear erroneous, perhaps arising from confusion at the front and the difficulty of distinguishing Chinese-speaking Koreans, transferred at an earlier time, from fresh Chinese units committed in mid-October. If such instances did occur, they were so infrequent as to make it implausible that this type of deception was a matter of general policy.

29. Mao Tse-tung, *On the Protracted War, Selected Works.*

30. These excerpts do not exhaust the parallels, by any means. Whole portions of the political analysis of Japanese strength and weakness, and arguments for the "inevitability" of Chinese victory could have been placed alongside analysis of the Peking press in 1950, the only notable difference being the substitution of "U.S." for "Japan."

31. Teng Ch'ao in *World Culture,* NCNA, Oct. 31, 1950, in *SCMP,* No. 1.

32. Prisoner-of-war interrogations offered limited evidence of CPV disillusionment with Mao's military doctrine, at least at the company level. While it is difficult to distinguish between criticisms of field tactics and those directed against general strategy, there is suggestive evidence that at lower levels the war was "fought by the book" and this book was Mao's *On the Protracted War*.

33. NCNA, Nov. 4, 1950, in *SCMP*, No. 3–4. On Oct. 30, according to NCNA, the British Consul in Mukden refused to permit shelter construction in his compound and because of this was subsequently expelled from his residence.

34. Special Report of General MacArthur to the U.N. Security Council, Nov. 5, 1950, in *Military Situation in the Far East*, p. 3493.

35. For details on these engagements, see Cagle and Manson, *op. cit.*, pp. 228–229.

36. K. M. Panikkar, *In Two Chinas*, p. 108.

37. "Comrade Mao Tse-tung on 'Imperialism and All Reactionaries Are Paper Tigers,'" *Jen Min Jih Pao* Editorial Department, Oct. 27, 1958, reprinted in *Imperialism and All Reactionaries Are Paper Tigers* (enlarged edition), Foreign Language Press, Peking, 1958, pp. 19–20. This version differs somewhat from that offered by the American journalist Anna Louise Strong, in "A World's Eye View from a Yenan Cave: An Interview with Mao Tse-tung," *Amerasia*, April, 1947, p. 126. Her ellipses at this point in the interview may explain some of the differences.

38. Panikkar, *op. cit.*, p. 108.

39. Raymond L. Garthoff, in *Soviet Strategy in the Nuclear Age*, Frederick A. Praeger, New York, 1958, p. 64, notes, "Although three articles had appeared in the Soviet military periodical press in late 1945 and in 1946, not a single article on atomic energy or atomic weapons is known to have appeared in the period from 1947 through 1953 in the Soviet military daily and periodical press, open or restricted in circulation."

40. Herbert Dinerstein, in *War and the Soviet Union*, The RAND Corporation, Report R-326, 1958 (also published by Frederick A. Praeger, New York, 1959), pp. 174–177, notes that in 1949 open congressional hearings indicated a small stockpile of atomic bombs in the U.S. and suggests that Soviet leaders "believed in the importance of the new weapons but did not consider that the nature of warfare had changed." In addition, the Russians may have passed on information gained from their intelligence network in the U.S.

41. Mao Tse-tung, "Concerning Several Important Problems in the Present Party Policy," directive to CCP Central Committee, Jan. 18, 1948, in *Imperialism and All Reactionaries Are Paper Tigers*. Mao continued, "If we overestimate the strength of the enemy, taking the overall situation, in every specific struggle, we do not adopt a careful attitude, do not attach importance to the art of struggle, do not concentrate all our efforts on the struggle . . . then we will commit the mistake of 'left' opportunism."

42. *Military Situation in the Far East*, pp. 2492–2493.

43. Radio Korea from Sinuiju, in Korean, Nov. 7, 1950.

44. Supplement to *People's China*, Vol. II, No. 11, Dec. 1, 1950.

45. *Military Situation in the Far East*, pp. 757 and 1233; also Cagle and Manson, *op. cit.*, pp. 223–229. Whitney, *op. cit.*, p. 407, claims the amended

restrictions were so severe as to make destruction of the bridges impossible, although Cagle and Manson give detailed reports of damage inflicted on six spans, two of which were destroyed. Whitney further asserts, p. 408, "It was at this time, when the first clear warning was sounded by MacArthur, . . . that the bridges played their most important role." However, more than two-thirds of the troops which took part in the massive CPV attacks of late November had already crossed the Yalu by Nov. 6.

46. Radio Peking, NCNA, in English Morse to Europe, Oct. 26, 1950. This new committee merged the former Chinese Peace Committee, of the so-called Stockholm Peace Appeal, with the Chinese People's Campaign Committee Against American Aggression in Taiwan and Korea, formed in early July.

47. *Jen Min Jih Pao* and *Kuang Ming Jih Pao*, both of Nov. 2, 1950, reported letters from students offering to volunteer for the war, as well as meetings of civic and educational groups on the same subject.

48. See, for instance, Wen-hui C. Chen, *Chinese Communist Anti-Americanism and the Resist-America Aid-Korea Campaign*, Series I, No. 4 (1952), of "Studies in Chinese Communism," Air Force Personnel and Training Research Center, Lackland Air Force Base, Texas, May 1955. For a compilation of key items, see the 1,300-page volume, *Wei-ta ti k'ang-Mei yuan-Ch'ao yün-tung* (The Great Resist-America Aid-Korea Movement), Peking, 1954.

49. *Jen Min Jih Pao*, Nov. 6, 1950, from NCNA, Nov. 6, 1950, in *SCMP*, No. 5. A less authoritative statement along this line came from the editor in chief of the Shanghai *Ta Kung Pao:* "There can be only two consequences: either the war will be stopped; or else, the war dangers will be further aggravated when the Americans refuse to give up. . . . [They can] seek a peaceful solution . . . or fight it out." The latter contingency would bring "an early peace" because of alleged U.S. weakness in Korea; see Hong Kong *Ta Kung Pao*, Nov. 10, 1950, in *SCMP*, No. 8. The editor's "peace terms" went well beyond those in more responsible media, including (1) withdrawal of all foreign troops from Korea and an all-Korean government, (2) withdrawal of the Seventh Fleet from the Taiwan Strait, and (3) a disarmed Japan which would sign a Sino-Soviet-Japanese peace treaty.

50. Hu Sheng, "Resist-America Must Help Korea" (in Chinese), *World Culture*, Vol. XXII, No. 19, Nov. 11, 1950.

51. Fu Ying, "Resist-America Aid-Korea Must Win!" (in Chinese), *World Culture*, Vol. XXII, No. 20, Nov. 18, 1950, p. 34.

52. *Jen Min Jih Pao*, Nov. 23, 1950, directive of Chinese People's Committee for World Peace and Against American Aggression.

53. *Jen Min Jih Pao*, Nov. 20, 1950, from NCNA, Nov. 20, 1950, in *SCMP*, No. 14.

54. *Current Affairs Journal*, Nov. [? 22], 1950, from NCNA, Nov. 22, 1950, in *SCMP*, No. 16.

55. Western speculation at the time focused on the North Korean power plants as a possible Chinese Communist concern because of their role in Manchurian industry. The total absence of references to these plants in the November propaganda does not prove they did not concern Peking, but it does reduce the likelihood that this factor played a part in determining intervention.

56. Earlier in this chapter we reviewed material evidence of possible Chinese Communist concern over the likelihood of U.N. air attacks across the Yalu River.

57. Although the Stockholm Peace Appeal signature campaign was worldwide and antedated the Korean War, its implementation in China coincided with the war and so óverlapped propaganda on U.S. atomic bombs. An official summary of the campaign claimed it was "closely knit with the Chinese people's struggle to oppose American aggression on China and Korea," and defined its "three stages" as (1) mid-May to the end of June, (2) early July to mid-August, and (3) mid-August to mid-November (NCNA, Nov. 22, 1950, in *SCMP*, No. 16). These "stages" paralleled developments in the war. A close examination of the campaign and consideration of its content and timing in relation to the main focus of this study has persuaded the author that it coincidentally supplemented propaganda directly related to the war. Basically, however, the campaign was independent of the events discussed in this study.

58. "How to Understand the United States," *Current Affairs Journal*, Vol. I, No. 2, Nov. 5, 1950, in *CB*, No. 32, Nov. 29, 1950.

59. *Jen Min Jih Pao*, Nov. 11, 1950, carried a front-page account by an eyewitness of the Hiroshima bombing who told of grass growing within one month of the atomic attack, concluding: "A baby was born in 1949 to a fellow-student who at that time was more badly hurt than I was. When you can get into a well-constructed air-raid shelter before the release of the bomb and put on a suit of white clothing, and make sure to get to a place ten kilometers away immediately after the explosion, nothing shall happen to you. Look at myself. I have gone through the explosion of an atomic bomb and I am still growing strong as before. The atomic bomb is in fact not half as dreadful as American imperialism points it out to be." Translation from NCNA, Nov. 11, 1950, in *SCMP*, No. 11. See also NCNA, Nov. 12, 1950, for detailed editorial discussion of atomic bombs together with disparaging comments on their effectiveness taken from Western spokesmen of World War II.

60. *Ibid.*, "Vyshinsky has recently warned the imperialists 'a bomb can be answered by a bomb.' He also said that in the unfortunate event of an atomic bomb being needed, the Soviet Union could have as many atom bombs as were necessary." Although the source for this statement has not been found, Vyshinsky did call for outlawing the atomic bomb, for branding as "war criminals" the first nation to use it in future war, and pointed to U.S. "failure" to maintain "atomic monopoly," noting: "For many years they banked on the atomic bomb— and lost out. Now they are banking on the hydrogen bomb . . . and will lose out here too." Speech to the First Committee of the General Assembly, Oct. 23, 1950, in *New Times*, No. 45, Nov. 7, 1950, Supplement, p. 3. In his U.N. statements, Vyshinsky did not threaten Soviet countermeasures in the event of U.S. atomic attacks in China or elsewhere.

61. During the informal talks of Security Council members in August, Malik at one point attempted to identify Sir Benegal Rau as a sympathetic collaborator in organizing the talks. Rau immediately denied the inference that he acted in anything but a neutral capacity. After failing in these talks, Malik rejected an earlier compromise proposal by Rau which he had previously treated favorably. Malik's manner convinced the Indian delegate of Soviet insincerity in peace talks

and that Malik was using the Council as a sounding board. In September, Malik rejected a proposal whereby a two-man commission, of Indian and Swedish representatives, would have investigated charges of U.S. bombing over Chinese territory, claiming that "under cover of the commission—on its staff if not as a member of it—it [the U.S.] is trying to send its own trusted representatives to make a spying reconnaissance of the situation in China." *UNSC*, 500th meeting, Sept. 12, 1950, No. 42. Rau immediately countered Malik's insinuations as a slight upon his government's integrity.

62. *World Culture*, Vol. XXII, No. 13, Sept. 30, 1950; see also *Jen Min Jih Pao*, Sept. 23, 1950, editorial comment and Ministry of Foreign Affairs statements, Sept. 26, 1950.

63. Compare, for instance, Sir Benegal Rau's statements in the General Assembly debate of Sept. 19–20 with the aforementioned treatment of the debate in the Chinese press. See also *Jen Min Jih Pao*'s selective quoting from a press conference by Nehru in its issue of Sept. 23, 1950.

64. K. P. Karunakaran, *India in World Affairs, February 1950–December 1953*, p. 28; also Margaret W. Fisher and Joan V. Bondurant, *Indian Views of Sino-Indian Relations*, Indian Press Digests—Monograph Series, No. 1, University of California, Berkeley, February 1956, pp. 10–12.

65. According to Peking, it responded to an Indian *aide-mémoire* of Aug. 26, 1950, by informing Panikkar on Aug. 31 that the PLA would soon enter west Sikang or the Kham area of Tibet, and that the Indian government might assist Tibet authorities to arrive in Peking by mid-September "to begin peace negotiations." (Official note of the People's Republic of China to the Republic of India, Nov. 16, 1950, in *People's China*, Vol. II, No. 11, Dec. 1, 1950, Supplement, p. 9.) The note claimed that the delegation had been warned to make haste by PRC diplomats in Delhi "in early and middle September," as well as "in mid-October." According to the Indian notes of Oct. 28 and Nov. 1 (*ibid.*, pp. 10–13), the Tibetan mission was delayed by its inability to secure visas in Hong Kong.

66. Fred W. Riggs, "Tibet in Extremis," *Far Eastern Survey*, Vol. XIX, No. 21, Dec. 6, 1950. Riggs cites Radio Peking of Nov. 2 as well as the Tibetan complaint to the U.N. of this date.

67. Panikkar, *op. cit.*, p. 112.

68. The Indian notes came on Oct. 21 and Oct. 28, the Chinese reply on Oct. 30, 1950; *People's China, loc. cit.*

69. See for instance the issues of Nov. 2 and Nov. 16, 1950; also Yu Sha, "The 'Sun of Happiness' Is Rising in Tibet," *People's China*, Vol. II, No. 11, Dec. 1, 1950. Actually, the main advance of the PLA did not penetrate Tibet proper, perhaps because of impending negotiations with the delegation from Lhasa, local resistance, logistical difficulties exacerbated by oncoming winter weather, or a combination of these factors.

70. Note of Oct. 30, 1950, in *People's China, loc. cit.*

71. In addition to standard U.N. and Chinese Communist sources, this draws upon I. F. Stone, *The Hidden History of the Korean War*, Monthly Review Press, N.Y., 1952, p. 186.

72. In voting for the invitation, Malik expressed his opposition to the lateness

of the date, Nov. 15, but explained his vote as necessitated by the requirement of seven affirmative votes for procedural matters.

73. Lengthy discussion of the date for PRC participation on the Taiwan matter was linked in the U.S. press with speculation on the duration of hostilities in Korea. The delegate from Ecuador justified inviting Peking but not Pyongyang on the ground that the latter had "aggressed against the United Nations." However, he warned, "If, before the date for the discussion of the question of Formosa such an action should take place [i.e., Chinese aggression against the U.N.], we should have to reconsider our position." *UNSC,* 505th meeting, Sept. 28, 1950, No. 47, p. 13.

74. *New York Times,* Sept. 21, 1950. Remarks attributed to British and Indian delegates hinted willingness to grant Peking's demands on admission and Taiwan if it refrained from combat in Korea.

75. The resolution was sponsored by Cuba, Ecuador, France, Norway, the United Kingdom, and the United States; for text, see U.N. Document S/1894, Nov. 10, 1950.

76. Text in *People's China,* Vol. II, No. 11, Dec. 1, 1950, Supplement, p. 3.

77. Ministry of Foreign Affairs spokesman in *People's China,* Vol. II, No. 11, Dec. 1, 1950, Supplement, pp. 3–8.

78. Fu Ying, "Resist-America Aid-Korea Must Win!" (in Chinese), *World Culture,* Vol. XXII, No. 20, Nov. 18, 1950.

79. Kuo Mo-jo, Nov. 18, 1950, from NCNA, Peking, Nov. 24, 1950, in *SCMP,* No. 16.

VIII. Motivations behind Intervention

1. Space has precluded more attention to this theme. The writer has benefited from discussion of this problem with Alice Langley Hsieh.

2. On Oct. 26, 1950, John Foster Dulles, as Adviser to the Department of State, transmitted to Jacob Malik a U.S. memorandum on the Japanese peace treaty including provisions for U.S. administration, under U.N. auspices, of the Ryukyu and Bonin Islands; for final determination of the status of Taiwan, the Pescadores, South Sakhalin, and the Kurile Islands, by the U.K., U.S.S.R., China, and the U.S.; and a rationale for the maintenance of U.S. bases in Japan.

3. Lynn Montross and Captain Nicholas A. Canzona, USMC, *The Chosin Reservoir Campaign,* p. 353, quoting from translation of captured document of 26th Army, CPV. This unit suffered 90 per cent frostbite injuries. The 27th Army, CPV, reported more than 10,000 non-combat casualties; 70 per cent of its shells were said to have failed to detonate because of the effect of the severe cold upon weapons and ammunition.

4. *Ibid.,* p. 355, quotes a Dec. 7, 1950, interrogation: "Missions of the four (4) armies in 9th Group are to annihilate the 1st Division which is considered to be the best division in the U.S. After annihilating the 1st Marine Division they are to move south and take Hamhung."

IX. IN RETROSPECT

1. For an authoritative, detailed account see Lynn Montross and Capt. Nicholas A. Canzona, *U.S. Marine Operations in Korea,* Vol. III. An excellent presentation of the incredible fight of a single unit down "Nightmare Alley" is contained in Capt. Russell A. Gugeler, USA, ed., *Combat Actions in Korea,* Combat Forces Press, Washington, 1954.

2. Montross and Canzona, *op. cit.,* p. 382; see also pp. 351–359.

3. For a thorough examination of the assumptions underlying American policy toward China, see John W. Spanier, *The Truman-MacArthur Controversy.*

BIBLIOGRAPHY

※

Books and Government Documents

Appleman, Roy L. "The Korean War: From the Naktong to the Yalu," in "The U.S. Army in Conflict with the Communist Powers." Unpublished document. Office of the Chief of Military History, Department of the Army. Washington, D.C.

Beloff, Max. *Soviet Policy in the Far East, 1944–1951.* London: Oxford University Press, 1953.

Brandt, Conrad, Benjamin Schwartz, and John K. Fairbank. *A Documentary History of Chinese Communism.* Cambridge: Harvard University Press, 1952.

Cagle, Malcolm W., and Frank A. Manson. *The Sea War in Korea.* Annapolis, Maryland: U.S. Naval Institute, 1957.

Chen, Wen-hui C. *Chinese Communist Anti-Americanism and the Resist-America Aid-Korea Campaign.* Human Resources Research Institute, Research Memorandum No. 36, Lackland Air Force Base, Texas, May, 1955.

Chiang Kai-shek. *China's Destiny.* New York: Roy Publishers, 1947.

Common Program and Other Documents of the First Plenary Session of the Chinese People's Political Consultative Conference, The. Peking, 1950.

Communiqué of the State Statistical Bureau of China on the Development of National Economy and the Results of the Implementation of the State Plan for 1954. Peking: State Statistical Bureau, September 21, 1955.

Cressey, G. B. *Land of the 500 Million.* New York: McGraw-Hill, 1955.

Davison, W. Phillips. *The Berlin Blockade.* Princeton, N.J.: Princeton University Press, 1958.

Dinerstein, Herbert S. *War and the Soviet Union.* New York: Frederick A. Praeger, 1959.

Eighth National Congress of the Communist Party of China. Peking, 1956.

First Five Years of Victory, The. Peking, n.d.

Fisher, Margaret W., and Joan V. Bondurant. *Indian Views of Sino-Indian Relations.* Indian Press Digest—Monograph Series. Berkeley: University of California, February, 1956.

Garthoff, Raymond L. *Soviet Strategy in the Nuclear Age.* New York: Frederick A. Praeger, 1958.

Goodrich, Leland M. *Korea: A Study of U.S. Policy in the United Nations.* New York: Council on Foreign Relations, 1956.

Gugeler, Russell A., ed. *Combat Actions in Korea.* Washington: Combat Forces Press, 1954.

Hate America Campaign in Communist China, The. Washington, D.C., n.d.

Huang Ts'ao-liang. *Chan-hou shih-chieh hsin-hsing-shih.* (*New Aspects of the Postwar World*). Shanghai, 1950.

Hu Hua. *New Period of Sino-Soviet Friendship and Cooperation.* Tientsin, 1950. [In Chinese]

Hu Sheng. *Ti-kuo chu-i i Chung-kuo cheng-chih.* (*Imperialism and Chinese Politics*). Peking, 1949.

India. Ministry of Information and Broadcasting. *Jawaharlal Nehru's Speeches, 1949–53.* Calcutta, 1954.

Karig, Walter, Malcolm W. Cagle, and Frank A. Manson. *Battle Report: The War in Korea.* New York: Rinehart and Company, Inc., 1952.

Karunakaran, K. P. *India in World Affairs, 1950–53.* London: Oxford University Press, 1958.

Kautsky, John H. *Moscow and the Communist Party of India.* New York: John Wiley and Sons, Inc., 1956.

Kierman, Frank A., Jr. *The Fluke That Saved Formosa.* Communist Bloc Program, China Project, B/54–3, Cambridge, Mass.: Center for International Studies, Massachusetts Institute of Technology, June 1, 1954.

Korolenko, A. S. *Torgovliye dogovory i soglasheniya SSSR s inostrannyme gosudarstvami* (*Trade Treaties and Agreements of the USSR with Foreign States*). Moscow, 1953.

Kundra, J. C. *Indian Foreign Policy, 1947–1954.* Gronigen, Holland: J. B. Wolters, 1955.

Leites, Nathan. *A Study of Bolshevism.* Glencoe, Ill.: The Free Press, 1953.

Liang Ch'un-fu. *Hsin-Chung-kuo ti wai-chiao* (*New China's Foreign Relations*). Canton, 1950.

Lindsay, M. *China and the Cold War.* New York: Cambridge University Press, 1955.

Liu Shao-ch'i. *On Internationalism and Nationalism.* 2nd ed. Peking, 1952.

McVey, Ruth T. *The Calcutta Conference and the Southeast Asian Uprisings.* Interim Reports Series, Modern Indonesia Project, Southeast Asia Program. Ithaca, N.Y.: Cornell University, 1958.

Mao Tse-tung. *Imperialism and All Reactionaries Are Paper Tigers.* Peking: Foreign Languages Press, 1958.

———. *On Contradiction.* Peking, 1952.

———. *On People's Democratic Dictatorship.* 3rd ed. Peking: Foreign Languages Press, 1950.

———. *On the Protracted War.* Peking, 1954.

———. *Selected Works.* New York: International Publishers, 1956. 4 vols.

Marshall, S. L. A. *The River and the Gauntlet.* New York: Morrow and Co., 1953.

Montross, Lynn, and Nicholas A. Canzona. *The Chosun Reservoir Campaign,* vol. III of *U.S. Marine Operations in Korea, 1950–53.* Washington: Historical Branch, U.S. Marine Corps, 1957.

New China's Economic Achievements, 1949–1952. Peking, 1952.

North, Robert C. *Kuomintang and Chinese Communist Elites.* Stanford: University Press, 1952.

Operations Research Office. *China: An Area Manual*, ORO-T229, Chevy Chase, Md., 1954.

Panikkar, K. M. *In Two Chinas*. London: Allen and Unwin, 1955.

Poats, Rutherford M. *Decision in Korea*. New York: The McBride Co., 1954.

Quigley, Harold S., and John Turner. *The New Japan: Government and Politics*. Minneapolis: University of Minnesota Press, 1956.

Rigg, Robert B. *Red China's Fighting Hordes*. Harrisburg, Pa.: Military Service Publications Co., 1951.

Rostow, W. W. *The Prospects for Communist China*. New York: Wiley and Sons, 1954.

Schnable, James F. "The Korean Conflict: Policy, Planning and Direction." Unpublished document. Department of Defense, Washington, D.C.

Shabad, Theodore. *China's Changing Map*. New York: Frederick A. Praeger, 1956.

Shih Ch'eng-shih. *People's Resistance in Mainland China, 1950–1955*. Hong Kong: Union Research Institute, 1956.

Snow, Edgar. *Red Star over China*. New York: Random House, 1944.

Spanier, John W. *The Truman-MacArthur Controversy and the Korean War*. Cambridge: Harvard University Press, 1959.

Stein, Gunther. *The Challenge of Red China*. New York: McGraw-Hill, 1945.

Steiner, H. Arthur. *Maoism: A Sourcebook*. Los Angeles: University of California, 1952. Mimeo.

Stone, I. F. *The Hidden History of the Korean War*. New York: Monthly Review Press, 1952.

Strong, Anna Louise. *Dawn Out of China*. Bombay: People's Publishing House, 1948.

Truman, Harry S. *Memoirs*. Garden City, N.Y.: Doubleday and Co., Inc., 1956. 2 vols.

United Nations General Assembly. *Official Records*.

United Nations Security Council. *Official Records*.

United States. Department of State. *United States Relations with China*. Washington, D.C., 1949.

———. Department of the Army. "Chinese Communist Forces: Army Histories." Unpublished document, Order of Battle Branch, Office of the Assistant Chief of Staff, G-2, U.S. Eighth Army, December 1, 1954.

———. Department of the Army. *Korea 1950*. Washington, D.C., 1952.

———. Senate. *Hearings Before the Committee on Armed Services and the Committee on Foreign Relations*. Eighty-second Congress, First Session. Washington, D.C., 1951.

———. Senate. *Military Situation in the Far East, Hearings Before the Committee on Armed Services and the Committee on Foreign Relations*. Eighty-second Congress, First Session. Washington, D.C., 1951.

van Aduard, E. J. Lewe. *Japan from Surrender to Peace*. The Hague: Martinus Nijhoff, 1953.

Wei-ta ti k'ang-Mei yuan-Ch'ao yun-tung (*The Great Resist-America Aid-Korea Movement*). Peking, 1954.

Whitney, Courtney. *MacArthur: His Rendezvous with History.* New York: Knopf, Inc., 1956.

Wu Yuan-li. *An Economic Survey of Communist China.* New York: Bookman Associates, 1955.

Articles

Acheson, Dean G. "Crisis in Asia: An Examination of U.S. Policy," *Department of State Bulletin,* XXII (January 23, 1950), 111–18.

Almond, E. M. "What Happened in Korea When Chinese Marched In," *U.S. News and World Report,* XXXIV (February 13, 1953), 40–42 +.

Berzhkov, B. "Foreign Policy Maneuvers of Indian Reaction," *New Times,* No. 22 (May 31, 1950), 30–31.

Chang Ming-Yang. "The Korean People's Just War for Unifying the Fatherland and Independence," *Shih Chieh Chih Shih (World Culture),* XXII (July 7, 1950).

Chao Yi-ya. "Kuo-chi chu-i hsüeh-hsi t'i-k'an" ("Study Principles of Internationalism"), *Hsüeh Hsi,* I (December, 1949), 7–9.

Chen Lien-tuan. "None Shall Starve," *People's China,* I (February 16, 1950), 21–22.

Ch'en Yün. "Report on the Financial and Economic Situation," in *The First Five Years of Victory.* Peking, n.d.

———. "The Problem of Commodity Prices and the Issuance of Government Bonds," in *New China's Economic Achievements, 1949–1952.* Peking, 1952.

Ch'ien Chün-yui. "Kuo-chi chu-yi te chu-yao piao-chih tuei Ssu-lien te you-yi" ("The Hallmark of Internationalism"), *Hsüeh Hsi,* I (December, 1949), 4–6.

Chou En-lai. "China Protests," *People's China,* II (September 16, 1950), 26–27.

———. "Chou En-lai's 2nd Message to UN," *People's China,* II (September 16, 1950), 27.

———. "Chou En-lai on Truman's Statement," *People's China,* II (July 16, 1950), 4.

———. "The First Year of People's China," *People's China,* II (October 16, 1950), 4–9 +.

Clubb, O. Edmund. "Chinese Communist Strategy in Foreign Relations," *The Annals of the American Academy of Political and Social Science,* CCLXXVII (September, 1951), 156–66.

Dubin, Wilbert. "The Political Evolution of the Pyongyang Government," *Pacific Affairs,* XXIII (December, 1950), 381–92.

Fu Ying. "Resist-America Aid-Korea Must Win!" *World Culture,* XXII (November 18, 1950).

Hsü Tsai-tan. "Northeast China Sets the Pace," *People's China,* I (April 1, 1950), 8–9+.

Hu Sheng. "Resist-America Must Help Korea," *World Culture,* XXII (November 11, 1950).

Ke Chia-lung. "Manchuria's Economic Victories," *People's China,* I (June 1, 1950), 7–9.

K'o Pai-nien. "Hsin-min chu-yi ti wai-chiao cheng-tse" ("The Foreign Policy of the New People's Democracy"), *Hsüeh Hsi,* I (October, 1949), 13–15.

Liao Kai-lung. "Kuan-yü chan-cheng yi h'o-p'ing wen-t'i" ("Problems of War and Peace"), *Hsüeh Hsi*, II (August 16, 1950), 17–22.

Lu Ting-yi. "Explanation of Several Basic Questions Concerning the Postwar International Situation," *Emancipation Daily*, January 4–5, 1947.

Mao Tse-tung. "On New Democracy," in United States House of Representatives, *Communism in China (The Strategy and Tactics of World Communism. Supplement III C)*. Eightieth Congress, Second Session. Washington, 1949.

———. "On the People's Democratic Dictatorship," in Conrad Brandt, Benjamin Schwartz, and John K. Fairbank, *A Documentary History of Chinese Communism*. Cambridge: Harvard University Press, 1952.

———. "Report to the Party Plenum," *People's China*, II (July 1, 1950), 4–6.

———. "Turn to Production," in H. Arthur Steiner, *Maoism: A Sourcebook*. Los Angeles: University of California, 1952. Mimeo.

Po I-po. "The Draft Budget for 1950," in *New China's Economic Achievements, 1949–1952*. Peking, 1952.

———. "The 1953 State Budget of the People's Republic of China," *People's China*, No. 6 (March 16, 1953), Supplement, 3–16.

Riggs, Fred W. "Tibet in Extremis," *Far Eastern Survey*, XIX (December 6, 1950), 224–30.

Strong, Anna Louise. "The Thought of Mao Tse-tung," *Amerasia*, XI (June, 1947), 161–74.

———. "World's Eye View from a Yenan Cave: An Interview with Mao Tse-tung," *Amerasia*, XI (April, 1947), 122–26.

Su Yü. "The Liberation of Taiwan in Sight," *People's China*, I (February 16, 1950), 8–9.

Ti Ch'ao-pai. "The Meaning and Method of Sino-Soviet Economic Cooperation," in Hu Hua, *New Period of Sino-Soviet Friendship and Cooperation*. Tientsin, 1950. [In Chinese]

Tien Huo-nung. "China's Agriculture in Speedy Rehabilitation," *People's China*, I (February 1, 1950), 7–9.

Tsai Ying-p'ing. "The Road to Final Victory," *People's China*, I (February 16, 1950), 6–7+.

Ward, Robert E. "The Constitution and Current Japanese Politics," *Far Eastern Survey*, XXV (April, 1956), 49–58.

Whiting, Allen S. "Communist China and 'Big Brother,'" *Far Eastern Survey*, XXIV (October, 1955), 145–51.

———. "Rewriting Modern History in Communist China: A Review Article," *Far Eastern Survey*, XXIV (November, 1955), 173–74.

———. "The New Chinese Communist," *World Politics*, VII (July, 1955), 592–605.

Yeh Mang. "The Criminal Act of American Imperialist Aggression in Taiwan," *World Culture*, XXII (July 7, 1950), 11–12.

Yu Shah. "The 'Sun of Happiness' Is Rising in Tibet," *People's China*, II (December 1, 1950), 8–9+.

Newspapers and Periodicals

Central China Post. Hankow, daily.
Changsha Hsin Hunan Pao. Changsha, daily.
Chin Pu Jih Pao. Shanghai, daily.
Current Background. Hong Kong, American Consulate General, irregular.
Current Digest of the Soviet Press. Ann Arbor, Mich., weekly.
Department of State Bulletin. Washington, D.C., weekly.
Emancipation Daily. Yenan, daily.
Hsin Hua Yüeh Pao. Peking, monthly
Hsüeh Hsi. (Study). Peking, monthly.
Izvestiia. Moscow, daily.
Jen Min Jih Pao. Peking, daily.
Kuang Ming Jih Pao. Peking, daily.
Minju Chosun. Pyongyang, daily.
New Times. Moscow, weekly.
New York Times. New York, daily.
People's China. Peking, fortnightly.
Pravda. Moscow, daily.
Shih Chieh Chih Shih (World Culture). Peking, fortnightly.
Survey of the China Mainland Press. Hong Kong, American Consulate General, irregular.
Ta Kung Pao. Shanghai, daily.

INDEX

※

Acheson, Dean G., 48, 98, 110, 169; on nature of UN, 39; on US defense perimeter, 40; reaction to Nehru proposal for PRC admission to UN, 60; emphasizes US defense aims, 96

Afghanistan, China frontier on, 3

Air violations (of PRC), US charged with, 95, 97–100, 106–07, 149. *See also* Limited war

Albania, question of recognition of PRC by, 25

Aleutian Islands, in US defense perimeter, 39, 96

Almond, E. M., 123, 130, 164

Altai Mountains, 3

Anderson, Orvil A., suspended from Air War College, 96

Antung, 43–44, 106–07; US machingunning of, 97

Asia, PRC interest in, 15; communist goal in, 30, 36, 40–41; PRC view of declining US power in, 45–46; US fear of communization of, 50; PRC concern for setback in, 88–89; PRC concern for effect of DPRK defeat on role in, 157–158; PRC Korean intervention affects status in, 166. *See also* individual countries

Atomic bomb. *See* Nuclear weapons

Austin, Warren, 69, 75, 111, 170; rebuts Malik's August 4, 1950, UN resolution, 78–79; UN speech of August 17, 1950, 86; outlines UN goals in Korea, 88; warns PRC against involvement in Korean conflict, 96; expresses concern over PRC military deployment, 98; August 16, 1950, UN speech, 103; warns PRC against involvement in Korean conflict, 105; declares for complete defeat of DPRK, 111; acts against Indian UN compromise move, 113

Australia, 71

Berlin, 40

Borneo, 4

British Labour Party, 61

Burma, 31–32, 40–41; as factor in historical Chinese expanionism, 2; China border on, 3–4; recognizes PRC, 25; opposes unification of Korea by force, 114

Capitalism, 6–7. *See also* Imperialism

Central People's Government Council (PRC), 107

Chamdo, PLA occupation of, 145

Chang Han-fu, talks with K. M. Panikkar, 59

Changjin Reservoir, 130–31, 163

Chang Wen-t'ien, 86

Ch'en Yi, 64

Chiang Kai-shek, 3, 5, 20–21, 26, 35, 37, 50–51, 54, 68–69, 83, 153, 159; xenophobic attitudes of, 4; US support of, 10–12, 49; US Democrat support of, 63; USSR-UN resolution tacitly accepts representation of, 74; meets with MacArthur, 81–82. *See also* Kuomintang; Taiwan

Ch'ien Tuan-sheng, denounces US, 127

China, expansionist and xenophobic tendencies of, 2–6; lack of natural frontiers, 3–4. *See also* People's Republic of China and Taiwan

China, Republic of. *See* Taiwan

Chinese Communist Party, historical expansionist component in policy of, 1; ideological component of, 6–7; distorted world view of, 9–13; provides

lations with Tito, 25. *See also* Chiang Kai-shek; Taiwan
Kuo Mo-jo, mission to Pyongyang of, 80; attacks UN, 149–50
Kurile Islands, 38

Li Chin-chuang, 100
Lie, Trygve, 49, 147
Li Hung-chang, 35
Li Li-san, mission to Pyongyang of, 80
Limited war, effect of lack of communication in, 168–72. *See also* Nuclear weapons
Lin Piao, 21, 45, 64
Liu Ning-i, 25
Liu Shao-ch'i, on reconquest of Taiwan, 18; on Asian revolutionary movements, 30–31

MacArthur, Douglas A., 37, 69, 117–18, 130, 148–50, 159, 170–71; excludes ROK from US defense perimeter, 39–40; visits Taiwan, 81–82; PRC propaganda image of, 83; demands aggressive Korean policy, 87; PRC fears power of, 89; claims Taiwan part of US defense perimeter, 92; charges PRC complicity with DPRK, 93; advocates militant US policy, 96; as figure in US domestic controversy, 96–98; PRC propaganda uses statements of, 100; September 29, 1950, recapture of Seoul by forces of, 103–04; demands surrender of Pyongyang, 104; charges PRC complicity with DPRK, 105; demands surrender of Pyongyang, 108; given authorization to engage PRC forces, 111; demands surrender of Pyongyang, 114; issues statement to UN on PRC belligerency, 137; given permission to attack on Korean side of Yalu, 138; "win the war" offensive of, 141–42; removed from post, 167
Malaya, 31, 157
Malik, Jacob, 65, 70–71, 88, 91, 95, 112–13, 170–71; demands UN recognition of PRC, 26; boycotts Security Council, 39; ends boycott of Security Council, 61; terms Korean conflict "civil war," 69; abusive behavior in UN of, 72–73;

introduces UN resolution to include PRC, ROK, and DPRK in Security Council discussions, 74–77; faces rebuke by Austin in UN, 78–79; mid-August 1950 moves of, in UN, 84–87; attempts to deter UN military action, 98; fails to secure PRC UN representation to discuss Korean action, 101–03; on PRC representation in UN, 146–47; proposes cease-fire talks, 165
Manchu Dynasty, 1, 35; xenophobic attitude of, 4
Manchuria, 11, 38, 43–44, 53, 152, 164; Czarist practices in, 5; 1950 budget of, 18; industrialization of, 19; 1950 PLA assignments to, 23; 1950 Sino-Soviet agreements regarding, 28–29; vulnerability of, 50; PRC strategic thinking on, 64; PRC military build-up in, 111; as PRC sanctuary, 138; as PRC industrial base, 159 '
"Mandate of Heaven." *See* Irredentism
Mao Tse-tung, 1, 16, 20, 34–35, 37, 58, 81, 160, 166–67, 170; as spokesman of Marxism-Leninism, 6–8; distorted world view of, 9–12; on declining PRC economy, 16–17; demobilizes PLA, 17–18; 1950 negotiations with Stalin, 27–30; on Asian revolutionary movements, 30–32; on asymmetry of power in Sino-Soviet alliance, 51; role in evolving strategy on Korea, 52; lack of concern for Korean conflict, 61; doctrine of numerical superiority of, 122; "protracted war" thesis of, 132–34; depreciates strategic significance of US atomic bombs, 135–36; statement on consideration of enemy forces, 137; "second stage" doctrine of, 139; fears US support of Taiwan, 153; relies on USSR, 154; fears effect of DPRK defeat, 157–58
Mao Tun, 99
Marianas, in US defense perimeter, 96
Marshall, George C., 134; becomes Secretary of Defense, 96
Marxism-Leninism, as creed of PRC, 6–8
Masan, 71
Matthews, Francis B., 92, 98, 159; demands aggressive Korean policy, 87, 96; PRC propaganda uses statements of, 100